Why Kids Hate School

Steven P. Jones

Cathy J. Pearman

Eric C. Sheffield

Academy for Educational Studies
Missouri State University

KENDALL/HUNT PUBLISHING COMPANY
4050 Westmark Drive   Dubuque, Iowa 52002

Chapter 2: From *Quiet Storm: Voices of Young Black Poets* by Lydia Omolula Okutoro.
Copyright © Hyperion Books for Children. Reprinted by permission.

Chapter 10: Excerpts *From Experience and Education: The 60th Anniversary Edition* by John Dewey.
Copyright © 1998 by Kappa Delta Pi, International Honor Society in Education. Reprinted by permission.

Chapter 11: Excerpts reprinted by permission of the publishers and the Trustees of the
Loeb Classical Library from *Quintilian: Volume I*, Loeb Classical Library ® Volume 124,
translated by H.E. Butler, pp. 19–20, 31–33, 57, 211–213, 215, 249, 297, 189,
Cambridge, Mass.: Harvard University Press, 1920.
The Loeb Classical Library ® is a registered trademark of the President and Fellows of Harvard College.

Chapter 12: Excerpt from "The Vindictives" from *The Poetry of Robert Frost*
edited by Edward Connery Lathem. Copyright 1969 by Henry Holt and Company.
Copryight 1936 by Robert Frost, copyright 1964 by Lesles Frost Ballantine.
Reprinted by permission of Henry Holt and Company, LLC.

(guy on front)
Image © Mark E. Stout, 2007 Under License from Shutterstock, Inc.

(school building, front/back)
Image © Lynne Furrer, 2007 Under License from Shutterstock, Inc.

(girl on back)
Image © Junial Enterprises, 2007 Under License from Shutterstock, Inc.

(girl on front)
Image © Anita Patterson Peppers, 2007 Under License from Shutterstock, Inc.

Copyright © 2007 by Kendall/Hunt Publishing Company

ISBN 978-0-7575-4432-3

Printed in the United States of America
10 9 8 7 6 5

**Academy for
Educational Studies**

Missouri State University

The mission of the Academy for Educational Studies is to foster a community of inquirers and provide a public space for debate and dialogue about important questions in education. The Academy encourages those interested in education, teaching, and learning to engage in thoughtful reflection, discussion, and critique of educational theory and practice. Involving people from across the state, region and country, the Academy promotes this vital dialogue by arranging education conferences and symposia and by creating publishing opportunities connected with Academy events. The Academy supports research efforts of graduate and undergraduate students and assists in the design and delivery of teacher education courses at both the graduate and undergraduate level.

Table of Contents

Why Do Kids Hate School?

PREFACE

Every teacher longs for students who come to school ready and eager to learn. But there is hardly a teacher in grades K-12—and especially in middle school and high school—who cannot look up in his or her classes and find students who are disaffected, disengaged, alienated, or "turned off" to the whole enterprise of learning in school. Or they are bored, or uninterested, or resigned to failure. Some resent having to go to school, and they are unresponsive to attempts teachers make to get them to learn or join in the activities of the class. Some students have perfected the look that says *"Don't even try to teach me anything."* Others are so far removed from the culture of the school that they are simply bodies keeping a seat warm until they are released. It is fair to say that some students hate school.

This collection of essays is a result of the Second Annual Conference of the Academy for Educational Studies at Missouri State University. The purpose of the Academy is to foster a community of inquirers and to provide a public space for debate and dialogue about important questions in education—questions like "Why do kids hate school?" It is a raw, pull-no-punches question that forces educators, administrators, parents, and communities to take a long, hard look inside school walls.

The following essays explore various reasons and viewpoints regarding the increasing disengagement of our students in public schools. They provide a vehicle for more sustained deliberations and discussions on the subject among any who care about teaching and learning. To facilitate these discussions, the book is arranged into five sections with three to five essays of a similar theme in each section. At the end of each essay are questions to check for comprehension or to encourage the types of dialogue mentioned above. The sixth section provides a summary and offers a set of questions that explore how we might help students like school.

SECTION I: THE POLITICAL LANDSCAPE

We begin to explore the question of why kids hate school in Section I by looking at the political landscape with essays by Philip Cusick, David Owen, and Susan Ohanian. Cusick discusses the shift in the role of responsibility from the student to the institution and the subsequent burgeoning of bureaucracy. He makes the observation that while one goal of reform efforts was to increase equity, in actuality, there may be an increasing difference in social distance between students with which schools cannot keep pace. Susan Ohanian also touches on social differences in our public schools and how some students are misfits. She posits that the educational environment, in conjunction with standardized testing, removes the student from the center of education. She suggests a Happiness Index which involves asking students themselves what they want, what they need, and what makes them happy. The educational environment, and the contexts shaping it, is also a theme in the concluding essay of Section I by David Owen. Owen suggests that teachers are asked to prepare students to be critical thinkers and life-long learners while they themselves must function in an anti-intellectual environment. He provides historical, sociological, cultural, political, and educational contexts to strengthen his position. He rounds out his composition by offering suggestions to classroom teachers on practices and strategies to help circumvent anti-intellectualism.

SECTION II: HEARING THE VOICES OF STUDENTS

Ohanian's question of happiness is also found in Section II: Hearing the Voices of Students. Lynda George begins her essay with at-risk students' responses to the question "How does your school contribute to your happiness?" These same students are then led through discussions on virtue and justice while George documents their candid responses. The dissatisfaction of George's students mirrored many of the attitudes found in a study funded by the Bill and Melinda Gates Foundation. While reviewing this study and other literature, Emmett Sawyer and Judith Gregg point out that students want a more real-life based education. Sawyer and Gregg discuss how lack of relevance, cultural norms, parental interaction, grade retention, and motivation impact students' persistence to graduate high school. They also highlight sociological and economic factors that force many students to become drop-outs. Factors leading to high school drop-outs are also the theme of Karen Scott's essay. She refers to the factors of economics, family problems, and personal problems that pull students out of school and suggests that many of these factors are beyond the control of the school. However, Scott also identifies push-out factors within schools that create barriers for certain students and lead them to drop out.

SECTION III: ARGUMENTS FOR STUDENT-CENTERED TEACHING

The importance of learner-centered education is the theme for Section III. Don Hufford contrasts standardized systems and student freedom and their impact on students' "courage to be." The concept of student freedom continues in the essay by Karla Smart-Morstad and Sara Triggs. These authors believe freedom is foundational for the development of potential and engagement of mind, and they suggest students may hate school when their potential is dismissed. Adam Harbaugh and Jeffrey Cornelius-White report results on a meta-analysis which reviews the relationship between positive learner-centered teacher-student relationships and comprehensive student success. These results are then used as a basis for suggestions for teachers and students on how to increase the likelihood of learner-centered relationships in the classroom.

SECTION IV: PHILOSOPHICAL CONSIDERATIONS

Exploring the philosophical considerations of why kids may hate school, Eric Sheffield examines and explains John Dewey's theory of experience as presented in his 1938 book, *Experience and Education*, paying particular attention to the notions of continuity and interaction and how they might influence educational practice. A look at educational practice is also provided by Pauline Nugent as she discusses the principles of pedagogy expounded by Quintilian and relates them to contemporary topics in education. She makes the point that many of the same topics that engaged the thoughts of ancient philosophers and teachers also occupy the minds of modern educators. In the closing essay of this section, Steve Broidy looks at the role of educational ideals which contribute to student attitudes toward school. He concludes that there are many reasons why students may hate school, but one of the most important factors is a lack of purpose within the school.

SECTION V: SUBJECT-MATTER CONSIDERATIONS

A child's educational experience may very well be a sum of its parts. In Section V, student dislikes, disinterest and dissatisfaction in the areas of special education, reading, language arts, and science are examined. Thomas Deering begins the section with an overview of the American curriculum, teaching practices, and assessment along with suggestions for bringing about much needed changes. Jerry Whitworth offers historical information on the development of special education and the evolution of current special education laws. He then contrasts the ideal with the reality of modern special education. The reality of current educational practices is also found in the essay by Debbie Landry, Bonnie Giese, and Roxanne Fillmore. They discuss the long-term effects, the impact on the educational environment, and the unreliable research on the results of the reading program, Accelerated Reader. The authors posit misuse as a possible reason why Accelerated Reader has fostered negative student attitudes. Susan Carlson also reports negative student attitudes toward reading among college students. She found systematic avoidance of complex reading at the university level. She also discusses the lack of confidence the United States government, via the Spellings Report, has in the ability of higher education to adequately address low student achievement. Carlson concludes with three suggestions to combat the issue of student illiteracy. Roy Fox also writes about a dislike for reading, writing, speaking, and language study. He argues that students do not like these because they do not see the importance of this kind of education in their lives, they are not provided choices in their work, and teachers emphasize products over processes. The loss of interest in science during the middle and high school years is the topic of Jill Black's essay. She reports the results of a study which suggests that individual concept understanding might be facilitated by the development of spatially-oriented curricula that addresses specific misconceptions.

SECTION VI: FINAL THOUGHTS AND FUTURE DIRECTIONS

In the concluding essay, Steven Jones suggests a tri-partite model to explain why kids hate school. The three factors of teacher mistakes, individual student factors, and school/cultural realities may work in combination to produce a negative school experience for some students. Jones then proposes a further three-part action plan of political change, structural change, and instructional change if educational institutions are to respond to the reasons kids hate school. He does not propose specific actions in these categories but, rather, opens dialogue for a discussion on future directions for educational change.

CONCLUDING REMARKS

There are no simple or magical solutions to the problems uncovered in this book. The problems are too complex and too profound for that. Teachers, prospective teachers, teacher educators, and the public at large have to engage in careful reflection about this complicated problem and engage in honest dialogue with one another to affect change. To shy away from such discourse is to say that our educational system works for most of the students most of the time, and that is good enough. It then becomes our purpose in education to teach those students that fit our model, or can be molded to fit our model, and marginalize those who do not. Educators are fond of the phrase "One size doesn't fit all." Maybe it is time to walk the walk and not just talk the talk. Hopefully, this book will promote active thought and discussion of factors that contribute to student disengagement and perhaps, through combined efforts, ameliorate their effects.

Steven P. Jones

Cathy J. Pearman

Eric C. Sheffield

ACKNOWLEDGEMENTS

We wish to thank a number of people for their assistance with this project. Dr. David Hough, Dean of the College of Education at Missouri State University, offered encouragement and provided support for the Academy for Educational Studies and continues to make it possible for us to host the annual conferences. We wish to thank Dr. Fred Groves and his office staff for all their help and support. Our keynote speakers, Philip Cusick, Susan Ohanian, and David Owen, provided thought-provoking addresses and sparked comments and discussion among conference attendees, and we thank them for an excellent job. We also wish to thank Jaafar Gassid, Lori Wickman, and the staff at Kendall Hunt for their patience and professionalism as we worked through this process. Last, but most importantly, we wish to thank all those who attended our conference who engaged in dialogue, asked questions, uncovered truths, and offered suggestions on "Why Kids Hate School."

SECTION I

The Political Landscape

"You cannot group kids; you cannot put them into a category; you have to find out what works for them . . . because if you don't give them a chance, there are lots of other places where they will get the opportunity and maybe not the best opportunity."

—MISSOURI BOYS AND GIRLS CLUB INSTRUCTOR

"The school don't got no money for lunch and stuff . . . we can't wear what we want to wear and it's all because we're poor . . . we're poor."

—16-YEAR-OLD FLORIDA HIGH SCHOOL STUDENT

"I believe everyone hates school because they are forced to do it. If people could choose to go to school, then they would take it as a privilege instead of a hindrance."

—12-YEAR-OLD MISSOURI MIDDLE SCHOOL STUDENT

"That the teachers should deliberately reach for power and then make the most of their conquest is my firm conviction. To the extent that they are permitted to fashion the curriculum and the procedures of the school they will definitely and positively influence the social attitudes, ideals, and behavior of the coming generation. It is scarcely thinkable that these men and women would ever act as selfishly or bungle as badly as have the so-called 'practical' men of our generation—the politicians, the financiers, the industrialists."

—GEORGE S. COUNTS, DARE THE SCHOOL BUILD A NEW SOCIAL ORDER (1932)

Why Do Kids Hate School? Why Do We Care?

PHILIP A. CUSICK

MICHIGAN STATE UNIVERSITY

INTRODUCTION

Our question is specifically, "Why do kids hate school?" But allow me to ask three related questions: "Why do we care if they hate school?" "When did we start caring?" and, "What have we done about it?" Let me begin with a personal story. I started teaching in 1962 at Thomas K. Beecher Junior High School in Elmira, New York. At that time the educational establishment that I joined did not get upset over the fact that a fair number of students, at Thomas K. and other schools, were not interested in school, academic knowledge, or institutionalized instruction. Many of the students were pushing 15 and 16 years old, and while their behavior was rarely terrible (they did not want a confrontation, possibly a physical one, with Principal Netsky), they resisted the enticements of schooling and left as early as they could.

Did that bother the staff? Yes, in the sense that all teachers want receptive students—they allow us to do what we came to do—but we did not blame ourselves, or the institution of schooling, for student disinterest, recalcitrance, and occasional bad behavior. In our open and egalitarian schools, it was assumed that any student could—to some degree—succeed in school if she or he chose to do so. As we saw it, the students who resisted schooling were following their own volitions, values, beliefs, inclinations, or family histories. It was their problem, not ours. We—the staff, the school, and the system—had opened the doors and provided a warm, dry, and reasonably humane and orderly environment. We gave them instruction, athletics, pencils, pens, paper, field trips, and ice cream socials. We regarded as axiomatic that the amount of learning that a student brought to school and took away was her sole responsibility. And we had varying explanations as to why Bucky or Melody or Harry or Kathleen behaved in ways that made them difficult to reach and why they were inclined to leave as early as they could. Please note that our goal at that time was not equality, but equal opportunity. And while backgrounds, abilities, and inclinations varied, in our open and egalitarian school, it was assumed that any student could succeed. Our unit of analysis was the student—singular—not the institution.

But in the 1960s, there began a series of events that changed the unit of analysis from the individual student to the school organization. Catholic Worker Michael Harrington (1963) argued that for 40% of Americans, poverty was an inherited condition, and that federal intervention was necessary to break its cycle. President Kennedy became interested; and later, President Johnson, a long-time advocate for equality, reasoned that "the primary reason poor children do not escape from poverty is that they do not acquire basic cognitive skills" (Jencks et al., 1972, p. 7). Johnson's proposed solution was to put educational opportunities for poorer students on a par with those of more affluent students. The resulting Elementary and Secondary Education Act (ESEA) of 1965 was designed to "equalize educational opportunity" with federal funds directed toward schools serving disadvantaged students. Successful lobbying by the Chief State School Officers got the ESEA money distributed through state departments of education, with the latter keeping five percent for administration (Bailey & Mosher, 1968). Five percent of 15 billion dollars, in just the first year, was a lot of money. So the effort to equalize educational opportunity was paralleled by an expansion in the size of and the resources available to state departments of education.

Accompanying those resources was a requirement of "accountability": Please note the word. In the early 1960s, Robert McNamara, then Secretary of Defense, initiated a program to hold defense contractors accountable for federal funds received. President Johnson became a convert to McNamara's measures, and the notion of accountability raced through federal and state programs, including those directed toward education. Soon one could not attend an educational conference without hearing thirty times that "the public is demanding accountability."

Add it up: Expanded federal funding, enlarged and empowered state departments, and the doctrine of accountability. What do you get? State standardized tests. In states such as my own, Michigan—where local property taxes made up 75% of school costs—the state department had constitutional power over schools, but few tools with which to actualize that power. However, the newly-created state tests given to all 4th, 7th, and 10th graders gave the state a tool with which to examine the interior workings of schools. Moreover, students' test scores—probably for reasons of intelligibility and convenience—were averaged by schools, and the averages showed glaring differences among schools, particularly those serving more and less affluent students. Thus was born the notion of good schools vs. bad schools, effective schools vs. ineffective schools, and succeeding schools vs. failing schools. We always knew there were differences in schools' average scores. We knew at Thomas K. Beecher that our test scores were probably the lowest of any junior high in the area. However, because the unit of analysis was the individual, and because we had many successful students, we did not think of ourselves as a less-than-successful school—certainly not as a "failing" school.

But the events described above changed the focus from the individual and perhaps under-performing student, to the school. Whereas the prior discourse was about Thomas K. Beecher having some "hard-to-reach kids," the new discourse started with, "Thomas K. Beecher's scores are low. What is wrong with Thomas K. Beecher?" And what is more, as James Coleman pointed out in 1968, the expectation changed: schools—which had long been asked to offer equality "in"—were now expected to offer equality "out." So for the last 40 years, the educational establishment has been searching for institutional answers to what were formerly thought to be individual problems. As Karen Scott reminds us in her discussion included in this collection, our job is to "improve the school experience" and stop "pushing students out of school."

IN SEARCH OF WHAT MATTERS

Allow me to review some of the mile-markers in our search. I remember an early one because it began at Michigan State as "effective schools." These schools developed after Coleman et al. (1966) and Jencks et al. (1972) examined the effects of family on schooling. Coleman argued that schooling accounted for only about ten percent of the variance in student achievement. The remainder was accounted for by students' ability/aptitude, socio-economic background, and home environment. And in 1972, Jencks questioned popular assumptions about poverty, the notion that school reform could influence poverty, and the place of the school in reducing inequality. He concluded that

1. Poverty is not primarily hereditary; there is as much economic inequality among brothers as in the general population. 2. The primary reason some people end up richer is not that they have more adequate cognitive skills; equalizing everyone's reading scores would not apprecia-

bly reduce the number of economic "failures." 3. There is no evidence that school reform can substantially reduce the extent of cognitive inequality, as measured by verbal fluency, reading comprehension, or mathematical skills. Neither school resources nor segregation has an appreciable effect on either test scores or educational attainment. (Jencks et al., 1972, p. 7)

Coleman's and later Jencks' report set off a "storm of political controversy" (Chubb & Moe, 1990, p. 15). Educators were upset. Moreover, most economic studies of the direct relationship between educational resources (especially money) and student outcomes have reached conclusions similar to Coleman and Jencks (Shavelson & Towne, 2003, p. 42).

Among those upset was Michigan State sociologist Wilber Brookover who was fond of recalling how his poor and rural school in Indiana had vastly improved his own, and his classmates' lives. Brookover et al. (1982) embarked on a series of studies in schools serving economically poor students where test scores were high, and concluded not only that "achievement...is highly related to the organization" (p. 78), but that "any child can learn if we provide the appropriate teaching-learning environment" (p. 2). Brookover and his later associates, Larry Lezotte and Ron Edmonds (Lezotte & Passalacqua, 1978), created the"effective schools" movement which advocated for a stronger, more focused school organization.

Later researchers, Rowan, Bossert and Dwyer (1983) questioned the effectiveness of "effective schools," suggesting that the research had "failed to present models of school effectiveness that can adequately guide the process of school improvement" (p. 25). Similar work by Purkey and Smith (1983) concluded that the effective schools research was "weak in many respects, most notably in its tendency to present narrow, often simplistic, recipes for school improvement derived from non-experimental data" (p. 426). But the educational establishment had decided that the school was the unit of analysis, and cautionary notes by academics did not slow the search for an "effective" school organization that would neutralize student differences.

Another widely heralded effort was stimulated by Coleman, Hoffer, and Kilgore' s (1982) study, *High School and Beyond*, which noted that students in private—mostly Catholic—schools scored higher, had fewer discipline and attendance problems, and attended college at higher rates, independent of their parents' social and economic status. Loosely translated, better schools are like communities, a concept supported by Sara Lawrence Lightfoot's (1982) *The Good High School*, Gerald Grant's (1988) *The World We Created At Hamilton High*, and Michael Rutter' s (1984) *15,000 Hours*, all of which noted that students in ethically-based and community-like schools did better than students in schools that were less so.

Continuing in the restructuring vein, Ted Sizer—based on his earlier work (Sizer, 1982)—wrote in his late 1980s' book *Coalition of Effective Schools*, that schools were too large, bureaucratic, busy, filled with extraneous activities, and inattentive to the task of training minds. Sizer argued for a simpler structure, team teaching, fewer distractions, no more than 80 students per teacher, and a "culture of civility" that would both equalize opportunity and increase achievement. Sizer offered a different kind of school, smaller, more focused, less busy, with fewer offerings, more locally run, and less bureaucratic.

But despite isolated successes, the major school thrust was by states that asked schools for more accountability and greater coordination between what was taught and what was tested. There was a supporting parallel effort to reduce property taxes, a move stimulated by voter dissatisfaction with inflationary increases, and evidence that reliance on local property taxes made school funding inequitable. The solution was to equalize school funding and, however it was accomplished—with more or less reliance on property taxes—the states were generally called on to play a greater role in distributing school funds. Please note: I began at Thomas K. Beecher where the student was the unit of analysis. I described ESEA and accountability testing as turning the school into the unit of analysis, and now I suggest that accountability tests combined with property tax relief—read here "more centralized funding"—was turning the state into the unit of analysis.

A word of caution about the term "state." Most often it refers to the state department of education. But in the mid-1990s, two Michigan superintendents, Wayne Peters (1995) and Diane Sheerhom (1995), concerned about the number of directives coming from the state capitol toward their offices, added up the number of directives that came to schools from the Michigan Department of Education, the Michigan Legislature, the Governor's office, and state attorney general in 20 years. The total was 289 separate initiatives coming from the state capitol to the schools. Moreover, most of them had several—up to 50—separate provisions. The point is that the states—qua states—were quite free to intervene in schools whenever they saw fit.

There was, however, an alternative view to greater state control. Stimulated perhaps by the early 1990s Republican resurgence, Chubb and Moe (1990) argue that the more effective schools were the more autonomous schools, and that the problem was with the moving of authority, upward into the state rather than downward into the schools. As they argued,

> In the private sector, where schools are controlled by markets—indirectly and from the bottom up—autonomy is generally high. In the public sector, where schools are controlled by politics—directly and from the top down—autonomy is generally low (p. 183).

Less directly, Chubb and Moe's argument was that the large and gluttonous educational bureaucracy is more interested in sustaining itself than in serving students. Those years were characterized by efforts to dissolve the bureaucracy, abolish the U.S. Department of Education, move the system to "choice, charters, and vouchers," as Michigan's then-State Board President used to say, and turn responsibility back to schools and their local constituencies.

But such efforts, while having some success at encouraging charter schools and greater student choice, were paralleled by federally funded efforts—Goals 2000 most notably—that gave increasing power to states. The efforts were supported by educationists, arguing for a systemic reform that would more closely connect parts of the educational bureaucracy, thought at that time to be too loosely coupled. As stated by Smith and O'Day (1990), a systemic reform would create "challenging and progressive curriculum frameworks, a supportive organizational environment and instructional content directed toward complex thinking and problem solving" (p. 235). Again, the result was a larger, more powerful, more centralized state apparatus. Most recently—and with the encouragement of the No Child Left Behind Act—systemic reform has morphed into "comprehensive school reform," with fiscal and policy instruments, uniform content standards, performance standards at all levels, professional development, more scrutiny of everything, and with underlying and unstated elevated levels of bureaucratic authority. The entire effort has been fueled by dire predictions of our country being left behind in the global economy and a stream of invidious comparisons between the performances of American students with their peers from around the world.

All these reforms, I note, are based on the assumption that if the organizational elements or variables can be properly controlled, then appropriate and predictable teacher and student behavior will follow. And the reforms of the last 40 years have been directed at controlling the structure, all in the hope that the school or state—now national—educational system can be developed in ways that neutralize differences in students' backgrounds and give all a greater chance. I certainly would not question the intent; I merely point out that the primary result of 40 years of good intentions has been a larger and larger educational machine.

Has it Helped?

Now the question I would pose—and this is not a rhetorical question because I don't know the answer: "Have 40 years of organized efforts, 40 years of elevating the unit of analysis from the individual to the school to the state (even to the nation) improved learning?" Some things are definitely better—high school graduation rates have improved; minority attendance and achievement have improved; there is more equitable treatment of women, children with special needs, alternative-minded students, people of color, and immigrants. We are now asking ourselves questions about social justice and engaging in direct action to assist students who—at Thomas K. Beecher 40 years ago—we were happy to see the last of. Overall, we have a more equitable educational system.

But there are a few caveats. Educational reform became organizational reform. And despite the advice of people like Ted Sizer who say "make it smaller," our more libertarian friends who say "get rid of it," or more conservative philosophers like Frederick Hayek (1988) who say "because you think you can understand reality does not mean you can control it," we have vastly increased the educational bureaucracy. We did not reform "education." We reformed the delivery system, the bureaucracy. And when bureaucracies have a problem, they often hire another specialist to take care of the problem. That is what we have done. Thus, while 30 years ago we had one professional teacher for every 27 students, we now have one professional teacher for every 18 students. And while 30 years ago, 70 percent of the people in education were teachers, now that figure is 49%.

Who are these other people? Secretaries, aides, cooks, bus drivers, coaches, counselors, psychologists, researchers, technicians, computer repairers, testing experts, administrators at all levels, and specialists assigned to translate the 674 pages of No Child Left Behind Act. In other words, while the ostensible conversation has been about quality and equality, test scores and standards, the system has responded by building a more specialized, differentiated, and expensive educational enterprise. Now I do not recommend that we go back to how Thomas K. Beecher was in 1962, but there are a few observations.

The first is that everything is more expensive in terms of money, people, and time. We have created a much denser, demanding, and differentiated educational system. A corollary of this is that authority is moving—not down to the school level as recommended by reformers such as Sizer and scholars such as Chubb and Moe—but up to policy makers, legislators, and administrators at distant levels. Despite the romantic talk of moving decisions down to the school and classroom level, we are following a long tradition of reform by moving authority to the state—even the nation—up the bureaucratic ladder and away from schools, students, and teachers.

The second observation is that transaction costs—the "costs of doing business"—the time and effort it takes to attend, not to productive work, but to the running of the institution, has vastly increased. Not only do we have 51% of the people assigned to non-teaching functions, the enterprise is taking greater amounts of time even from teachers. I have watched this for several years—and I invite teachers in the field to ask yourselves if this is the case—are you spending more time on organizational as opposed to instructional matters? In-service meetings, testing and test training, reporting, special education meetings, answering inquiries from someone up the ladder, dealing with forms and demonstrating that one is doing what is required, all take a large amount of the school day. The percentages of time directed toward these and similar tasks run from 25 to 40% with a (conservative) average of 30%. So if we added the efforts of the 51% of the people who do not teach and 30%

percent of the time of the 49% who do teach, one might conclude that more than 60% of the human energy in education is going toward "running the machine." It is a sobering thought.

The third observation concerns equity. Our goal has been to decrease social distance, to run schools in ways that will overcome the disadvantages that students bring through the door. But that goal might be moving away from us at a greater rate than the system can keep up. The importance of education at all levels, the increasing notion of education as a private good with exchange value, the anxiety of the already well-off and those who want to be well-off to get their children into better schools in order to enhance their life-chances, the fact that educational credentials are more and more used to legitimate social distances, are all increasing. We educators view our enterprise as a collective good. Our thinking is egalitarian. What we do not account for is that education is also an intensely private good, and that at the other end of the social scale are ambitious parents and students who are competing for society's preferred places, whose educational aspirations far exceed the institution's, and to whom equity is an abstraction, and averaged scores, a matter of indifference.

As a recent reporter in *The Economist* noted:

"... the bounds of society are being strained. A new aristocracy of talent is retreating into golden ghettos, and running the global economy in their own interests. The logic of talent is meritocratic; the logic of democracy is egalitarian. The two are bound to conflict" (Woolridge, 2006, p. 64).

Now I would ask you: in the face of what we have done in the name of equity, in the directions we have moved, the organization we have created, and in the ability of the organization to do what we want it to do, are we moving along a trajectory that will, in the long run, serve our intended purposes?

REFERENCES

Bailey, S. K., & Mosher, E. (1968). *ESEA: The Office of Education Administers a Law*. Syracuse, NY: Syracuse University Press.

Brookover, W., Beamer, L., Efthim, H., Hathaway, D., Lezotte, L., Miller, S., Passalacqua, J., & Tornatzky, L. (1982). *Creating Effective Schools*. Holmes Beach, FL: Learning Publications, Inc.

Chubb, J. E. & Moe, T. M. (1990). *Politics, Markets and America's Schools*. Washington D.C.: The Brookings Institute.

Coleman, J. S., Campbell, E. Q., Hobson, C. J., McPartland, J., Mood, A. M., Weinfeld, F. D., & York, R. L. (1966). *Equality of Educational Opportunity (FS 5.238.38001)*. Washington, D.C.: U.S. Department of Health, Education and Welfare.

Coleman, J. S., Hoffer, T., Kilgore, S. (1982). *High School Achievement: Public, Catholic, and Private Schools Compared*. New York: Basic Books.

Grant, G. (1988). *The World we Created at Hamilton High*. Cambridge:Harvard University Press.

Harrington, M. (1963). *The Other America: Poverty in the United States*. Baltimore, MD: Penguin Books.

Hayek, F. (1988). *The Fatal Conceit: The Errors Of Socialism*. Chicago: University of Chicago Press.

Jencks, C., Smith, M., Acland, H., Bane, M.J., Cohen, D., Gintis, H., Heyns, B., & Michelson, S. (1972). *Inequality: A Reassessment of the Effect of Family and Schooling in America*. New York: Basic Books.

Lezotte, L. W., & Passalacqua, J. (1978). *Individual School Buildings do Account for Differences in Measured Pupil performance*. East Lansing: Michigan State University, Institute for Research on Teaching.

Lightfoot, S. L. (1982). *The Good High School*. Boston: Houghton Mifflin.

Peters, W. (1997). *The Effects of State Directives on Local Schools and School Superintendents*. Unpublished PhD dissertation. East Lansing, MI: Michigan State University.

Purkey, S. C., & Smith, M. S. (1983). Effective schools: A review. *Elementary School Journal* 83: 426–452.

Rowan, B., Bossert, S. T., & Dwyer, D. C. (1983). Research on effective schools: A cautionary note. *Educational Researcher* 12(4): 24–31.

Rutter, M. (1984). *Fifteen Thousand Hours: Secondary Schools and their Effects on Children*. Cambridge, MA: Harvard University Press.

Shavelson, R.J. & Towne, L. (Eds.) (2003). *Scientific Research in Education*. Washington, D.C: National Academy Press.

Sheerhorn, D. (1995). *The Effects of State Directives on Local Schools and School Superintendents*. Unpublished PhD dissertation. East Lansing, MI: Michigan State University.

Sizer, T. (1982). *Horace's compromise*. Boston: Houghton Mifflin.

Smith, M. S., & O'Day, J. (1990). Systemic school reform. In S. H. Fuhrman & B. Malen (Eds.), *The Politics of Curriculum and Testing* (1990 Politics of Education Association Yearbook, pp. 233–266). Philadelphia: Falmer Press.

Wooldridge, A. (2006). The battle for brainpower. *The Economist* 380(8498):48–66.

SUGGESTED READINGS

Chubb, J. E. & Moe, T. M. (1990). *Politics, Markets and America's Schools*. Washington D.C.: The Brookings Institute.

The Chubb and Moe studies are all classics, learning particularly toward the conservative side in education, economics, and politics.

Coleman, J. S., Hoffer, T., Kilgore, S. (1982). *High School Achievement: Public, Catholic, and Private Schools Compared*. New York: Basic Books.

A classic statistical comparison between the three types of schools regarding extra-curricular as well as academic issues.

Jencks, C., Smith, M., Acland, H., Bane, M.J., Cohen, D., Gintis, H., Heyns, B., & Michelson, S. (1972). *Inequality: A Reassessment of the Effect of Family and Schooling in America.* New York: Basic Books.

Sizer, T. (1982). *Horace's Compromise.* Boston: Houghton Mifflin.

Sizer is known for his controversial suggestions for school reform as well as his work with teacher unions.

MULTIPLE CHOICE QUESTIONS

1. The author relies on his experiences gained while teaching at

    a. Martin Luther King High School

    b. Thomas Jefferson High School

    c. Thomas K Beecher Junior High School

    d. Susan B. Anthony Junior High School

2. Catholic Worker Michael Harrington suggested in 1963 that what percentage of Americans in poverty had "inherited" that poverty?

    a. 34 %

    b. 40%

    c. 27%

    d. 80%

3. Who was president when "the notion of accountability raced through federal and state programs?"

    a. John F. Kennedy

    b. Ronald Reagan

    c. Bill Clinton

    d. Lyndon Johnson

4. Who created the "Effective Schools" movement?

    a. Wilbur Brookover

    b. Sara Lightfoot

    c. John Dewey

    d. Steven P. Jones

5. Ted Sizer suggested in *Coalition of Effective Schools* (1982) that

    a. school should start later in the day

    b. public schools could never be as good as private schools

    c. schools were too large and bureaucratic

    d. schools can fix any of our social problems

6. Chubb and Moe (1990) suggested that the more effective schools were

    a. only to be found in northeastern states

    b. the more autonomous ones

    c. those who were under the control of the state, rather than locally

    d. racially mixed

7. According to the author, the reforms he describes are

    a. based on the idea of organizational control

    b. never going to work

    c. unconstitutional

    d. similar to those he experienced in his early career

8. According to the author, educational reform became

    a. teacher education reform

    b. political reform

    c. monetary reform

    d. organizational reform

9. What percentage of education employees are teachers?

    a. 10%

    b. 28%

    c. 49%

    d. 70%

10. The author argues that what percentage of human energy in education goes to "running the machine?"

    a. 60%

    b. 45%

    c. 30%

    d. 10%

Hey, All You Data Crunchers: What Schools Need Is a Happiness Index

SUSAN OHANIAN

The first rule in evaluating schools should be to check the vomit index: What practices and procedures annoy and infuriate students? In an informal poll of students in grades 3–12, students reported what they most dislike about school:

1. Getting up before dawn and waiting for the bus in the dark

2. Excessive homework

3. Can't get a drink when you're thirsty

4. Assigned seats

5. Dirty, unsafe bathrooms, often without toilet paper, towels, or soap

6. Teachers and principals ignore bullying

7. Mindless memorization and worksheets

8. Disappearance of recess

9. Shortening of lunch time—students have no time for social exchanges

10. Disappearance of choice—learning centers in elementary school, electives in high school

11. Total focus on high stakes tests, eliminating every other aspect of schooling

12. Too many different classes, making the mind jump from one topic to another. In one student's words, "Schools try to teach a million things at once. It hurts my head."

One sixth grader offered this poignant observation, "Teachers think I'm dumber than I am. They don't listen to what I say. If they did, they might be surprised." In a school culture dominated by relentless standardized test questions, a tenth grader observed that the right questions are missing. This tenth grader suggested, "Why don't teachers ever ask students, 'How are you doing?' Ask what's good, what's bad. Ask what students need." As every real teacher knows, this type of information, ignored by data crunchers, is crucial to the student's well being.

In a poetry anthology compiled by Lydia Okutoro, *In Quiet Storm: Voices from Young Black Poets* (2002), a young Texas student, Amy Auzenne, speaks for many:

The Question

You never asked about

my favorite color,

my first love,

the holes in my heart,

the state of my soul,

or the weight of your words upon me.

"They never asked" is a refrain Steve Orel has heard many times from young people in Birmingham, Alabama. Working in an adult education GED program, Steve was surprised by the number of teenagers trying to get into the program. When he asked them why they weren't in high school, they all showed him the same official termination papers. The reason for termination was identical for all: *Lack of interest*. Steve wondered just how much "lack of interest" there could be when the students were actually trying so desperately to get back to school. Upon investigation, he discovered that 522 African American students had been terminated for "lack of interest" between the last day rated for average daily attendance monies and the administration of the high stake's state tests. Birmingham schools were in danger of being taken over by the state if they didn't improve their scores, and as every educator knows, the easiest way to raise test scores is to eliminate the probable low scorers. It ain't pretty but it's life in the Standaristo universe.

Because he asked the questions that so many school folks, intent on test scores, don't find time to ask, Steve discovered all sorts of reasons for the World of Opportunity (WOO) student failures in regular schools: family illness, lack of appropriate clothing, inability to cope with the curriculum, and so on and on. Given appropriate support, many WOO students have flourished. One of the early WOO enrollees, dismissed from regular high school for "lack of interest," scored 100% on the GED literacy section and immediately enrolled in the University of Alabama honors program. Since then, many students have gone on to college after earning their GEDs through the WOO program.

Education activists from around the country traveled to Birmingham to pay tribute to the WOO and to work with the students. Gathered around a table, trying to figure out a way to support the WOO, they came up with the idea of a CD: *No Child Left Behind? Bring Back the Joy: 15 Songs of Resistance*. Through the CD, they hope to promote the idea that across the country, teachers and students have a lot in common, and we can lift their voices together in these songs of resistance to government interference. The CD is priced at $15, and all proceeds go to the WOO. For more information, see: http://susanohanian.org/bbtj.html

LOOKING AT STUDENTS

To prepare for this conference, I looked through many disciplinary referral forms. Some popular ones are listed:

Reasons for detention:

- Tardiness

- Excessive talking

- Disrespect

- Sleeping

- Eating

- Failure to complete assigned work

- Lack of material

- Poor attitude

- Mischief

- Littering

- Phone violation

- Restlessness

What would happen if the tables were turned and this very checklist were applied to teachers during required in-services? Of course, looking at discipline policies in New York, Chicago, and Los Angeles renders these reasons quaint. Even regions we might consider bucolic seem to eye students harshly. Take, for example, the Beaufort County Schools. According to their district's Discipline Referral Form, folks in South Carolina are on the lookout for sexual harassment, possession of drug paraphernalia, habitual truancy, gambling, counterfeiting, bribery, intimidation, burglary, extortion, fraud, homicide, kidnapping/abduction, prostitution, vehicle theft, and weapons (Type 0, Type 1, Type 2, and Type 3).

When a student walking through the school door is viewed as a potential criminal, how does this affect the education he receives? Have we ever considered what a checklist for positive attributes might look like? What if we issued referrals for expressions of kindness, courtesy, helpfulness, humor, and ingenuity?

LOOKING FOR CONNECTIONS AT AN ALTERNATIVE HIGH SCHOOL

When I taught in an alternative high school—kids excluded from the 'regular' high school but required to attend school because of their age or as stipulation of their probation—I was surprised to discover these kids' common complaint about regular school. What these kids hated most about regular high school were the bells. Not algebra, not essays for English—it was the bells that drove them to despair. As Mike put it, "You'd just get into something and then the bell rang and you'd have to go start something else."

Our alternative school was part of the BOCES (Board of Cooperative Educational Services), a New York State agency formed to encourage local school districts to pool their resources. With community recommendations,

BOCES came up with 220 things a student needs to know to get a high school diploma (algebra was not on the list). We teachers came up with the curriculum to validate these 220 concepts. We put the list in file drawers. Students had free access to these file drawers and could choose whatever they wanted to work on. More often than not, a student would work on, say, a social studies requirement for a couple of weeks and then switch to something else for a while. Schools might do well to consider why they are so devoted to timetables. What difference does it make in which order a student learns what the school wants him to learn?

Then there was Jack. We had three rules at our school: no drugs, no swearing, and read (non-academic material) for half an hour. He ignored rule three and his swearing quickly taught me to turn a deaf ear to him. One day I brought in a *Harper's* article about Scrabble hustlers in New York City, and Jack was immediately impressed by the money they made. The article mentioned that serious Scrabble players liked the *Funk and Wagnall's Dictionary* because it had lots of extra word lists, words beginning with the same prefix, and so on. Jack began pestering me for that dictionary. I told him I was sure our *American Heritage Dictionary* would be adequate for his needs, but he wouldn't agree. To tell the truth, I felt pretty good about telling my supervisor that a student had requested a dictionary recommended in *Harper's*. After all, everybody has certain preconceptions about *those* students.

Jack then retired to a corner of the room with the Scrabble board and the dictionary for six months. I think his solitary game playing may have started because he was so obnoxious that nobody else would play with him, but soon he was locked into a battle of wills with himself. My supervisor deserves credit. Having hired a teacher after extensive interviewing, he then allowed that teacher to be completely responsible for her students. He would nod over at the corner and say, "Jack still playing Scrabble?" And I would smile and say, "Yes, Jack is still *working* at Scrabble." Frank Smith's wise observation is my credo: When a student persists at the same activity over and over again, he is not wasting time. He is getting out of that activity what he needs. Students don't set out to be weird. Students want to be "regular." We need to allow them space and time to come to grips with their own personal demons, and time and space to learn how to be as regular as they can be.

I won't pretend that my smile didn't become forced by the third or fourth month and that I didn't become fairly desperate by the fifth, but no one can *make* a high school student study anything. One can only provide an environment of possibility. Somewhere along this Scrabble marathon, Jack agreed to start reading half an hour a day, a period that he soon extended to two hours or more. Still, he did no "work," that is, no assignments which would lead toward his high school graduation. Then one day, after six months of solitary Scrabble, Jack challenged me to a match. After beating me soundly, he settled into working his way toward a high school diploma.

Years later I read *Word Freak: Heartbreak, Triumph, Genius, and Obsession in the World of Competitive Scrabble Players* by the *Wall Street Journal* writer Stefan Fatsis (2002). Fatsis says that scrabble is about mastering the rules; it is about a balance between risk and reward. Scrabble is also about linguistics, psychology, and mathematics. It throws light on such notions as brilliance, memory, competition, failure, and hope. And, Fatsis observes that, that at the national competition level, Scrabble is also about weirdness.

I would say that all of this applied to Jack. I would say that one of my greatest strengths as a teacher is the ability to accommodate weirdness. But weirdness is a concept—and a reality—unacknowledged in Standardisto documents, in state standards, and in NCLB. Bill Gates does not fund programs to provide time and space for weird kids.

KNOWLEDGE WITHOUT CONSCIENCE

In Tennessee, an adult monitor reported to the principal that a first grade teacher talked to two crying children who didn't understand a test question. The teacher consoled the crying children, saying, "Don't worry. Just do your best." The teacher received a written reprimand because conversation with students is forbidden during test time. The reporter assured the public reading the paper, "Test results were not affected and will remain valid in the system's bank of testing data."

Bank of testing data!? What about a 6-year-old's tears? A teacher is reprimanded for stopping for tears? What have we come to? Knowledge without conscience is the ruin of one's soul. What good are statistics about children if our hearts are cold? There are two types of people in the world. Those who stop for tears and those who don't. Who do you want teaching *your* children?

Slavish obedience to state mandates can do terrible things to people. Take what happened in Indianapolis on September 11 and September 12, 2001. Despite the nation-wide alarm, school officials required students to continue the scheduled state testing on those days. They reasoned that students should be able to compartmentalize their emotions. This meant that Indianapolis students were asked to shove aside the emotions engulfing everyone else in the country and concentrate on doing the work required by the state.

For me, the moral absolutes about teaching always center on individual students. That's why every time I give a talk I read a letter that a former student, Michael, wrote to me . It represents who I am as a teacher and the values I hope to exemplify for students. First, a little background to introduce Michael. My team-teaching partner and I lobbied to be assigned the worst readers in the school—if we could have them two periods a day. This meant that Michael was my student two periods a day in both 7th and 8th grade. If such a thing as dyslexia exists, Michael could have been its poster child. He had all the classic signs and also all the classic complaints about school. A bright boy from a concerned, loving family, popular with his peers and just discovering girls, Michael had experienced years of school failure. He approached the printed page with evasion, bluff, and eventually, panic. When I asked my seventh and eighth graders to fill in the blank in the following sentence: *I would rather read than___; I would rather write than____*, Michael wrote, "I would rather read than write; I would rather write than DIE." I can't say I was surprised. For Michael, in his eight years of school, reading and writing had been a kind of slow death . While many students pretend and play that school game of lugging books home from school, checking books out of the library, and claiming to spend the weekend reading, Michael was candid in his dislike of books.

When I first told Michael's class that we were going to exchange daily notes, he was not shy about telling me his opinion of the idea: "Why would we write to you when you're standing right there?" But once he recognized my intransigence, recognized that his charming wheedling wouldn't move me, Michael gradually became an avid note-writer. His notes were messy and horribly spelled, but they revealed a humor, wit and compassion that was lovely to behold. In January, when I complained about the snow, Michael advised that, "I just take the months as they come."

As spring approached, I began to ask students to describe what they thought were the first signs of spring, confessing that for me, the asparagus ads in the newspaper are a sure sign that winter is loosening its strong grip. The kids, of course, thought that this was a hoot, surely it was a teacher thing—paying attention to asparagus. But they too began to watch the papers, leaving ads on my desk, competing for who would find the best asparagus bargain for Mrs. O.

Michael won the contest, announcing one day that he would type his note:

Dear Mrs. O,

As you no I want to Boston firday. It was a lot fo fun. Wen I first got to Boston we drov aron looking for a parking plas. We fon one and then we got out of the car. We walkt to a fance market and had a bite to aet.

Then we went to the aquarium and that was eciting. There was a shoe with dolphins and seals. Wan we got out we want by a fruit markt. I thogt of you and chekt the pric of asprgus. It isi $1.00 a lb in Boston and 3 heds of letis for $1.00. Boston is a long way to go for asprgus tho.

Your friend,
Michael

Not long before Michael graduated from eighth grade, his mother wrote to me, "I like to think I would have written to thank you on my own, but I am writing this letter because Michael asked me to. We both want to thank you. Michael was very emphatic that our thanks should be in a letter, in words that would last. He says that when you want to tell someone something important, you put it in a letter. I know where he learned that, and I thank you." This is what is scary about teaching: We can only teach who we are.

I share Michael's asparagus letter almost every time I give a talk. I share it to remind teachers of what really counts in the work that we do. Fifteen or so years after Michael wrote that letter, I gave a talk at the State University of New York at Albany. Afterwards, a teacher from my old district came up to greet me. She was Michael's first-grade teacher and still lives next door to his parents. Michael is now a famous chef in an up-scale restaurant in Connecticut. I wonder if our asparagus connection gives me the right to claim partial credit for his success. I don't remember his achievement test scores, but I do know that Michael learned something important from me. He learned that words count, that words can give information and joy; he learned that carefully chosen words can make a difference. He learned that when you care about someone you send them a letter.

If Michael were in school today, he'd be denied a high school diploma, and then he wouldn't have been able to get work as a chef. Or as an auto mechanic; barber; bus driver; draftsman; baker; broadcast technician; cardiology technologist; communications dispatcher; electro-neurodiagnostic technologist; fingerprint classifier; forklift operator; graphics designer, heating, air conditioning, and refrigeration mechanic; hotel desk clerk; land surveyor; legal secretary; medical transcriptionist; numerical control machinist; optometric technician; paramedic; plumber; robotics technician; sheet metal worker; shorthand reporter/court reporter; solar energy system installer; small appliance repairer; surgical technician; tool and die maker; translator/interpreter; veterinary technician; ward clerk (medical); webpage designer and so on.

Read the list again. How many of these occupations would you like to eliminate as not being necessary or useful in your life? And how about butchers, bakers, candlestick makers, gardeners, and stone wall builders?

The danger of leaving no child behind, as it is currently being pursued by many schools, is that an entire generation will be left behind, alienated from schools, trained to think, from the time they enter a school building, that they aren't good enough; they don't measure up. After mandatory summer school, Paige, 11-years-old and in the 3rd grade for the third time, told a reporter that other kids are "like little bitty ants." Asked why she was held back again and again, Paige grew quiet and then said, "I guess the teachers didn't like me." And now we're extending this concept to pre-kindergarten. After one four-year-old took a readiness test, he went up to his teacher and softly said, "Let's not tell Mommy. She thinks I'm smart."

18

PSYCHIC DISEQUILIBRIUM

In *Blood, Bread, and Poetry*, Adrienne Rich (1994) notes, "When someone with the authority of a teacher, say, describes the world and you are not in it, there is a moment of psychic disequilibrium, as if you looked into a mirror and saw nothing." As schools implement No Child Left Behind, students experience long school days filled with psychic disequilibrium. Scott Howard, Superintendent of Perry, Ohio, public schools, puts it this way: "The ESEA [No Child Left Behind Act] is like a Russian novel. That's because it's long, it's complicated, and in the end, everybody gets killed."

Imagine being in kindergarten and asked to read this list, a test of Nonsense Word Fluency for kindergartners:

hoj	rij	ad	bol	em
buv	haj	en	wof	loj
tuc	ful	vab	fum	han
hol	mun	yud	dav	dub
paj	jav	lak	diz	nom
viv	kon	juf	miz	vuv
zep	yac	dac	jom	rej
zuz	vum	zes	tej	zub
qob	jec	oc	rit	def
neb	kif	wab	ov	ruj

This subtest is part of the *Dynamic Indicators of Basic Early Literacy Skills 6th edition* (Good & Kaminski (2003) Kindergarten Scoring Booklet DIBELS Benchmark Assessment http://dibels.uoregon.edu

Think about it: Five-year-olds who come to school already knowing how to read are asked to 'read' nonsense words that make no sense. Five-year-olds who don't know how to read are labeled deficient if they can't read those same nonsense words. As fingerpaints, play house, blocks, and recess are eliminated from kindergarten, we need to realize that much of the 5-year-old's day is now based on fear of failure. In February 2006, L. J. Williamson wrote in the *Los Angeles Times*, "My son already hates school and he's just halfway through kindergarten." Williamson listed a litany of drudgery. And the misery doesn't end in kindergarten. Children in K-3 are graded throughout the year on how many of these nonsense words they can read in one minute, and the curriculum gets deformed to prepare children for such tests.

My little education group in Vermont has launched an offensive against DIBELS with the publication of *Examining DIBELS: What It Is and What It Does*, edited by Ken Goodman (2006). We also have a website, http://www.vsse/dibels, whose mission is to inform teachers and parents of the dangers of DIBELS . Besides putting too much emphasis on one aspect of the reading skill, DIBELS represents the current mania for pushing academics on younger and younger children. Some four- and five-year-olds are ready to learn to read. Others are not. And labeling those who need more time as deficient is sure to turn them into children who hate school.

It is worth noting that the Finns, whose students score highest in international tests, put a great emphasis on play in the early school years, not introducing reading instruction until children are eight years old.

HAPPINESS INDEX

What would happen if, instead of viewing children as being deficit or criminal, we began to look for happiness in them? Why does it seem like such a radical idea, asking school children: Are you happy? We could start each day with this suggestion, "Think of one thing that could increase the possibility for this being a good day for all of us." Then end the day with the question, "Was today a good day for you? What added to (or took away from) your happiness?

Surely schools can steal a few minutes away from the Standardisto curriculum each day and devote them to happiness. Operating, as so many schools do now, on the principle articulated by the Athenian lawmaker Solon: "Count no man happy until he is dead," seems, at best, counter-productive. At worst, it results in the Beaufort County School District Discipline Referral Form.

Jeremy Bentham, the Eighteenth Century political theorist, put forth the Greatest Happiness principle, declaring that the best society is the one where the citizens are happiest—All citizens. This means that the right moral action is that which produces the most happiness for all the people. Can you imagine the Standardisto outrage if a school superintendent proposed this as his district's mission statement? But is it such a radical idea? Maybe it is past time for us all to take another look at the opening passage of our Declaration of Independence: *We hold these truths to be self-evident, that all men are created equal, that they are endowed by their Creator with certain unalienable Rights, that among these are Life, Liberty and the pursuit of Happiness.* It doesn't say pursuit of happiness everywhere except in school.

In 1972, the king of Bhutan declared that his small Himalayan country (which is the size of Switzerland) would henceforth measure progress by gross national happiness instead of gross national product. With our present hysteria over test scores, I wonder if any school board in the land would have the nerve to declare that a school is as good as its students' Happiness Index. Declare it and then work to raise the level of happiness. After all, even McDonald's and Kentucky Fried Chicken are trying to figure out if their cows and chickens are happy. This offers schools a radically different corporate model to consider than the standard Business Roundtable/neutron Jack Welch approach. If McDonald's and Kentucky Fried Chicken are sponsoring research to find out answers to such questions as *Are cows ever happy? Do pigs feel pain? What do chickens really want?*, can our schools do less?

Put aside, for the moment, the question of whether McDonald's and KFC are being somewhat disingenuous. Just consider the new territory they are entering: asking scientific questions about an animal's feelings. That's worth repeating: asking scientific questions about an animal's feelings. Now, consider how far schools have been driven away from this territory. The fact is that it is inconceivable to imagine the current U. S. Department of Education sponsoring research to find out answers to such questions as:

- What causes kindergartners to feel pain?

- Are 5th graders ever happy?

- What do 7th graders really want?

These questions should give parents and teachers pause. And it should give them a cause for which they can join hands and march together. Why aren't such questions taken seriously any more? Why isn't a kindergartner's Happiness Index taken as seriously as his phonemic awareness score? Why don't we ask high schoolers this question: *What do you really want?* Ask that—and shut up and listen to the answer—instead of issuing rules such as nobody gets a high school diploma without passing a high stakes math test based on algebra, geometry, statistics, and probability and a literacy test requiring deconstruction of a sonnet and the use of the semicolon.

Questions about children's happiness are neither frivolous nor rhetorical. The cruelty of No Child Left Behind puts childhood at grave risk, setting schools on a course that will produce very, very angry children who grow up to be adults whose values are very skewed and who are mad as hell to boot. Let's judge NCLB by Jeremy Bentham's standards. He declared that a law is good if it increases the happiness of the citizens and decreases their misery. If it does not, it is bad.

I call for a nation-wide commitment to working for the Happiness Index in our schools. In the June 29, 2003 *New York Times* David Barboza wrote that "Some food retailers have introduced labels indicating that an animal was raised with care." Can schools do any less? Every teacher, every year, must be able to testify that every child was educated with care. Childhood is short; it is our obligation to make sure it is also sweet.

Scandinavian countries score at the top of the charts on international tests. On many measures, the Scandinavian countries are also among the happiest and they have the clearest concept of the common good. Here's the percentage of children aged 11 to 15 agreeing that "Most of the students in my class[es] are kind and helpful":

Switzerland 81

Sweden 77

Germany 76

Denmark 73

France 54

United States 53

Russia 46

England 43

In "Solving for Patterns,", an essay in *The Art of the Common Place*, Wendell Berry (2002) opens with the observation that "Our dilemma in agriculture now is that the industrial methods that have so spectacularly solved some of the problems of food production have been accompanied by 'side effects' so damaging as to threaten the survival of farming." He notes that he could as well be talking about school systems. Berry discusses three kinds of solutions: solutions that cause new problems, solutions that make things worse and good solutions. Of his 14 good solutions, I zero in on two points: *A good solution should be cheap* (not enriching one person by the distress or impoverishment of another) and here is Number 10:

Good solutions exist only in proof, and are not to be expected from absentee owners or absentee experts. Problems must be solved in work and in place, with particular knowledge, fidelity, and care, by people who will suffer the consequences of their mistakes. **There is no theoretical or ideal *practice*.** Practical advice or direction from people who have no practice may have some value, but its value is questionable and is limited. The divisions of capital, management, and labor, characteristic of an industrial system, are therefore utterly alien to the health of farming—as they probably also are to the health of manufacturing. The good health of a farm depends on the farmer's mind; the good health of his mind has its dependence, and its proof, in physical work. The good farmer's mind and his body—his management and his labor—work together as intimately as his heart and his lungs. And the capital of a well-farmed farm by definition includes the farmer, mind and body both. Farmer and farm are one thing, an organism.

If we are ever to have happy children, we must throw out the federally-sanctioned absentee owners and absentee experts, profiteers and their lackeys who will first smother our public schools and then bury them. Instead, we must look to the particular knowledge, fidelity, and care of **local remedies**. John Adams wrote that "The happiness of society is the end of government." Let us return to our radical roots: let us bring the founding principle of the American Revolution to the communities served by our schools and ask if it isn't a worthwhile end to aim for.

Because I run a website that advocates for children, I get a lot of mail from desperate parents and grandparents. This mom's note shows what happens when schools ignore Adams' principle of the happiness of society as the end of government.

> My son is now 15 and in the 9th grade. He doesn't do anything but put his head down in class and sleep. This is the extent of his work. He is in high school with all new teachers who were poorly informed about Matthew. I have to go up to the school and explain what needs to be done. In the past 2 days I have received emails that he has zero for not doing his work. This means totally nothing to him. We have lost him. I just don't know what to do anymore.

A 10th grader taught me an important lesson in my first year of teaching. Although I had not trained to be a teacher, with an emergency credential, I found myself in a New York City high school larger than my hometown. I was lucky to have a very helpful department chairman who offered me a lot of practical advice. When it was time for the official observation, I did a show-and-tell lecture on Julius Caesar. The chairman said I did pretty well, but he was concerned about the girl in the back of the room who was reading a newspaper throughout the lecture. He told me that at one point he leaned across the aisle and asked her, "Don't you think you should put away that paper and pay attention to what your teacher is saying?" He was startled and discomfited when she replied, "Who the hell are you? If she wants me to do that, let *her* tell me."

After a long pause, I took a deep breath and told him, "Well, when you think about it, who the hell are you? I was in error by not introducing you. That girl didn't know who you were, coming in with your briefcase, writing your notes. But more importantly, you don't know who *she* is. She had been truant for half the year and now she comes to class to read the *Daily News*, which I buy for her. This isn't where I plan to leave her, but it is a start."

I'm proud that first year teacher had such good instincts. We are in danger of losing our very professionalism—and our students—if we continue to let classroom authority be stolen from us. All educators should read "Antigone," who does not flinch from the moral need to bury her brother, despite her king's command that she must not. Antigone chooses family over king. We must choose children over state.

My favorite story ever about teaching and learning and standards and values appeared in the *New York Times'* "Metropolitan Diary" for November 1, 1989. A woman driving in mid-town Manhattan made an illegal right turn and was pulled over by a stern-looking cop. He took her license and registration and explained the error of her ways. Then he let her go with a warning. As she started to drive off, the officer queried, "Aren't you going to ask why I didn't give you a ticket?" When she nodded, he grinned and replied, "You were my first-grade teacher."

Surely no teacher can read that story without both jubilation and terror. I spent three days making lists of students who I thought would have let me off and students who would have gleefully thrown the book at me. If we could go into our classrooms every day with the thought that these kids are tomorrow's traffic cops, the world would be a better place.

REFERENCES

Barboza, D. (2003, June 29). Development of biotech crops is booming in Asia. *The New York Times*. p. A3.

Berry, W. (2002). *The Art of the Common Place: The Agrarian Essays*. NY: Counterpoint.

Good, R. H., & Kaminski, R. A. (2003). *DIBELS: Dynamic Indicators of Basic Early Literacy Skills*. Longmont, CO: Sopris West/Scott Foresman.

Goodman, K. (Ed.) (2006). *The Truth about DIBELS: What it is, what it does*. Portsmouth, NH: Heinemann.

Fatsis, S. (2002). Word Freak: *Heartbreak, Triumph, Genius, and Obsession in the World of Competitive Scrabble Players*. New York: Penguin.

Okutoro, L. O. (2002). *Quiet Storm: Voices of Young Black Poets*. New York: Jump at the Sun.

Rich, A. (1994). *Blood, bread, and poetry: Selected prose 1979–1985*. New York: W.W. Norton and Company.

SUGGESTED READINGS

Bruner, J. (1997). *The Culture of Education*. Boston: Harvard University Press.

Garan, E. M. (2004). *In Defense of our Children*. Portsmouth, NH: Heinneman.

Goodman, K., Shannon, P., Goodman, Y., & Rapoport, R. (2004). *Saving our Schools: The Case for Public Education, Saying no to "No Child Left Behind."* Muskegon, MI: RDR Books.

Kohn, A. (2000). *The schools our children deserve: Moving beyond traditional classrooms and "tougher standards."* Boston: Mariner Books.

Meier, D., Kohn, A., Darling–Hammond, L., Sizer, T. R., & Wood, G. (2004). *Many Children Left Behind: How the No Child Left Behind Act is Damaging our Children and our Schools*. Boston: Beacon Press.

Nelson, J. (2003). *Critical Issues in Education: Dialogues and Dialects*. New York: McGraw-Hill.

Ohanian, S. (1999). *One Size fits Few*. Portsmough, NH: Heinnemann.

Ohanian, S. (2002). *What Happened to recess and why are our Children Struggling in Kindergarten?* New York: McGraw-Hill.

MULTIPLE CHOICE QUESTIONS

1. According to Ohanian, what is the moral absolute of education?

   a. adherence to standards

   b. focus on individual students

   c. working cooperatively with students' families

   d. helping every child achieve grade level

2. In this essay, what does Ohanian consider to be one of the gravest dangers of No Child Left Behind?

   a. teachers will become overwhelmed with paperwork

   b. assessment will become the school's main objective

   c. an entire generation will be left behind and alienated

   d. federal funds will be withheld from struggling schools

3. Ohanian quotes Wendell Berry as saying "A good solution should be cheap." What is Berry's definition of "cheap?"

   a. not enriching one person by the distress or impoverishment of another

   b. application for federal and state resources does not place undue burdens on school faculty and administration

   c. no one—faculty, student or student's family—bears direct cost

   d. solutions should be as simple and straightforward as possible

4. According to Ohanian, what may happen if teachers lose authority over the classroom?

   a. teacher pay will become based on student performance in standardized tests

   b. teachers will be come "puppets" of federal/state/local government

c. teachers will leave the education field in vast numbers

d. teachers will lose their professionalism

5. Jeremy Bentham puts forth that the best society is one where citizens are:

    a. most productive

    b. educated

    c. happy

    d. vested in societal norms

6. What did Steve Orel discover when he investigated "lack of interest" as the reason listed on termination notices for several Birmingham, Alabama students?

    a. students were interested but had behavior problems

    b. district test scores were down

    c. only African American students had been terminated

    d. school districts were not receiving state funds for these students due to truancy

7. Ohanian feels one of the dangers of tests such as DIBELS is that it pushes academics on increasingly younger children. What does she feel is so negative about this?

    a. children learn early on that they are failures

    b. teachers are not prepared in early grades to administer standardized tests

    c. parents may demand tutoring at increased cost to the school district

    d. private, learner-centered schools may pull students out of public schools

8. Along with discipline referral forms, Ohanian believes schools should develop what other type of form?

    a. checklist for positive attributes

    b. checklist for mitigating factors

    c. form for student self-evaluation of offending behavior

    d. referral form to appropriate community agency to support and/or counsel student

9. Adrienne Rich suggests that when students do not feel a connection to the environment they must function in, they may experience:

    a. traumatic stress disorders

    b. clinical depression

    c. psychic disequilibrium

    d. misplaced locus of control

10. If we are to have happy children in our public schools, Ohanian feels we must:

    a. educate legislators on factors contributing to student happiness

    b. develop curriculums which adhere more closely to educational theory

    c. privatize education

    d. rely on local remedies

Why Do Kids Hate School? A Question of Context

DAVID B. OWEN

IOWA STATE UNIVERSITY

* More than four hundred years ago, in the famous balcony scene of Shakespeare's *Romeo and Juliet*, the young Romeo, longing for Juliet, sighs:

> Love goes toward love, as schoolboys from their books:
> But love from love, toward school with heavy looks.
> Act II, Scene 2, lines 156–57

So, the reality expressed in the theme of this conference—Why do kids hate school?—is not really new. However, such recognition does not imply that this reality is an inevitable condition which releases us educators from an obligation to strive continually to find ways to reduce or even eliminate that obdurate experience of childhood. Obviously, the last four hundred years have witnessed a vast alteration in the circumstances of education, and the sources of children's antipathy toward formal education, too, have shifted over time. Thus, we need to search unceasingly for ways to make their educational experience richer, more creative, and more helpful to them. This conference provides an excellent opportunity for all of us, in a spirit of communal analysis and mutual help, to think through anew the educational issues involved in schooling.

Let me briefly indicate the perspective I hope to bring to our common investigation. I am an academic and, thus, have the luxury of being critical without bearing the responsibility of actually having to teach in any public preK–12 setting. Moreover, my area of primary interest and training is the history and philosophy of education, especially the latter. Obviously, then, I am well removed from the pressing practical problems of the classroom teacher. To top it off, I view the No Child Left Behind Act (NCLB), increasingly the central fact of American public education, to be a virtually unmitigated disaster, at best a misguided attempt to correct past inequities but, in my judgment far more likely, both in intent and in result, an attempt to destroy public education. Yet due to this historically unprecedented legislation, all of us are "in this together" and, thus, must attempt to support one another. Consequently, I truly wish to be of help to practicing teachers, to whom my heart goes out, as they bravely face what I view to be almost insurmountable odds against teaching successfully in the current American context. So, I will try to offer whatever I can in the hope that what I say may be of

---

* I want to thank Robert Hollinger, Jeff Kuzmic, Joanne Olson, and Chris Snethen for generously reading and providing most helpful criticism of an earlier draft of this paper.

at least some little help to those directly involved in solving today's problems of schooling. I know that despite the frequently un-workable limitations put on them, numerous teachers are making creative responses to the demands of their workplace and are somehow succeeding in helping prepare children to become thoughtful adults. Nonetheless, perhaps the character of my perspective may suggest a different framework within which to search for possible ideas to aid in assessing the current situation on a basis broader than immediate experience, in formulating and reformulating the problems that truly need to be solved, and in suggesting novel solutions to novel circumstances. I make no claim that my observations are the unarguable, "objective" truth because I do not think such statements are possible with regard to a social activity as complex as public education. Rather, regarding the issues I intend to discuss, I will try to present my best judgment based on decades of studying such issues, and nothing more.

THEME

Early in my career I shared an office with an elderly professor who had studied with John Dewey. He told me the following story. Late in Dewey's career, practicing teachers would come to him at Columbia University and request help in improving their teaching. Their archetypal question was, "What should I do Monday morning?" Surprisingly for the questioner, given the great pragmatist that Dewey was, he would invariably respond, "Think about it!" Great question: great answer. Let me follow his advice and suggest several things we might like to think about. I will divide my comments into two halves, the first regarding a few aspects of the contexts within which schooling occurs in the U.S. and the second suggesting several ideas that might be used to deal with those circumstances.

So, let me begin. In attempting to give a partial answer to the question this conference asks, I would encourage us to locate any answer to that question in the largest framework, exploring it from historical, economic, sociological, cultural, political, and higher education contexts, in order to see some of the complexity of circumstances prevalent in elementary and secondary schooling. I will attempt to undertake this sketchy overview from the practicing teacher's perspective—someone who, given all the demands, limitations, frustrations, even contempt (both explicit and implied) he or she faces daily when trying to teach, may well be driven to ask, "What's going on here? What am I up against?" To provide some coherence to my selective and disparate comments on the current context, I want to organize my comments around a particular focus in American education: anti-intellectualism.

Anti-intellectualism in America is a powerful and frequently explored theme with numerous variations going back to the Colonial period (Hofstadter, 1963). So what I offer here will be neither original nor exhaustive. Moreover, to prevent misunderstanding, I would like to preface my remarks with two qualifications of this term. First, a word about the term itself. The word "intellectual" is frequently used in a quite narrow sense as referring to ideas as entities existing independently of human cognitive activity and having a reality "truer" than any material referent—an orientation going back to Plato in ancient Greece. Thus, "anti-intellectual" is a charge frequently leveled at those who do not take a Platonic approach to experience. In contrast, I will be using the term "intellectual" in a much broader sense to refer to *any* thinking that is more than a mechanistic, reductive procedure—more than just a technique. Thus, any attempt to be aware of one's own and others' thinking, about the context and alternative possibilities of ideas, can, for our purposes, be viewed to be intellectual (Wegener, 1978). The charge of anti-intellectualism, then, implies an unwillingness to review the character of ideas under consideration, to take a critical stance with respect to them, to call at least into question the ideas of authority, of tradition and habit. My second qualifications has to do with the fact that the charge of anti-intellectualism is one frequently raised with regard to the teaching profession itself. I wish to dissociate my remarks here from that charge. In the current climate, teachers are being blamed inappropriately, even unconscionably, for educational results over which they have increasingly limited or even no control. I consider the blame heaped upon teachers today as being, for the most part, morally akin to blaming the victim for the behavior of others. In short, then, my thesis here is that, taken together, these two qualifications imply a profound paradox that teachers face today, namely, that they are asked to prepare children to be "critical thinkers" and "lifelong learners," yet both teachers and students function in contexts which overwhelmingly militate against such thoughtful behavior—ones which are profoundly anti-intellectual. Let me briefly point out some examples from a variety of contexts.

CONTEXTS

The Historical Context

One of the most striking national features of our period is the attempt to frame an increasingly broad range of issues, both domestically and internationally, in Manichean terms. You may remember that around eighteen hundred years ago, the Mani took the position that the world was radically divided between the spirit and flesh, soul and body, good and evil. The current form of this either/or view of the world has undergone rapid change. Initially, after the attacks on September 11, 2001, the nation was encouraged to engage in a military war on "terror," a battle between those who are moral and "play by the rules" and those who are not and do not "play by the rules." This, then, soon evolved rhetorically into a political struggle between democracy and those opposed to it. Most recently, it has become increasingly characterized as a conflict between Judeo-Christianity and what the President calls "Islamic Fascists," Such a view of our times as an epoch best seen as embodying a "clash of civilizations"—Samuel P. Huntington's phrase (1996)—really calls up a millennium-old idea, the Crusades (which were, in fact, alluded to by the President almost immediately after the 9/11 attacks). What is important here for my purposes is the progress of ideas represented in the evolving rhetorical portrayals. What began as a question of method of inappropriate behavior (terror) became one of the proper form of government (democracy) and has culminated in an englobing disagreement on the question of faith (essentially, Christianity versus Islam). Now, if history has any "lessons" to teach, certainly the testimony of millennia indicates that conflicts of religion tend to be resolved by force and not by reasoned argument and compromise. To the extent that our time is—or, at least, is widely said to be—one that embodies a conflict over faith, where individuals must chose one of two sides with no other alternatives possible, the status of reason, where reason is broadly taken to be reflective thought and judicious engagement with ideas, argumentation, and evidence, is bound to suffer. Faith has been, is, and ever will be a potential source of suspicion of, and in certain contexts even an antithesis to, questioning, doubt, and critique. Put bluntly, blind faith is the enemy of critical thought.

Given this current context of increasing anti-intellectualism growing out of the age-old argument between faith and reason, the current power of a revivified Calvinism in the United States takes on increased importance. I am referring to the Calvinistic doctrines of predestination and the division of humanity into the elect and all others, into the saved and the damned—again, a form of Manicheansim. These beliefs, of course, go back to American Puritanism and have, at various times throughout our history, powerfully reasserted themselves in our national consciousness. In the last decades they have once more come to the fore. Insofar as they have, they tend to represent a powerful anti-intellectualism which argues that faith is what matters in *all* facets of life and that questioning is a sign of lack of faith. This fundamental orientation towards life has also had broad consequences in non-religious contexts. For instance, when allied with evolutionary theory, the belief in a deterministic world, and consequently necessary human behavior within it, has led, since the British philosopher Herbert Spencer in the 1850s (even before Darwin's publication of *The Origin of Species*) and the American sociologist William Graham Sumner a decade and more later, to a Social Darwinism which holds that successful individuals are successful by nature and those who are not deserve to fail, based on the principle of "the survival of the fittest." When pushed, as it frequently is, this conception of Social Darwinism ends in the belief that since nothing *can* be done about human or social problems—they are all the consequence of natural evolutionary laws—nothing *should* be done about them (Cremin, 1961). This orientation holds rich possibilities for anti-intellectualism in that it is not individual effort and reflection that produce success but the "hidden hand" of evolutionary laws, or, transferred into economic terms, of the market place.

A second instance appears in the belief in American "exceptionalism," an idea which goes back to the Puritans' self-professed belief that they were founding in *new* England "a city on a hill" to which all other humans should aspire—a place which, if not heaven on earth, was at least the highest human approximation of that ultimate goal for those who had been "saved." In the current form, such a belief implies that merely *because* one is American, that is, one of the elect, one's beliefs, ideas, and actions are inherently true, good and beyond rational analysis of others. Especially ironic here is that when others make similar claims to being in some regard above others or "elect" or "saved," they are considered to be clearly not only wrong but also, frequently, adherents of "evil." This position embodies a religious idea that, like Manicheanism, the Roman Catholic Church historically treated as a heresy, namely, Antinomianism. Antinomians asserted that through Christian faith alone, and God's consequent grace, an individual is above all law, namely, the law of the Old Testament and, even more so, positive law or the law of the state, a position that by definition is opposed to reasoned argument. Antinomianism has increasingly been the position taken by the current administration when it argues in favor of, for instance, Presidential Signing Statements as expressing the President's constitutional authority to choose, in the face of terrorist threat, what part, if any, of a piece of legislation which he has himself signed into law that he and the agencies of his government will execute. In essence, the President is arguing, as Louis XIV did, "L'état, c'est moi." The American Bar Association, a traditionally quite conservative professional organization, at its recent August annual meeting voted unanimously that this position fundamentally denies the power of the United States Constitution by placing the President above the law and called upon the Congress to challenge this position.

The Economic Context

Two different aspects of economics, one abstract and the other experienced directly day by day, are worth mentioning here. On the one hand, much (most?) of U.S. public thought and expression can be summed up by the bumper sticker: "The one who dies with the most toys wins!" The pervasiveness, even predominance, of the idea that the accumulation of wealth is the purpose of life deeply colors attitudes toward learning. Since wealth is the accumulation of things, the acquisition of goods and not *"the* good," it implies a materialistic and mechanical conception of human circumstances and activities. Mental activity, as a consequence, becomes rule-based, routinized behavior, something that must be "shaped up" by the application of pleasure and pain in education. The value of any idea, then, is judged by economic profit, not by any broader benefit such as social good, creativity, mental richness or insight. This leads to an attitude whereby, if someone suggests that reflection is required upon some proposed course of action, they can be dismissed as merely encouraging "analysis paralysis."

On a more concrete level occur the economic realities of life today. At the individual level, the average worker's pay, after being adjusted for inflation, has essentially not increased in three decades, despite vast increases in his or her productivity. At the level of class, the separation between the rich and all the others is greater than at any time in the nation's history, and the disparity between the two is also increasing at a rate greater than at any time in the nation's history. You all know these statistics; you all know the effects of such economic inequalities and uncertainties on children. The vast majority are at the bottom of this mountain of pressures, both physical and psychic. What parents experience, influences the children for whom they are responsible. In numerous cases, that influence passes beyond the indirect to the direct in the form of abuse—physical and psychological. The increasing pressures now to "get a living," faced by the middle class as they were earlier faced by the lower class, fundamentally undermine the conditions required for thought and reflection, for the "play of ideas," namely, the condition of some degree of leisure. A perfect demonstration of this change is the new conception of "play" as either a business or, at least, a preparation for a job—of "sport" as a profitable enterprise.

In general, this reduction of the conception of human life to economic behavior is having a profound impact on education. The trend toward an economic conception of education has, of course, a long and rich history. As Raymond Callahan (1962) has so carefully documented, post-Civil War industrialization in America occurred at the same time as the expansion of public education to include the whole country and both elementary and secondary education. It was probably inevitable that some individuals would see in mass manufacture a model for mass education. This movement away from education in its more traditional, European view as cultivation of the individual to generate, at its best, a truly liberal education gained momentum before the First World War—thanks, to a significant degree, to the enthusiastic support of professors of education (sic) in the then-new American universities—and transformed public elementary and secondary education into the institution we recognize today as devoted to "Fordist" principles and "the cult of efficiency." Significantly, given that Ford (the automotive company that modeled such principles) is currently flirting with bankruptcy, the Fordist model of education is itself evolving further into one that, to accord with the new conception of the U.S. economy, is characterized as a "service" industry where the student is a "customer" and, as the cliché goes, "the customer is always right." And since, under the economic theory of humans, the customer is motivated entirely by profit, students are viewed as being interested solely in the profit of immediate pleasure or of longer-term utility, that is, of entertainment or of job training as an instrument for accumulating the means of consumption. What is ironic about this whole approach is that, when told that they must go to school to "get a good job," most students—and virtually all in the earlier years—find such a rationale wholly unmotivating, leaving only entertainment as a conceivable inducement to attend to what goes on in school. Under such an assumption, the teacher is left with few resources to engage students meaningfully in significant learning (Goodlad, 1984).

The Sociological Context

We all know the clichés regarding the institution of education in our society and of the individuals who inhabit it at all levels. "Those who can, do; those who can't, teach"—and by extension, of course, "Those who can't teach, teach teachers" (myself!). University professors are often seen to be inhabiting an "ivory tower" divorced from the realities of the "real" world; as being (derogatorily) "egg-heads" (an epithet going back at least as far as Illinois Governor Adlai Stevenson in his run against Dwight Eisenhower for President in 1952) or "pointy-headed intellectuals" (an attack famously launched by Richard Nixon's Vice President Spiro T. Agnew, who compounded the insult by repeatedly calling such individuals "nattering nabobs of negativity"—before he was ousted from office and sent to jail for fraud!). For close to a century, sociologists have characterized school teaching as a "passing profession," that is, a form of employment usually to be inhabited by children of so-called blue-collar workers attempting to move into the lower middle class so that *their* children might, in turn, fully enter the middle class in a more respectable form of work, such as business or even a profession like engineering (Waller, 1932). Much of this American disrespect for teaching has a history which goes back centuries, but for over a century it has clearly been influenced by the profession being largely dominated, at least in the classroom, by women—though, before the Civil War, such teaching was largely done by men. Not only is school teaching especially at the elementary level, "women's work," but it also has the additional social liability in America of working full time with children. Thus, those who opt for a teaching career are frequently viewed as being individuals who cannot function effectively in "the grown-up world." Teaching is widely viewed as being a low-level, little-valued, non-professional job. This social stereotype has had a deep and enduring influence on the character of those who have chosen to enter teaching (Lortie, 1975). This American social attitude toward teaching at any level of the institution of education, but especially at the pre-collegiate level, implies a society profoundly distrustful of ideas, of their investigation and expansion, and, consequently, of those who seek to help future generations enter into that world of reflection and inquiry. I would argue that this structural position of education in American society has a powerful anti-intellectual influence on children which affects how they perceive everything that is involved in the sole formal institution dedicated to helping them grow up.

The Cultural Context

Anyone who teaches today recognizes the profound influence culture has on everyone in the United States, including the young. Studies have repeatedly shown that children spend substantially more time per day engaged with the media of television, movies, the computer (internet, games, communication), and electronically reproduced music, various forms of "virtual reality," than with any other waking activity, whether in the family, school, or the natural world (Steyer, 2002). This has led to widely recognized consequences, such as not only children's increased demand for an "entertaining" environment and immediate reward for engaged activity but also their decreased "attention span" and willingness to use books, magazines, and newspapers as an enrichment of personal experience. Possibly less widely recognized is the media's power in shaping children's values, including the value of thinking, not only regarding their own prejudices relative to consumption but even their acceptance of the media's apparent preference for force rather than mediation (reasoning) in the resolution of conflict. I have personal experience with the difficulty of suggesting that young adults in a collegiate teacher-preparation program—the students being, obviously, products of the present media culture—reflect upon how powerfully and unquestioningly their view of themselves and their world is shaped by media. In teaching a course in media literacy with a colleague, I found that students prided themselves on their media "savviness" and grew increasingly angry as they were stimulated to confront how thoroughly their lives were being shaped by subtle influences in the media. For instance, we faced an emotional crisis one day in class in the late 1990s when we had all the students whose hair styling reflected Rachel's in the television comedy "Friends" stand and a third of the class stood. As instructors, we had clearly violated the boundary over which teachers should not pass in engaging the students' personal lives. After six years, my colleague and I had to discontinue teaching the class due both to student complaints that such subject matter was "not relevant" to preparing future teachers as well as to a lack of faculty support for a course in media literacy, even if it were to be taught by others who might be more skilled than the two of us in negotiating this emotionally charged material (Owen and Silet, 1997; Owen et al., 1998). In short, the media, even if just one among a number of cultural influences on students, exert to a considerable extent an anti-intellectual influence that inhibits, even prevents, students from cultivating a reflective view of themselves and their world.

The Political Context

What are the political conditions that help set up an overwhelmingly anti-intellectual climate that teachers have to face with their students? "No Child Left Behind"—need I say anything more? No—but, also, yes. Although some supporters of the original legislation thought it would assist disadvantaged students if properly funded—which, of course, due mainly to the cost of the war in Iraq, it never has been and almost certainly never will be—much of the main support arose from individuals and organizations who were consciously and publicly hostile to state-supported schools and intended the legislation to be a way to destroy public schooling in the U.S. and thereby restructure, probably through vouchers, all education as being private—and for many, hopefully religious (Bracey, 2003, 2004). But beyond that specific motive driving much or most of the support for NCLB, one can say much more. It is worth remembering that NCLB has a lineage that goes back through the Goals 2000 legislation, which was supported by both Presidents Clinton and the first Bush, to its original parentage in the Presidential Commission of President Reagan that issued the report entitled *A Nation At Risk* (National Commission, 1983). This quarter-century movement clearly expresses all the various contexts—historical, economic, sociological, and cultural—mentioned above and politically codifies them into public policy. What we have, then, in essence, is what I would describe as *legislated philosophy*; in particular, through the exercise of political power, as translated into legislative enactment, a particular philosophy has been imposed nationwide on public education—a philosophy fundamentally reductionist and, in its most common, materialistic and mechanistic formulation, explicitly anti-intellectual. In education it draws together a vast variety of tendencies into a particular expression of the nation's character. It is an expression that claims to be "objective" and, thereby, definitive, brooking no question, argument, or alternative. It alone defines what is "true" and excludes all other orientations as false.

From one point of view, NCLB is an expression of the American character that is surprising, even historically unique, in that it directly and explicitly denies what has often been described as what is most typical of America, namely, its belief in individuality and pluralism. Yet, from another viewpoint, it brings to fruition a host of tendencies, a few of which were suggested above, which have frequently been observed in our national life. For me, a perfect example of this national trait of anti-intellectualism is reflected in Presidential politics over the last thirty or so years. President Carter was widely criticized publicly in the late 1970s because of his deep immersion in the details of governmental management, making him what would later become known as a "policy wonk"—someone deeply knowledgeable about issues of legislation and governance. President Clinton ran for office in both campaigns as "a good ol' boy," distancing himself as far away from his Rhodes Scholarship as he could get and obviously following the example of President Reagan, who was widely reported to be innocent of the details of governance, even in his second campaign. Presidential aspirant Gore, however, the son of a long-time senator and someone who had spent his entire professional life in public service and who was widely acknowledged in 2000 as the individual in Washington, DC, with the broadest understanding of issues of governing, was treated by the media as a "drugstore" or "wooden" Indian—someone of whom one would not want to ask a question because he would overwhelm you with his knowledge of what was at stake. These comments are not meant to reflect issues of party but of public perception. In other words, American political wisdom today appears universal that a candidate must appear to be "friendly," which really means he or she must not be especially intelligent or knowledgeable. Try to imagine Jefferson—or even better, Washington—running as someone with whom you would like to sit down and have a barbeque! Anti-intellectualism is apparently not just a necessity, it has become a virtue in the public, political life that shapes our nation (Postman, 1985).

The Educational Context—the University

In dealing with the broad circumstances within which schooling takes place today, we should not omit the issue of the university's transformation as a factor having anti-intellectual consequences on K–12 education. Many not directly involved in higher education may not be aware that universities in the U.S.—and around the world, largely as a result of American influence and pressure—are experiencing a thorough-going and fundamental transformation. Given the various circumstances suggested above, it should not be surprising, if one thinks about it, that colleges and universities are increasingly not only being thought of as businesses but also being run as such—all the way down into the selection of faculty to staff them and the classes being offered and required for the students in attendance (Readings, 1996). Especially at research institutions—though it is happening at four-year institutions, too—faculty are under increasing pressure to bring money into the institution, rather along the lines of a sales force whose employment and compensation depends upon product sold. Accounting is broken down to the individual departmental or major level. Those that generate money, either through student fees or outside money brought in, flourish; those which do not, such as service departments like literature, art, history, philosophy, sociology, or anthropology either must change the nature of their subject—frequently transforming themselves into a "consulting" business, as English has by becoming business writing, art by becoming graphic consulting for media, or philosophy by reducing itself to ethics for technologists or businesses—or lose standing, resources and even potential existence, within the institution.

Coupled with this radical re-creation of the purpose of learning—the mantra these days is "education *means* business"—is a separate dynamic which is helping to define the nature of institutions of higher education. That is the re-definition of the nature of knowledge along reductionist—technically, positivist—lines, namely, from liberal arts into fields of specialization, a re-definition that started in the U.S. around the time of the Civil War with the founding of the university, most notably the Johns Hopkins University, to convert the traditional English college model's emphasis upon liberal education into preparation in German-inspired research (Flexner, 1930). The position that all knowledge is specialist knowledge has, since the Second World War, come to dominate almost wholly the conception of post-secondary learning, both collegiate and university, overwhelming even that "liberal" education which had, under pressure, disguised itself as "general" education (Bell, 1966). As the Harvard sociologists Jencks and Riesman (1969) were already able to point out by the 1960s, graduate programs in universities were so able to dominate the college curriculum that "university college" became an institution for preparing specialists and pre-professional academics. This is of considerable importance for preK–12 education because school teachers were increasingly trained in this specialist view of knowledge, and they were the ones institutionally designated to introduce *their* students to the world of knowledge. This led, for instance, to the view that even in kindergarten, children were "researchers on the forefront of knowledge" (Bruner, 1962) and to the idea, popular in the 1990s, that even first-grade teachers should be majors in some specific subject matter in college, not just broadly prepared as "education" majors, on the assumption that teaching first-grade children required a degree, say, in physics (Boyer, 1992). In collegiate teacher education programs, too, as the doctorate became required for employment, faculty were required to become specialists in a subject matter, not only in "education." This development has led to the current situation in academic careers where research is more important than teaching experience, where methods teachers may have had *no* experience in teaching, and where educational technologists, including those writing software, may never have had exposure to children. In all this, educating as a complex, serious, subtle, and indeterminate action is denigrated and, viewed instead as a rule-based behavior and, as such, reducible to mechanistic law and rote memorization—a view Dewey (1929) argued eighty years ago to be fundamentally untenable. In fact, a number of institutions, including the one from which I graduated (the University of Chicago in 1999) and the one at which I currently work (Iowa State University in 2005), have gone so far as to close their schools, colleges, or departments of education (Clifford and Guthrie, 1988).

In the increasing transformation of the study of teaching and education from a practice into a science, it must be recognized that its context within the university is significant. As the university has increasingly been managed on business principles, so, too, has its proclaimed chief value, namely, its research. The re-definition of research as a "value-added" activity—meaning profitable—has had, and is having, profound consequences for society, including education. Since researchers are increasingly having to find their own financial support for their work, businesses seeking to expand the goods and services on which they can profit are more and more providing the funding essential for that research and are thereby defining what questions will be asked, what methods will be employed, and what results will be shared publicly—facts of the deepest import for the development of knowledge.

I recently ran across a tiny, but telling, education example of this transformation of research in a Letter to the Editor in *Rethinking Schools* (Polacco, 2006). In her letter, Patricia Polacco said that she had been invited to speak at the International Reading Association Conference to be held in Chicago on May 2–3 at a session sponsored by SRA/McGraw Hill. She states that her public position on NCLB is that it is "the most controversial and political lie that has ever been perpetrated on the American teacher" and that it embodies a "destructive path that is laying waste to our schools." She adds that, evidently, when SRA/McGraw Hill found out that this was her position , they asked her to "guarantee" that her speech would be "upbeat, non-controversial and non-political." She declined, and her invitation was withdrawn. Most telling to me is that even at an international professional conference where individuals are supposed to present their research and discuss its implications, the influence of business is so great that profit-making is becoming the criterion for the discussion of ideas.

To sum up the circumstances of research today, then, we cannot, either as a nation, as professionals, or as individuals, look to university research as we once, to a significant extent, could, namely, as a source of arm's-length judgment regarding issues of knowledge, of policy, of culture. The researchers all too often have financial interests, both overt and covert, in shaping their results to their own and their sponsors' profit. Further, within the university itself, this vast re-orientation of research to business purposes has so changed the nature of the institution that even the long-time President of Harvard University, Derek Bok (2006), has noted the decimation of its traditional role as educator and called for a re-balancing in favor of the latter. Possibly his most devastating argument is that, contrary to conventional wisdom, research does not, in balance, bring money into the institution, if one takes into account all the indirect costs involved in the activity.

Conclusion

Such , then, are a few of my individual observations on various problems of context within which public education takes place. When one looks at the above as a whole interconnected nest of contexts—and I have obviously omitted numerous crucial issues, such as those of gender, race, and class, partly because they will be amply addressed by others at this conference, as well as the whole host of topics related to the subject of psychology, which has historically been the "mother" discipline of educational research, a tradition which is itself a problematic issue—one would be justified in concluding that it is nothing short of astonishing that any serious educational benefit is observable in public schooling. Yet such benefit does exist. As individuals like Gerald Bracey (2003; 2004) have repeatedly pointed out, American public education is in many ways surprisingly successful, especially if one takes into account that it really is comprised of two systems, one rich and one poor. On the whole, for example, national standardized test scores have *never* "plummeted," and international comparisons such as TIMMS and PIRLS show, when reflectively interpreted, that American results are at or near the top of those of industrialized societies. In short, when all the forces working against serious education are taken into account, American public school teachers should on the whole be praised, not vilified, for their successful contributions to children.

SUGGESTIONS

Now, then, to the second half of my remarks—those having to do with suggestions for improvement in the current circumstances. Although, like Bracey, I do not believe the public school system is "broken," I do believe that it has a number of problems that require urgent attention. As implied above, I hold that a variety of ways of conceiving of education exist, ones at odds with the currently dominant mode; and that if our culture were willing to overcome its anti-intellectualism, tools and actual examples exist which could help us address our educational problems more creatively and effectively. So, given the constraints of time, I will stay with my theme and focus on what I see as potential improvements in the intellectual preparation of students, recognizing that a number of other important issues related to the contexts briefly discussed above, are also worthy of attention and action.

Let me quickly describe the general direction of my research. I have come to the conclusion that the most important fact in the history of ideas, including those on education, is the ongoing disagreement among individuals of great intellect, honesty, and humanity, both in the west and, insofar as I have been able to investigate, in the east. At their most fundamental level, these disagreements are enduring and take on a structural coherence and continuity, though the language and facts at issue may change over time. In this respect, I am a follower of the American philosopher, Richard P. McKeon, who lived from 1900 to 1985 and was a student of John Dewey. In an essay entitled, "A Philosopher Meditates on Discovery," McKeon (1990) commented that his central position grew out of an insight of the Roman orator Cicero, namely, that "the truth is one, though the expressions of it are multiple." McKeon spent his career tracing out this insight and ended up distinguishing four different "modes of thought," that is, distinct ways or methods of thinking, which endure over time and which are all present in any one period, though one or two dominate at any particular time. He called his approach intellectual pluralism (McKeon, 1990; 1994).

Based on McKeon's work, I have tried to explore the educational consequences of his position. In this I have been influenced by Joseph Schwab (1978), who was engaged in a similar undertaking. McKeon's modes of thought are not just different ways to explain Howard Gardner's theory of multiple intelligences (Gardner, 1983). Where Gardner distinguishes among logico-mathematico, spatial, kinesthetic, and a number of other intelligences, McKeon argues that with regard to *thinking itself*, a variety of ways of proceeding exist. The four different approaches to thinking emphasize, respectively, parts, wholes, problems (located midway between parts and wholes), and perspectives (the skeptical stance). Though I use terms derived from the four words just listed—respectively, the atomistic, the holistic, the problematic, and the perspectival—they can be thought of as equivalent to, roughly speaking, the analytic, synthetic, pragmatic, and relativistic approaches to thinking. The consequence is that, by using these four interpretive tools, one can understand the structure of disagreements and the continuity of debates over time regarding the interpretation of human thinking, acting, and making.

Rather than explore some of the abstract consequences of this approach to intellectual interpretation, including those in the field of education, we can look at several of the practical consequences of this pluralistic approach. For instance, in my view, the three most important schools of the twentieth century reflect three of the four different modes of thought listed above. Each of these schools was successful in practice, though the meaning of that "success" differs radically from school to school. Let me briefly describe them.

The first great school is A. S. Neill's Summerhill, a boarding school founded in 1923 and still in existence today, run by his daughter in Leiston, England, which embodies a perspectival mode of thought in its education (Neill, 1960). It is a truly free school, where children do not have to go to class if they choose not to go. In practice, as they enter their teens, students almost universally *do* choose to go to class and prepare either for the national high-school-leaving exam (traditionally called the "O-Level Exams") or the college-entrance exam (formerly the "A-Levels"). For me, the school is important because it has consistently demonstrated for eight decades that only two, at the most three, years of formal schooling are required for someone to graduate high school and, if interested and able, to enter college, including the best, like Oxbridge, as Summerhillians in fact have. The perspectival aspect is reflected in each child choosing what is *for her or for him* the best way to achieve happiness—the overarching purpose of Neill's school.

The second great school, the Dewey School at the University of Chicago, existed from 1896 to 1904, when John Dewey and his wife, who had been principal of the school, left the University and moved to New York to join Columbia University. Fortunately, we have an extended account, written in the 1930s by two sisters who were teachers at this school, which embodies what I would call the problematic mode of thought (Mayhew and Edwards, 1936). Here students worked in what Dewey characterized as "an embryonic community," learning as a group how to address the fundamental functions of human existence as reflected in the issues of food, clothing, and shelter, all taken in increasingly rich and complex meanings. For me, the school is important because it brilliantly shows as its purpose both a thoroughly integrated community that truly educates the student for an adult life of participatory democracy and, equally important, a thoroughly integrated curriculum leading to an adult who knows his or her own mind and feels empowered to solve the problems that arise in life.

The third great school, the Waldorf School, was founded in 1919 by the German philosopher Rudolph Steiner in Stuttgart, Germany, and has grown to be a world-wide educational movement, with over 300 schools and a college in the United States alone. Steiner's approach to schooling embodies the holistic mode of thought. In this instance, that means that his curriculum integrates the historically broadest conception of the human being—physical, emotional, intellectual, and spiritual—in a series of developmental stages (Harwood, 1958; Spock, 1985). For me, the school is important because its purpose is to explore the widest possible sense of what it means to be human and because it places art and aesthetics at the very heart of that educational exploration in childhood—a conception of educating that goes back as far as Plato's *Republic* (Plato, 1968).

Absent by design from this list of great educational innovations of the twentieth century are any of the schools embodying the atomistic mode of thought. The atomistic approach represents the last century's leading view of schooling, resulting in a mechanistic conception of thinking and schooling as expressed in the various traditions of behaviorism that have dominated the period, both those based on pain and the threat of pain or, as in Skinner's innovation in operant conditioning (Skinner, 1948), those based on pleasure and the desire for such. The atomistic mode of thought truly culminates in the behaviorism of NCLB, which is why I described it before as a piece of "legislated philosophy"—something which in its very nature stifles intellectual activity.

For our purposes here, these schools' radically different yet equivalently successful practices—children from each went on to become thoughtful, productive, creative adults—suggests several points worth considering. First, with respect to mental activity, children differ not just in degree but in kind. Consequently, to be successful at the beginning, education ought to reflect those differences and seek to match the learner with the mode of learning, the student's mode of thought with the classroom practice of thinking. Thus, students would be able to learn from the beginning that the world around them as embodied in subject matters "makes sense" to *their* way of thinking. Then, having secured a foothold in the world of ideas, a student could advance in understanding ways of knowing that differ from their native, initial form, possibly at the secondary level. (This last is a question subject to experiment, both in general and in individual cases.)

Second, the success of each of these radically different approaches demonstrates that one should not try to find a "best practice" or the "right way" in teaching. Rather, as there is a plurality of ways of thinking, so, too, should education reflect that plurality in a diversity of methods. One size does *not* "fit all."

Third, all three schools indicate a deep but usually overlooked truth: ultimately, it is curriculum, not the teacher, that educates. Here I am taking curriculum in a broad sense as, literally, the "course" around which the student "runs" (the word's etymological meaning). By this I mean that students develop habits of mind, or a "second nature," through continually acting intellectually in one way as distinct from another, that is, by "thinking about thinking"—a kind of activity which hopefully is encouraged not only by the structure of the subject matter and by the way the teachers teach but also by the circumstances, direct and indirect, obvious and hidden, of the educating institution (Wegener, 1978). This happens not under the tutelage of just one or two teachers over a limited period of time, say, a semester or even an academic year. Rather, it is engrained by numerous individuals in numerous situations over an extended time encouraging the learner to function intellectually in a common fashion so that by the end, he or she has internalized that way of operating and will spontaneously and repeatedly do so without external prompting.

Lastly, the importance of this educational pluralism is enduring. It is not an accident that the three modes of thought represented by the schools above can trace similarities of approach for each, including ones in education, back as far as we have records of intellectual activity. For instance, the perspectival approach represents an orientation expressed by Rousseau, who based his views on the ancient Roman orators, who, in turn, derived their position from that of the earlier Greek sophists; the problematic orientation so extensively explored by Dewey goes all the way back to Aristotle; and the holistic mode has been continuously explored by educators as far back as Plato, as noted above.

My point here is that, in thinking about how we should respond to the question of why children hate school, we should recognize that these three schools also faced circumstances in which anti-intellectualism was an important aspect of children's lives but that by means of a thorough-going working out of one of the modes of thought, a school and a curriculum were invented which more than offset the limitations of the context, which, in fact, cultivated the growth of individuals to become adults living rich and humane lives.

At this point, however, I can imagine a number of individuals in the audience objecting, "But I do not work in circumstances where such thorough-going transformation of the school is possible. I have to meet the demands of NCLB." Assuming that one recognizes that such limitations prevent the full cultivation of individuals that the three schools above embody, it is still possible to draw some "lessons" from these approaches which, to a greater or lesser extent, might inform current practice without the fundamental reform they all embody. Let me briefly list, then, several random suggestions for possible improvement of practice, even in current, unaltered circumstances.

From the perspectival mode of thought, one could try to enter empathetically into a child's view of the world and imagine what it looks like from the inside (Holt, 1974). On a more specific level, a teacher might consider ways of individualizing instruction. For instance, Carl Rogers (1969), a perspectival practitioner, suggests using individual contracts between teacher and student where some of the former's power is transferred to the latter, who then gets to decide when, how, and to what extent he or she will come to terms with the demands of a subject matter.

A host of individuals have explored the problematic mode of thought in the American context. For instance, one ought to begin by referring to the most important research project in the history of American education: the Progressive Education Association's Eight-Year Study of the 1930s (Aikin, 1942). This study examined fifty high schools that were released from the restrictions of standard college entrance examinations and, consequently, were able to experiment with their curricula. The results are still impressive: the graduates of these experimental schools performed, on the whole, *better* in college than did students of traditional—roughly equivalent to today's (Cuban, 1984)—high schools; and even more significant, the more experimental the curricula, the *more* successful the graduates were in college. In a more recent vein, William Glasser (1969) emphasizes the use of three different kinds of classroom meetings—social problem-solving, educational diagnostic, and exploratory—in order to encourage students to feel like respected members of the class, to reveal to teachers the degree to which their teaching has succeeded or not, and to help students see the relevance of what they are studying. Again, peer education, the powerful concept encouraged by Herbert Thelen (1960) that uses individual students to teach others in the same or lower grade—following the ancient truism, *docendo discimus*, "in teaching we learn"—has historically proven an effective educational tool. A third problematic technique that has proven successful for those like Deborah Meier (1995) and Theodore Sizer (1992) is to reconnect the disjointed subject matters so that problems running across disciplines can be studied in a form coherent to students and, thus, in a more meaningful and memorable fashion.

The holistic mode of thought can remind us of the centrality of art to every subject, not just because it is an expression of individuality (a perspectival interpretation) but also, more importantly, because it can sum up the essence of any subject being considered. Another superb expression of the holistic approach can be found in the brilliant reflections of one of our wisest teachers, Herbert Kohl (1984), who organizes teaching around a central idea (rather Platonic in conception), such as light, and engages the students in *Sprache*, in "thoughtful speech" regarding that idea, working it out in a multitude of directions and interconnections.

One interesting overview of the vast diversity of approaches that can successfully be made to teaching—one that explores different pedagogic "methods," is Joyce and Weil's *Models of Teaching* (1972). Though they do not use the exact distinctions reflected in the four modes of thought above, their taxonomy of the various "families" of teaching models can be easily related to what is being proposed here and provides a rich environment, including traceable origins of different members of each family, for exploring the plurality of orientations to teaching.

Finally, a more general observation regarding actions that individual teachers might take to transform the circumstances of their work. I have often thought that it would be immensely valuable to teachers and teaching if teachers' professional organizations, notably the National Education Association and the American Federation of Teachers, were to re-conceive themselves as being not the premier advocates of teachers—and thus rendering themselves to be easily dismissed as merely another "special-interest group"—but the principal defender of children in the United States, arguing in their behalf for health, for welfare, for safety, for child care, and so on, including education. I can foresee such a principled stand giving them a voice in national decisions of vastly more weight than they currently possess. And, along the same lines, might it not be possible for teacher educators to become the principle advocates for teachers and the improvement of teaching conditions?

So, we return to where we began—Why do kids hate school? Dewey's response is still fitting: "Think about it!"

POSTSCRIPT

I cannot over-emphasize the urgency of thinking most carefully about this issue of—let me be blunt—intellectual freedom in how we educate our children. U. S. Secretary of Education, Margaret Spellings has just delivered a speech on September 26th in response to the report of a commission on improving education that she had appointed last year. In her comments, Spellings indicated that she wants, one, to extend the provisions of No Child Left Behind to high school; two, to make colleges and universities subject to greater "accountability" in order to "improve standards" and increase financial "efficiency" (three criticisms that historically were at the heart of the movement that culminated in NCLB); and, three, to create a national database to track all college students' learning (*USA Today*, 2006a). This news appears the same day as a story about a report issued by six national higher-education policy groups which calls for the creation of a clearing house of "best practices" in teaching (*USA Today*, 2006b). The forces encouraging standardization, routinization, and administrative control of education, encouraging, in my view, a legislated philosophy of atomism, are at full flood, apparently sweeping all before them. I am reminded of a justly famous cartoon by Al Capp of a number of years ago in which a character remarked about the then-active Cold War, "We have met the enemy and they are us." It appears that the United States, having outlasted the Soviet Union, has increasingly decided to embody the latter's principle of governance: standardized, centralized rule. I am left to wonder: Whatever happened to what used to be considered America's greatest virtue, namely, its sense of individuality and pluralism?

REFERENCES

Aikin, Wilford M. (1942). *The Story of the Eight-Year Study*. New York: Harper & Brothers.

Bell, Daniel. (1966). *The Reforming of General Education*. New York: Columbia University Press.

Bok, Derek Curtis. (2006). *Our Underachieving Colleges*. Princeton: Princeton University Press.

Boyer, Ernest L. (1992). *Cornerstones For a New Century*. Washington, D.C.: National Education Association.

Bracey, Gerald W. (2003). *On the Death of Childhood And the Destruction of Public Schools*. Portsmouth, NH: Heinemann.

___. (2004). *Setting the Record Straight: Responses to Misconceptions About Public Education in the U.S.*, 2nd ed. Portsmouth, NH: Heinemann.

Bruner, Jerome S. (1962). *On Knowing: Essays on the Left Hand*. Cambridge: Harvard University Press.

Callahan, Raymond E. (1962). *Education and the Cult of Efficiency*. Chicago: University of Chicago Press.

Clifford, Geraldine Joncich, and James W. Guthrie. (1988). *Ed School: A Brief For Professional Education*. Chicago: University of Chicago Press.

Cremin, Lawrence A. (1961). *The Transformation of the School: Progressivism in American Education, 1876–1957*. New York: Knopf,.

Cuban Larry. *How Teacher Taught: Constance and Change in American Classrooms, 1890–1980*. New York: Longman.

Dewey, John. (1929). *The Sources of a Science of Education*. New York: H. Liveright.

Flexner, Abraham. (1930). *Universities: American, English, German*. New York: Oxford University Press.

Gardner, Howard. (1983). *Frames of Mind: the Theory of Multiple Intelligences*. New York: Basic Books.

Glasser, William. (1969). *Schools Without Failure*. New York: Harper & Row.

Goodlad, John I. (1984). *A Place Called School*. New York: McGraw-Hill.

Harwood, A. C. (1958). *The Recovery of Man Childhood: A Study of the Educational Work of Rudolf Steiner*. London: Hodder and Stoughton.

Hofstadter, Richard. (1963). *Anti-Intellectualism in American Life*. New York: Vintage.

Holt, John. (1974). *Escape From Childhood*. New York: E. P. Dutton.

Huntington, Samuel P. (1996). *The Clash of Civilizations and the Remaking of World Order*. New York: Simon & Schuster.

Jencks, Christopher, and Riesman, David. (1969). *The Academic Revolution*. Garden City, NY: Doubleday.

Joyce, Bruce, and Marsha Weil. (1972). *Models of Teaching*. Englewood Cliffs, N.J.: Prentice-Hall.

Kohl, Herbert. (1984). *Growing Minds: On Becoming a Teacher*. New York: Harper & Row.

Lortie, Dan. (1975). *Schoolteacher*. Chicago: University of Chicago Press.

Mayhew, Katherine Camp, and Anna Camp Edwards. (1936). *The Dewey School*. New York: D. Appleton-Century.

McKeon, Richard P. (1990). *Freedom and History, and Other Essays: An Introduction to the Thought of Richard McKeon*, ed. Zahava K. McKeon. Chicago: University of Chicago Press.

___. (1994). *On Knowing—The Natural Sciences*, ed. David B. Owen and Zahava K. McKeon. Chicago: University of Chicago Press.

Meier, Deborah. (1995). *The Power of Their Ideas: Lessons For American From a Small School in Harlem*. Boston: Beacon Press.

National Commission on Excellence in Education. (1983). *A Nation At Risk: The Imperative For Educational Reform*. Washington, D.C.: The Commission.

Neill, A. S. (1960). *Summerhill: A Radical Approach To Child Rearing*. New York: Hart Publishing.

Owen, David B., and Charles L. P. Silet. (1997). Changing perceptions, not just channels, in the Heartland: Teaching Television's Teaching. *Radical Teacher* 50:7–11.

___. Charles L. P. Silet, and Sarah E. Brown. (1998). Teaching television to empower students. *English Journal* 87, (no. 1 (January),):28–33.

Plato. (1968). *The Republic of Plato*, trans. Allan Bloom. New York: Basic Books.

Polacco, Patricia. (2006). Letter to the Editor. *Rethinking Schools, XX*, 4 (summer):7–8.

Postman, Neil. (1985). *Amusing Ourselves to Death: Public Discourse in the Age of Show Business*. New York: Penguin Books.

Readings, Bill. (1996). *The University in Ruins*. Cambridge, MA: Harvard University Press.

Rogers, Carl R. (1969). *Freedom to Learn*: A View of What Education Might Become. New York: Merrill.

Schwab, Joseph J. (1978). The Practical. In *Science, Curriculum, and Liberal Education: Selected Essays*, ed. Ian Westbury and Neil J. Wilkof. Chicago: University of Chicago Press.

Sizer, Theodore R. (1992). *Horace's School: Redesigning the American High School*. Boston: Houghton Mifflin.

Skinner, B. F. (1948). *Walden Two*. New York: Macmillan.

Spock, Marjorie. (1985). *Teaching As a Lively Art*, 2nd ed. Hudson, NY: Anthroposophic Press.

Steyer, James P. (2002). *The Other Parent: The Inside Story on Our Children*. New York: Atria Books.

Thelen, Herbert A. (1960). *Education and the Human Quest*. New York: Harper.

USA Today. 2006a. Sept. 27, sec. A, p. 1.

___. 2006b. Sept. 27, sec. D, p. 7.

Waller, Willard. (1932). *Sociology of Teaching*. New York: J. Wiley & Sons.

Wegener, Charles. (1978). *Liberal Education and the Modern University*. Chicago: University of Chicago Press.

Suggested Readings

Mayhew, Katherine Camp, and Anna Camp Edwards. (1936). *The Dewey School*. New York: D. Appleton-Century.

John Dewey's educational philosophy has inspired educators ever since his classic texts were published over a century ago. This text helps the reader understand how his ideas were put into practice in his own school. Written by two teachers in the school, it is a description of the curriculum and instructional practices from year-to-year.

McKeon, Richard P. (1990). *Freedom and History, and Other Essays: An Introduction to the Thought of Richard McKeon*, ed. Zahava K. McKeon. Chicago: University of Chicago Press.

___. (1994). *On Knowing—The Natural Sciences*, ed. David B. Owen and Zahava K. McKeon. Chicago: University of Chicago Press.

McKeon is an important thinker—a truly impressive scholar. These texts will deepen the reader's understanding and appreciation of "intellectual pluralism." For people who want to truly understand the sciences, the second book is a real treat—but be prepared for an intellectual challenge.

Neill, A. S. (1960). *Summerhill: A Radical Approach To Child Rearing*. New York: Hart Publishing.

This is a most interesting book to read: How could there be a school where students didn't have to come to class? How could one argue for such an approach? Neill answers all such questions.

Multiple Choice Questions

1. The perspective or point of view from which the author comments is that of

    a. a classroom teacher

    b. a school administrator

    c. a member of Iowa's State Board of Education

    d. an academic

2. Owen worries about the "anti-intellectualism" he sees. By "anti-intellectualism" Owen means

    a. the poor academic training of teachers

    b. the failure of teachers to stimulate the intellect of their students

c. a Platonic conception of experience

d. thinking that is mechanistic or reductive

3. In his discussion of historical contexts, Owen

a. mistrusts all religions, especially Islam

b. mistrusts either/or alternatives, some of which stem from religious sources, that stifle reflection and critical thinking

c. favors a Social Darwinism orientation that explains why certain people succeed in life and others fail

d. sees strong political power such as that wielded by President George W. Bush after 9/11 as necessary—even if it may temporarily limit the political and intellectual rights of citizens

4. According to Owen, No Child Left Behind (NCLB)

a. reflects the anti-intellectualism that he has found in the contexts he discusses

b. has nothing to do with the anti-intellectualism he discusses

c. is an appropriate response from educators to the anti-intellectualism he discusses

5. Owen argues

a. intellectual life in the university (but not in teacher education programs or departments) has remained vibrant and alive

b. universities have remained independent of big business and the business model predicated on profitability

c. universities have not remained independent of economics or the business model but have, on the contrary, changed in significant ways because of these influences

d. none of the above

6. Owen argues NCLB legislation is a natural outgrowth of

a. holistic approaches to education

b. problematic approaches to education

c. perspectival approaches to education

d. atomistic approaches to education

7. The three schools Owen discusses are important to his argument about anti-intellectualism because

    a. they represent an out-moded way of thinking about intellectual life it has taken us a long time to over-come

    b. they present powerful examples of ways of thinking that can through a prolonged school experience become habitual to the students

    c. they provide the historical context for NCLB which takes the best from all these schools and repackages it in new and interesting ways

8. Owen believes teacher unions should be

    a. Eliminated—bad teachers get too much protection

    b. Expanded—teachers need more help and protection

    c. Transformed—to be advocates for children even more than they are for teachers

    d. Combined—the two major unions (and other smaller unions or associations) should become one to give teachers a stronger voice

9. Owen believes

    a. kids hate school primarily because they have bad teachers

    b. kids hate school, and there is very little we can do about it because of the many different contexts (economic, historical, cultural, etc.) discussed in the first part of the essay

    c. kids hate school, but despite NCLB, this situation could be improved if curriculum and educational practices were informed or revised in light of the educational models he discusses

    d. kids hate school, and because of NCLB, there is very little we can do about it

10. Owen argues that anti-intellectual practices

    a. may be extended to universities in the increasing call for "accountability" and "improved standards"

    b. threaten American virtues of individuality and pluralism

    c. both a. and b

    d. neither a. nor b

SECTION II

Hearing the Voices of Students

"I hate school because of the fact that people are treated unfairly and unjust and discriminated against. For instance, I have friends who are 'freaks' or 'goths' who wear extremely baggy pants that cover their shoes and they get called out for it absolutely every time they wear it yet whenever I wear extremely baggy pants no one says anything about it … there's something wrong with that picture. I mean, I can have a conversation with the dean in pants that I can fit midgets in and no one says anything to me about it."

—15-YEAR OLD FLORIDA HIGH SCHOOL STUDENT

"I guess it's because when you are sitting in a room doing math or reading a textbook for nine months out of the year it gets really boring, you know there will never be anything new happening; nothing different, exciting, spontaneous. I wish we could do more things outside and hands-on-projects … things that boost our creativity."

—13-YEAR OLD MISSOURI MIDDLE SCHOOL STUDENT

"It's true what Rosa was talking about how teachers…in general, all think it's easy for us. Probably you all smoked some of this or did some of that, but it's not like, you all didn't grow up like we did. It is hard, [is] what she is saying, if you all come through where we live and you all hear a gunshot, you get scared. But if we hear gunshots it's like somebody flushed a toilet. I see people sell drugs every day. It's like a job to them, street pharmacists."

—AN URBAN MIDDLE SCHOOL STUDENT IN CONNECTICUT

"When parents are asked what they want for their children, they usually answer that they want their children to be happy. Why, then, is happiness rarely mentioned as an aim of education?"

—NEL NODDINGS, HAPPINESS IN EDUCATION (1997)

The Republic of Middle School: "At-Risk" Student Voices on Virtue, Justice, and Happiness and the Unhappiness Endemic to Education

Lynda George

Central Connecticut State University

This exploratory qualitative action research examines "at-risk" middle school students' perceptions of happiness within their urban school setting through a philosophical lens. To uncover their perceptions about happiness, students read sections from Aristotle's *Ethics* (1953/1976) regarding virtue, as well as his definitions of justice and happiness as they relate to virtue. Students responded to the text through discussion, interviews, and reflective journals. Their thoughts on happiness, virtue, and justice within their school brought forth a unique and telling understanding of student frustration regarding the lack of virtue and justice within their school, a lack which hampers their happiness. Their perceptions and stories provide insight into why kids hate school.

Critical theorists stress that the best means to promote an educated citizenry is through critical inquiry (Sirotnik, 1991). When offered the opportunity to think about and discuss virtue within their school, based on classical definitions, ten urban "at-risk" eighth graders applied the concepts to their experiences and quickly articulated their views and experiences. For this study "at-risk" refers to students considered by educators to be academically and/or socially in trouble within the school setting as evidenced by poor attendance, multiple suspensions, low standardized test scores, failing grades, and/or a negative attitude toward school rules/school authority. Three assistant principals selected the student participants. These administrators were provided the above definition of "at-risk" and were asked to select outspoken students. Those students selected were asked by the researcher to volunteer for the study as a means to help the researcher with her work and to have their voices heard. At the time of the study, 1,225 students attended the school (grades seven and eight). The teaching faculty numbered 87, with an administrative staff of five. The average class size was 21.6 students, and the ratio of students to support staff (including counselors, social workers, and the school psychologist) was 1:179.

The school district is a large urban system, which, at the time, included twenty-seven elementary schools, four middle schools, three high schools and two local charter schools. The district was taken over by a private-for-profit corporation. Following this change of hands, the system lost local control to a state takeover. The district is known for low test scores, a high drop-out rate, and poor leadership.

The student participants for this study included six girls and four boys. The ethnicity of the group, based on students' descriptions of themselves, included Jamaican, African-American, Puerto Rican and "I'm a lot of things." This action research incorporated elements of critical theorist Henry Giroux's (1983) model for citizenship education.

Giroux's pedagogical assumptions and practices are an attempt to promote civic courage through an emancipatory model for citizenship education. Giroux suggests that "the active nature of student participation in the learning process must be stressed.... Students are able to challenge, engage, and question the form and substance of the learning process" (Giroux, 1983, pp. 351–352). The discussion of classical texts using the Socratic method provided the means for active participation within this study. A nurturing, supportive and safe space for discussion was arranged by the researcher in order for students to challenge, engage, and question the substance of the materials they discussed. This was accomplished by sitting around a table with the researcher as part of the group, having only ten participants and with a brief discussion on confidentiality.

Giroux also argues that "...the development of a critical mode of reasoning must be used so as to enable students to appropriate their own histories, to delve into their own biographies and systems of meaning" (Giroux, p. 352). In this study, students' thoughts, ideas and experiences were expressed through discussion, and reflective journal writing was based on their experiences. The lens provided by Aristotle promoted a critical mode for reasoning. Students' stories were told and their voices authenticated. Thus Giroux's model, along with primary source philosophical texts on virtue, was used to uncover students' perceptions of happiness, virtue, and justice within their school. The use of these texts provided a scholarly foundation for thinking about virtue as well as a common starting point for discussion.

HAPPINESS IN SCHOOL

The discussion, following the reading of Aristotle, "On Happiness" (Appendix A) began with an opening question. "How does your school contribute to your happiness?" "There ain't no happiness here" was an immediate response. The second voice replied, "That is what I was about to say." Three others nodded in agreement. Thus began the dialog on students' perceptions of happiness within their school. A fourth student spurred the conversation onward into thoughtful deliberation with the initial lone voice of dissent, "There is happiness because when you do something good in the school, like, you get an award or if you get a good grade on your test you are happy. Right or wrong?"

Maya suggested Aristotle is "...trying to say that happiness is not about having fun and stuff. Amusement is like when you be relaxed, and you are calm and stuff and that you could have happiness. But when it comes down to life itself, you are going to have to have seriousness." (George, 2005, pg. 420)

Maya wondered philosophically, "...does happiness always have to be something good?" Rosa concurred: "That's what I'm thinking." Jesus, who is not an academically successful student, reiterated his initial belief about school and happiness, "I don't think school is happy at all (pg. 421)".

JOURNAL ENTRY

Jesus wrote: "I think goodness makes every one happy inside, like getting an A+ on your test or a teacher telling you, you did good. But when no one tells you how good you did then you don't feel so good."

* * * * * *

The students demonstrated their ability to read and discuss Aristotle and reexamine their definition of happiness to incorporate Aristotle's broader interpretation. Receiving praise and high grades were seen as a means for happiness, but for some students success and praise is rarely, if ever, received. Students who are not successful academically are not happy in school. Although there is a need for high standards and high expectations, there is also a need for happiness through success for all. This could be accomplished through smaller classes and more individualized instruction. These "at-risk" students were articulate and thoughtful in their understanding of Aristotle. Group discussion, and relating the learning to their experiences, promoted learning.

VIRTUE IN SCHOOL

At the start of this study none of the students could define virtue. Aristotle's definition of virtue as the good person, the good life and the good society (Virtue and vice, 1952) was given to them. They voiced a lack of connection between school and the rest of their lives that hindered having the good life in or out of school.

Jesus suggested that the requirements, expectations and pressures put on the students place them at-risk. "I think that pushes kids to drop out of school at an early age." Rosa stated some problems that exist within the community: "Well, where I live, there is a lot of drugs and a lot of violence. I hear gunshots almost everyday and I bet when they (teachers) were younger they didn't go through the things that we are going through right now. (George, pg. 423)"

A lack of understanding between and among teachers and students and/or teachers and the community further drives the disconnection or sense of alienation for some students.

JUSTICE IN SCHOOL

In "The Republic of Plato" Socrates described a series of scenarios where no matter what the virtuous person did his actions are perceived as wrong. Socrates argues that even though the virtuous person was punished and looked down upon he was happier than the person who lacked virtue (Plato, 1991 trans).

When the students discussed the idea of justice in relationship to virtue, eight students made use of language that suggested Platonic idealism. Words and terms such as "fairness," "right," and/or "rights" were used to describe justice. Rosa explained, "To me, it's like doing the right thing, like you have to do the right thing, to have a positive influence. That is how I define justice." Maya defined justice as, "figuring out the right and wrong of a thing."

Ruby and Rosa defined justice in terms of rights and opportunity. Ruby said, "Justice to me is something that makes things right. If I want justice, then I'm gonna have to fight for something right and that is justice." Rosa also expressed the need to struggle for justice. "I believe that's justice, for you to fight for your rights." Jesus described it in terms of the judicial system. "Justice is when people from the court system get together and decide are you right or wrong."

Justice according to Aristotle is "Anything that tends to produce or conserve the happiness of a political association... Justice in this sense, then, is complete virtue; justice, however, not unqualified but in relation to somebody else" (Aristotle, 1953/1976, p. 173). When asked to describe justice in action within their school, nine out of ten students articulated examples of injustice. Six students spoke of receiving suspensions they believed were not deserved. Ruby told a story that included a twist on Aristotle's idea of being in the right place at the right time in the cafeteria:

They didn't suspend the whole cluster. I know they couldn't have done that, but they didn't know exactly who really threw the food. They just assumed there was food in this part of the cafeteria; we should suspend this part and I was in that part...Two people who got suspended; they really did have something to do with the fight. But the other four, we all ran out being in the wrong place at the wrong time.

Tamika and Will both said there wasn't much justice at the school because their side of the story was not respected. "There is not much justice because...they listen to the teacher's side of the story and not your side of the story... and they don't even need any evidence, automatically the teacher is right. The teacher might not even know what really happened." Will said, "There ain't really no justice in 'Grove'...There is no justice at 'Grove' because if you get in trouble they will just believe the teachers..." Will described the lack of justice in terms of teachers versus students:

> There ain't no justice at "Grove" because usually the students will be out-ruled by the teachers because...the kids are defined as liars and what not. The students know when the teacher did something wrong. But then the students are wrong too because the students carry on doing something that gets them into trouble like cursing at the teacher...and then get suspended. Teachers sometimes blame students for something they didn't do.

Oliver also recounted a story about a suspension. "There's not that much justice. I got suspended...I got hit in the head with a (sunflower) seed, I told the teacher (a substitute) and he told me to sit down. I kept on explaining to him but he just told me to sit down. So I picked up a seed and threw it back. And then I got in trouble for throwing the seed...which really sucks."

Jesus spoke of a lack of justice regarding suspensions and offered a suggestion that reflected society's judicial system. "I think they suspend you for like anything. I don't think that's right. That is not good justice. They should put you through something like court in school with kids participating... I had a fight last year and the boy started it and we both got suspended for the same amount of days but I was just defending myself." Will, too, expressed hope in a broad social justice: "Well, I see there is more justice in society than in the school...Justice in society, you actually can use witnesses to say that you did or did not do something and prove that you did not do what you were accused of doing..."

Two examples were cited about not getting permission to use the girl's room. Tamika's response was:

> Justice, I don't think justice is at "Grove." I don't think it is fair. I had to go to the bathroom and I asked my vice principal if I could go and she said no. So somebody else asked her and she said OK. She let her go. So I got up again, after the girl came back, and she said no, and I had to go to the bathroom really bad, so I had to leave. I went to the bathroom and I got a five-day suspension.

Jesus spoke of another example of what he perceived as unfair treatment regarding a broken promise. "Last year I was supposed to get double promoted...and it was a promise and [later] they said I can't get double promoted because they didn't write it down on some paper...so the house principal said I couldn't get double promoted. What a mean person she is." (George, 2005)

*****

Justice was expressed as a means for determining what is fair and what is right. When asked to describe justice in action within their school, negative examples were given. Justice was perceived as hindered by unfair and unjust acts and actions toward students by the authority figures within the school.

CONCLUSIONS

Constructivist pedagogy builds on students' prior knowledge and provides them with the necessary tools for sustained inquiry into difficult primary source materials. Constructivist pedagogy within the context of this study shows that students appreciate relating experiences as a means to promote understanding and derive new meaning from difficult texts. The means for enlightenment through constructivist theory encourages learning and leads to insightful, intellectual, happy scholars. The ten students in this study demonstrated an ability to read and philosophically discuss Aristotle. They were able to re-examine their initial definition of happiness as well as incorporate and assimilate Aristotle's broader interpretation into their discussion.

Why do kids hate school? The students in this study perceived virtue as related to happiness, but found happiness to be only marginally evident within the school building. Receiving praise and high grades were seen as a means for happiness in school, but this was not readily obtained by all. Virtue in relationship to justice was expressed as a means for determining what is fair and what is right. But when asked to describe justice in action within their school, negative examples were given. The discussion of justice was a discussion of the injustice students found in the school. It is easy to hate a system that strictly enforces a school rule and thereby punishes a student for what was, in fact, a virtuous act. Without giving students a voice regarding an act/action that at first glance appears to be breaking a school rule, justice and hope perish.

These students believed that virtue, as reflected in the cultural milieu of the school, was hindered because teachers were not properly aware of the external community forces facing urban students. The voices of these students tell us, if we listen to them, that there is a need for democratic schools—not only to promote a democratic society—but also to encourage and connect the disenfranchised student as well. Students are taught the ideals of democracy and justice, but they do not see themselves participating in a fair and just school society.

APPENDIX A

Aristotle on Happiness

"Happiness is not a state...we ought rather to refer happiness to some activity... and such a description is thought to fit actions that accord with goodness... Happiness does not consist in amusement...Amusement is a form of relaxation, and people need relaxation because they cannot exert themselves continuously. But the happy life seems to be lived in accordance with goodness, and such a life implies seriousness and does not consist in amusing oneself...If happiness is an activity in accordance with virtue, it is reasonable to assume that it is in accordance with the highest virtue, and this will be the virtue of the best part of us. Whether this is the intellect or something else that we regard as naturally ruling and guiding us, and possessing insight into things noble and divine...It is the activity of this part, in accordance with the virtue proper to it that will be perfect happiness" (p. 326, 327, 328).

REFERENCES

Aristotle. (1953/1976). *The Ethics of Aristotle: The Nicomachean Ethics.* (J.A.K.Thompson trans.) New York, N.Y.: Penguin Press.

George, L. (2005) Moral development through thoughtful inquiry, discussion and reflection. In Forum on Public Policy, *Child Psychology*, vol. 1, no. 4.

Giroux, H. and Purpel, D. (1983). Social education in the classroom. In H. Giroux and E. Purpel (eds.). *The Hidden Curriculum and Moral Education.* Berkeley, CA: McCutchan Publishing Co.

Plato. (1991). *The Republic of Plato.* (Allan Bloom trans.) New York, NY: Basic Books.

Sirotnik, K (1991). Critical inquiry: A paradigm for praxis. In E.C. Short (ed.) *Forms of Curriculum Inquiry.* Albany, NY: State University of New York Press.

___ (1952). Virtue and vice. M. Adler and W. Gorman (eds.) *A Syntopicon of Great Books of the Western World.* Chicago, Ill: Encyclopedia Britannica, Inc.

MULTIPLE CHOICE QUESTIONS

1. Critical theorists propose that the best means to promote an educated citizenry is through

    a. civics courses to understand government

    b. critical inquiry to promote thinking

    c. criticism of students to motivate underachievers

    d. all of the above

2. Critical theorist Henry Giroux stated that "...the development of a critical mode of reasoning must be used so as to enable students to appropriate their own histories, to delve into their own biographies and systems of meaning." In this study this was accomplished by the students:

    a. discussing Aristotle's Ethics

    b. writing in Reflective Journals

    c. using examples from their lives as they related to Aristotle

    d. all of the above

3. Based on the students' thoughts and perceptions regarding justice in their school, what could/should administrators do to promote more justice?

    a. explain the rules to the students more often

    b. listen to the students and give them a voice regarding their behavior

    c. have more rules so students know what to do

    d. all of the above

4. Based on this study how might teachers promote a more virtuous school environment?

    a. inflate grades

    b. give fewer tests

    c. listen to the students about their lives

    d. all of the above

5. According to Aristotle, happiness is:

    a. having fun and enjoying life

    b. an activity in accordance to virtue

    c. only comes from hard work and study

    d. all of the above

6. The students showed their ability to use higher order thinking skills:

    a. by their discussion of Aristotle on happiness

    b. by their anger over the lack of virtue in their school

    c. by their concern for graduating high school

    d. all of the above

7. Democratic schools promote student involvement in the running of the school. What evidence is given by the students that this would be a good idea for their school?

    a. their poor behavior in the cafeteria

    b. their lack of appreciation for the school rules

    c. their examples of unfair treatment at school

    d. all of the above

8. The students appreciated the idea of virtue meaning the good person, the good life, and the good society. But when they were asked to give examples within their school negative experiences were expressed. From reading about this study, why do you think this was the case?

    a. it was easier for the students to come up with negative examples because there were more of them in their daily school experiences

    b. the students didn't know any better

c. the students were negative about everything because they behave poorly

d. all of the above

9. From listening to the voices of these urban middle school students, teachers should

a. listen to their students and appreciate their life circumstances

b. promote happiness and academic success through discussion

c. develop rules that are fair and just

d. all of the above

10. Students in this study revealed that they should be seen as "at-promise" rather than "at-risk":

a. because they can reason and think

b. because they, at times, have been treated unfairly

c. because they are articulate and capable of learning

d. all of the above

Why Kids Hate School What the Kids Say!

EMMETT E. SAWYER
JUDITH GREGG
MISSOURI STATE UNIVERSITY

INTRODUCTION

The theme for the steering committee of the 2006 Academy for Educational Studies Second Annual Conference was, "Why Kids Hate School." The debate was led by experts such as Susan Ohanian, David Owen and Philip Cusick and a host of other professors, practitioners and graduate students. Do kids hate school or do kids just hate certain aspects of the educational process? Is their discontent focused on certain subject areas? Is "hate" the right word to use to describe adolescents' attitudes toward school? Obviously, the questions are many and complex.

What we do know is that something is happening in our schools—something that leads thousands to continue disengaged throughout the system until they receive a diploma, or leads them to disengage completely even before that, which generally leads to confinement in the lower socio-economic levels or, worse still, to criminal activity. Either way, the consequences for a highly developed society and economy are discouraging at best and debilitating at worst.

We come to the conference concerned and puzzled. The conundrum is this: more and more students are disengaged at a time when no other nation in the history of the world has spent more dollars on education-related expenditures and espoused the noble belief that *no child will be left behind*. Despite numerous, well-intentioned, expensive initiatives at the local, state and national levels, little has happened to reverse this negative trend in public schools. While the overall rate of drop-outs has shown a slight decrease in recent years, analysis of disaggregated data for high school students reveals that certain ethnic and minority groups' rate of drop-outs remains alarmingly high. If "hate" is not the right word, then we need to discover what word or words might fit into the statement to replace it and, as part of the discovery process, learn more about how to engage disengaged students. In order to accomplish this task, we use a two-pronged methodology. First, we review literature that focuses on characteristics, attitudes and behaviors of high school drop-outs, which might lead us to a better understanding, promote more effective thinking and yield more permanent, broad-based solutions. Second, we talk to the experts—disengaged students in alternative school settings—in order to gain their perspective about the subject.

LITERATURE REVIEW

The most recent revelation regarding drop-outs is found in a study funded by the Bill and Melinda Gates Foundation. Hundreds of high school drop-outs were asked the reason why they dropped out. No surprises emerged to anyone who has worked with high school students: students were not interested in their course work, attendance and the need to work. What is surprising is that many of these students had passing grades, but they lacked the motivation to complete work, nor was it demanded, in their opinion, to work harder. But more revealing is the statement made by many that they should have stayed in school. Real-life experiences taught them that good job opportunities required a high school diploma. What is ironic is that these students had actually wanted a more real-life based education. One might predict that these students would not want their parents contacted by the school or vice-versa, nor would they want their parents involved in school, but the opposite was offered by many high school drop-outs (Bridgeland et al., 2006).

Nancy Beekeman's (1987) earlier work found many of the same reasons for dropping out. After reviewing studies conducted between 1959 through 1984, she found that drop-out students disliked school, found it boring and not relevant, experienced academic distress or failure, and needed money, which led to full-time work. These studies affirmed that dropping out of school actually led to higher unemployment rates or lower wage earning jobs. Interestingly, Beckman reported that earlier studies found that between a third and half of drop-outs interviewed indicated leaving school was a bad decision.

Rick Fry (2005) studied drop-out rates of foreign-born students in our nation's schools. He found that a disproportionate percentage of drop-outs were foreign-born students. The Pew Hispanic Center Study (2006) also found that students who had difficulty in school before they came to this country were more likely to have difficulty in school here and drop-out more frequently. This report obviously adds another layer of complexity as to why kids might not like school and suggests that a one-size-fits-all approach will be less than effective.

The work of Michael J. Strube and Larry E. Davis as reported by O'Conner (1997) appears to confirm the ineffectiveness of the dictum "one-size-fits-all." The principal investigators took an opposite approach from many other researchers in this area by conducting a study of African-American students in St. Louis, Missouri. They studied characteristics of African-American students who were completing high school requirements in order to use this information to create programs designed to strengthen the positive characteristics of at-risk African-American students. They found that the student's sense of empowerment to overcome barriers and his/her attitudes are far more important than factors at school or home in determining successful completion of high school. In some instances, students perceived it was not a black cultural thing to do to complete high school.

Other researchers believe that the process of dropping out or disengagement can be interrupted by parents' interaction with their children. Morse, Christenson and Lehr, (2004) suggested that students who received parental support in the areas of academics and motivation have higher levels of engagement. In other words, parents who are engaged in their children's lives by modeling positive behaviors, setting appropriate expectations, providing reasonable levels of structure and being adequately informed about activities in school, among other behaviors, are more likely to have children who are more engaged in the educational process and less likely to drop out. Students are then less likely to lose interest in or develop negative attitudes toward school.

Conversely, Vallerand, Guay and Fortier, (1997) examined parents' influence on less persistent or disengaged children. They found that parents' influence on their children is stronger than those of school personnel. Parents of less persistent or disengaged students appear to be more controlling, therefore, exacerbating the problem. Their children feel even less in control of their lives and tend to disengage or drop out more frequently.

The researchers believe that the role of the parent is crucial in addressing the drop-out issue. Teachers generally have contact with a student for one academic year, while parents have a long-term relationship with their child which increases the negative or positive impact they might have on the child (Vallerand et al., 1997).

Astone and McLanahan (1991) examined the relationship between children living in a single-parent household, or step-parent families, and school completion. The researchers analyzed data from the *High School and Beyond* study (National Center for Education Statistics, 1988) to examine the effects of family structure, parenting practices, grade point averages, attendance, aspirations and attitudes. Each of these factors could affect the child's ability to cope with and navigate a course for successful school completion. The researchers found, "Children from single-parent families and step-parent families are more likely to exhibit signs of early disengagement from school" (p. 318). However, the researchers cautioned that many other variables could be affecting their conclusions and encouraged better, more refined methods of data collection.

Understanding the effects of grade retention is critical to the understanding of disengaged students. The standards-based movement made grade retention an acceptable school response to poor or below grade-level performance. The complex environment influenced by teacher and administrator attitudes, school policies and the vagaries of making life-altering decisions regarding children as young as five years of age, makes retention a practice ripe for debate, especially in light of the literature regarding retention.

Roderick (1995) found in literature three strong messages regarding retention. Retention appears to be an ineffective solution to a complex problem; it communicates the negative message that the student's ability is inferior and removes a student from his or her peer group. The result is an increased probability that a student will disengage from school, a place he or she views with frustration and failure when compared to his or her peer group. While the results of studies regarding these three messages are mixed, retention may tell students that they are inferior, differences do not really matter and that the school is not about all children being successful.

Motivation is a key factor in understanding the high school student's decision to disengage or drop out of school. Vallerand, Guay and Fortier (1997) examined motivation and found that it is not a singular term, but a very complex concept, better understood by dissecting motivation into three types: internal, external and amotivation. They explained that if a student completes an activity because he or she personally finds value or interest in the activity, intrinsic motivation is being displayed. Extrinsic motivation is a more complex concept, but essentially focuses on factors outside the individual that prompt various behaviors. And, citing the work of Deci and Ryan (1985) on amotivation, they recognized that motivation can be absent in individuals—behaviors and consequences are not connected by the individual.

Given these differences in motivation, the researchers examined what factors could strongly influence motivation. One of the factors that could affect motivation was identified as social context—a broad term that includes individuals (i.e. parents, teachers and administrators known as social agents) interacting with the student and the climate of the school. The climate of the school is usually determined by individuals operating in the social context, especially school administrators. The major thought is that the social context affects the student's perception of his/her ability to exercise control of his/her behavior to produce desired results. The researchers do not make a direct relationship between the individuals operating in the social context and their effect on the student's level of motivation; rather, they emphasize the student's perception of how his/her competence and autonomy is influenced by the impact of the social context on the student's level of motivation. If a student's perception of his/her competence and autonomy is negative, more negative forms of motivation are prevalent (Vallerand et al., 1997).

While a form of external motivation can lead to positive outcomes for the student, particularly when he/she believes completing a course of study might lead to a better way of life or occupation, external motivation is generally viewed, along with amotivation, as producing negative results. Intrinsic motivation generally leads to positive outcomes. More important to the understanding of this complex subject is that persistence is more highly related to intrinsic motivation. The lack of persistence is evidenced more frequently in students who are only extrinsically motivated or who are not motivated at all to complete an activity. For the drop-out, discontinuing schooling is not usually a spontaneous decision, rather it is one he/she has considered for some time, and, therefore, he/she acts on this decision whenever it is legal for him/her to do so (Vallerand et al., 1997).

While the degree and type of motivation could be used to predict behavior, and, consequently, whether a student had a propensity to drop out of school, Ensminger and Slusarcick (1992) examined the long-term accumulation of factors that influence a student's decision to drop out by studying a cohort of African-American first grade students. They studied the relationship of school performance in the first grade and school dropouts in later grades. They also investigated the student and his/her family to determine if there were characteristics present that influenced school performance. The researchers found that first grade males and females who earned higher grades were more likely to persist toward graduation than students who earned lower grades. A more refined analysis of the data suggested that grades in mathematics might have some power in predicting graduation rates.

The researchers found additional factors interacting with persistence to graduation. Examples of these factors include the following findings. When family background was introduced, the researchers found that those students who earned higher grades were more likely to persist toward graduation regardless of how dysfunctional the family. The structure of the family appeared to affect the persistence to graduation of females more so than males . When testing for school behavior and performance, they found that the student's perception of how teachers rated his/her performance affected the student's persistence to graduation. The research indicated that parent involvement in school did not affect persistence to graduation in the early grades; however, this factor did interact with persistence to graduation when the student reached sixteen years of age. Surprisingly, the researchers found that reading to a child in the first grade did not interact with persistence to graduation; however, they did find that a child talking about school to the parent or completing homework with an adult family member interacted positively with persistence to graduation. One final factor of concern is the aggressive behavior of young children in school, especially in males. Aggressive behavior in young children appears to negatively affect the student's chances of graduating and must be controlled or altered to prevent more harmful behaviors in the future (Ensminger & Slusarcick, 1992).

Bhanpuri and Reynolds (2003) authored a report for Learning Point Associates on the high school drop-out age. Their work summarized research on drop-outs and offered ways to address issues such as raising the compulsory attendance age. One factor identified by the authors is truancy. As one would expect, truancy was identified as a negative behavior that increases the probability that a student would drop out of school.

Dunn (1990) and Dunn and Dunn (1993) attribute at-risk characteristics that influence a student's decision to drop out of school to the match, or mismatch, of instruction to the student's identified learning styles. Through studies of at-risk students, Dunn and Dunn found that, in general, drop-outs have strong needs for several learning style elements. These elements include: (1) mobility at frequent intervals; (2) tactual and kinesthetic learning; (3) variety rather than routines; (4) late afternoon or evening classes; (5) recognition of their high motivation levels; (6) collegial relationships rather than authoritative; (7) informal classroom design or settings; and, (8) low levels of lighting in the classroom. Emphasizing that the one-size-fits-all approach is detrimental to our schools and students, the researchers advocate a more rational approach firmly grounded in research that is based on the learning needs of the student. Critical to this approach is the re-training of teachers to provide them the expertise to deliver instruction through a variety of ways to address the student's learning preferences through matched instruction.

Marzano (2004) and many other researchers, including Bennett et al. (2004) and Payne (1996), recognized economic and sociological causes as reasons for students' academic distress. However, they more appropriately focused on the effect these factors have on the students' ability to learn, or on what they have not learned. In general, the primary assertion is that due to poverty and other related issues, many students enter kindergarten or first grade without the same amount of background knowledge as students from more advantaged homes and families. Students who traditionally start behind tend to stay behind, and the researchers maintain that school systems should focus on ameliorating this deficit in critical domains of learning that are well-known today as the achievement gap.

Finally, in a report to Congress (1999), transitions and mobility were identified as factors that increase the probability that a student would be at-risk socially and educationally, and, therefore, in danger of not completing school. Neighborhoods with high rates of mobility experience higher rates of negative community activities (i.e. crime, drugs).

SUMMARY

The literature review revealed the complexity of the factors that converge on the issue of high school drop-outs, including personal, economic, sociological and systems factors. Students' personal issues related to lack of interest, boredom, lack of empowerment, motivation and aggression. Economic issues contributed to high school drop-out rates as students left school to earn money because of family or personal situations. This factor leads to the long-term consignment of the student to lower socio-economic levels. Poverty also contributed to students entering the school system with a deficit in background knowledge, which if not addressed, left the student behind until he/she could make the decision to drop out. Sociological factors such as family structure, parent involvement, parent control and mobility affect the student's ability to complete his/her education. A systems approach indicated issues of relevancy, academic support, appropriate match of instruction to learning styles, immigrants and minority students, motivation, and the effects of early grades on achievement.

STUDENT INTERVIEWS

Reviewing selected pieces of literature is usually done to gain a more global perspective on why students disengage or drop out of school. It is also useful to look at actual data points—the students who are at-risk—to hear, in their words, why they disengaged from or dropped out of school. Three students who are enrolled in an alternative school in a large, urban school district were selected to be interviewed. Two of the students were actual drop-outs and were reclaimed, and the other had contiguous but troubled enrollment in the district high schools. The students ranged in age from 16 to 20 years old. Two students were female and one male. One female was Hispanic and the other two were white/Caucasian.

Karen was the oldest student. She was tall, pretty and seemed eager to be a part of the study . She was gregarious, which probably factored into her decision to quit school. Karen has specific goals in life and wants to attend college when she graduates. She is concerned about finances for college, but seemed encouraged when the interviewers gave her specific information regarding student loans and admission procedures. Karen will graduate this semester at the quarter. She was very excited at the prospect of completing school.

Judith is 18 years old and is Hispanic. She will give birth to a little girl within a few weeks— one who she has already named. She lives with her fiancé who is older and earns enough money so that she can concentrate on school and the baby. Even though she has had many problems growing up, she took control of the situation and found a way out on her own. She gives the impression that she is strong, mature and level-headed. She was pleasant and smiling throughout the interview. Judith and Karen answered as if they were appreciative that someone wanted to know what they thought.

Blake is a polite, clean-cut, nice-looking, 16-year-old white male. He seemed fidgety and somewhat guarded. Blake grew more comfortable with the interview situation as time went on. He slouched in his chair while replying to questions, while the other two sat up in the chair and seemed totally engaged . His answers, though, were direct, but not as in-depth as those of the other two interviewees. He has not had the life experiences to the degree that Judith and Karen have . He did express goals for the future, but did not seem to have all the details worked out about how to accomplish his goals.

A standard set of questions was asked of each student in a semi-structured format. This allowed the students to comment beyond the scope of the question and allowed the interviewer to follow-up with additional questions. The data will be reported in a question-and-answer format.

At what point in your educational career did you sense you were not making appropriate academic and social progress?

All three indicated that they began to have problems early in high school. Each participant gave a different reason for his/her problems. For Blake and Judith, it was their ninth grade year, while Karen said her problems began in her sophomore year.

To what do you attribute your lack of progress?

Blake does not like large classes and felt he needed individual attention in science and mathematics, which he did not receive. He indicated some behavior problems at school, and this, combined with his poor academic progress, resulted in him being suspended and sent to another alternative school for behavior problems before being sent to his current alternative school. Judith attributed her problems to her home situation, which affected her academic progress. She dropped out of school to earn money so that she could leave home. Her relationship with her father was very poor. She said emphatically, "I had to move out; I had to earn money." While Judith indicated social issues at home, Karen's social issues were at school. Karen attended a large high school that had many students from wealthy homes. She summarized her feelings regarding the culture of the school this way, "Unless you have money or you are doing something good for the school, no one pays any attention to you. It is an arena for stereotypes." Karen was from a blended family. She was much older than her siblings and was given the responsibility of taking care of them. She did not view her home life in a positive light. In her opinion, "Everything was bad."

How did your parents react to the lack of progress?

Blake said that his mother blamed the school for his lack of academic progress. Karen said that her parents told her to get her homework done, but did not really understand her or her problem. Judith's parents were a nonfactor at this point.

Did you ask for help from the school? Parents? What was their response?

Blake said he asked for help in his science and mathematics classes, but did not receive enough to make a difference. When asked if he had contacted his counselor or assistant principal, he said that he did not know how to contact them. Judith severed her ties with her family so they were not helpful. She was emphatic in not asking for help from the school because of how she thought the school perceived her. She said, "No, they thought I was a problem student." Judith said her friends were not aware of her problems. Karen, faced with little help from home, attempted to get help from her assistant principal and counselor. She liked her assistant principal, but said that he was too busy and that he referred her to her counselor. In summarizing her attempt to get help from school personnel, teachers, principals and counselors, she said that they were all "too busy!"

How did your issues at school affect your behavior?

Judith indicated that the issues she was dealing with affected her behavior. She was involved in several fights at school. Blake, too, was involved in discipline issues; however, he did not make any connections between his academic problems and his behavior. He gave the impression that even if he were performing well academically, he might still have been involved in inappropriate behavior at school. Karen started skipping school every day. She could not make up for the lessons missed so she quit school her sophomore year. Later, she did enroll again at the same high school, but with little success. The school finally referred her to the alternative program.

Have you changed school districts during your academic career? How many times?

Each student had moved from school to school, especially during his/her elementary years. However, as far as they could remember, they had stayed within the same school district.

What is your perception of school?

Blake's perception of school was related more to his body clock than to any other issues. He does not like to rise early in the morning. He would not like a job that started early in the morning, either, even if it paid good money. Judith said she took a lot for granted in her high school. She is more mature now and enjoys being back, especially at her current school. Karen said school is good, but emphasized again the concept that it is an arena for stereotypes. When we discussed the fact that she may confront the same problems out of school, she replied, "Society sucks!" Her opinion of her current school is strong and positive. She felt like it was her family—a huge family. Judith and Blake had similar feelings regarding their current school.

If you could change school, what changes would you make?

Blake's answer was predictable, "Start later." Judith and Karen agreed that classes should be smaller, and Karen added that group efforts were important for them to learn how to get along with others—an important life-long skill. Judith said more individual attention should be given to students as usually only those who demand attention get it. Even at her school "drama queens" were still present. She wished students would be more mature.

Do you see a value in learning information for the sake of knowledge or only learning information for potential careers/jobs?

Blake did not seem to understand this question—the potential power in knowledge. He talked about his future goals and that guided what he needed to know. Judith and Karen said yes to both aspects of learning knowledge; however, Karen, becoming more animated, added, "I am a student for life. Knowledge is power and it is essential to understand life."

What parts of school do you like?

Blake answered, "everything" about his current school. Judith said she likes sports and had she been more involved in school activities, she might not have dropped out. She did say, however, that working nights did prevent her from participating in sports. Karen likes being around people.

What parts of school do you dislike?

Blake responded, "Too strict, too many rules." However, in a follow-up question, he did seem to understand the importance of rules to the overall well-being of students and the operation of the school. Judith disliked the size of classes and Karen stayed consistent with her social theme, "Stereotypes!"

Do you plan to graduate?

Each student plans to graduate. Blake, still reserved, worried about being suspended from this school and having to attend a small, rural school while living with his grandmother. Judith, in a well-thought out response, indicated that she wants to graduate and enter the medical field. Karen simply but enthusiastically said, "Yes!" She expressed excitement about being able to graduate at the quarter. Her counselor had reviewed her coursework and told her that she could receive a diploma earlier than expected. Her face revealed her sense of pride at this accomplishment.

Did your parents/siblings graduate from high school?

Blake indicated that only one cousin in his family graduated from high school. No family member, to his knowledge, attended college. He would be the first, he said with a slight indication of pride. Judith said her brother was in college, but a sister did not graduate from high school. Her father had two years of college. Karen's biological parents did not graduate from high school, but her stepmother did. Karen revealed that her stepmother was very popular in high school, a status Karen deplored earlier in the interview. She did not know much about her biological mother.

Do you feel high school is important for future success/happiness?

All three interviewees emphatically declared that high school was important for their future success and happiness. Judith summed it up when she said, with a smile on her face, "Yes, you need an education to get the things you want in life!"

What are your future plans?

Blake indicated that he had watched a Discovery Channel show about demolition and rebuilding in cities. He thought that he might go into the demolition field, perhaps through the army, and then study architecture. Judith plans to enter the medical field, but her primary "future plan" is to be a great mother to her baby. Karen wants to be a writer for magazines like *National Geographic*.

Open comments from student regarding the topic?

Students were asked if students really hated school. Blake said that no, they only disliked the hours associated with the school day, which had been a consistent theme with him during the entire interview. Judith said that students do not hate school. She said that when students experience problems with school, they feel stupid, do not feel like they fit, and sit in classes in which they do not understand what is being taught. They develop the feeling, according to her, that "it is better to just not be there." Judith was chronically absent, fell farther behind in her coursework, and continued to repeat the cycle of being absent and lost in her coursework. She did not experience any intervention from the school, nor did she ask for help that could have broken the cycle. She indicated that even her best friends did not realize how lost she was in school. Karen said students do not necessarily hate school, they only hate conforming to a rigid structure. No one ever explains to them why he/she had to be in school.

Judith returned to the topic of being a good mother. She worried about providing a good home and life for her baby. She said that her relationship with her father was much better, and he was excited about the baby.

DISCUSSION

The purpose of the literature review was to provide an overview of the drop-out problem in a way that we might determine if students really do hate school. The review was not meant to provide a comprehensive look at the literature regarding drop-outs; rather, it was intended to give the reader a sampling of what might be found in the literature base. Much has been written regarding this issue in easily accessible formats for those who might want to pursue a more in-depth research. The interviews were meant to give life to the literature at the local level.

At this point in the discussion, the reader should understand the bias of the lead author regarding the topic. For approximately twenty-seven years, this author served as an assistant principal and principal at the high school level, associate superintendent, and department head of a K–12 laboratory school. During that time, much effort and time was devoted to the various issues discussed in the literature review. Opinions and beliefs were developed, refined, discarded and, in some cases, new ones adopted. These will permeate, with no apologies, the remainder of this discussion.

The literature review and the interviews revealed a complex set of factors affecting students' behavior in and out of school. Many of the papers defined the problem and offered simple to complex, common sense to utopian solutions to the problem. The solutions were based on the findings of the studies, which were limited by what the researchers determined as the scope of the problem or research questions. Reading the studies gives one the effect of putting a jigsaw puzzle together. Many researchers studied common variables or factors like attendance/truancy or family structure, while many added new variables or factors to the picture. But the picture, while complex in nature, reveals that the factors extend beyond the school to the home, community and government at all levels. In other words, it becomes a quality of life issue that is rarely discussed in that framework. Generally, the discussion focuses on parts, and, in many cases, blame—Who is not doing what to solve the problem. Therefore, responses to this problem were generally fragmented with mixed results.

Students' perceptions, attitudes and behaviors appear shaped by what happened to them both prior to entering school and after entering school. Students lacking early social, intellectual and family supports, many times related to generational poverty, enter a system disadvantaged. The students are probably not aware of their disadvantage until they enter a system that begins to measure them against accepted, and sometimes arbitrary, standards of behavior and intellect, which is often imposed from the outside. Students quickly become aware, through interactions with teachers and administrators, whether or not they meet the standards. A shy student assumes a role in the shadows of the classroom; whereas an aggressive student, especially an aggressive male student, assumes a role that leads to confrontation with the teacher and administrator. Both roles could have serious consequences when addressed by the parent.

As students progress through the grades, they receive mixed messages. Students hear messages that the school wants everyone to learn and succeed and that the school will meet everyone's needs. However, students soon learn that they will be treated as individuals just as long as they are achieving at grade level in order to enter the next grade together.

Young students experiencing difficulty in the classroom might not understand the word "competent," but they soon become aware that they are different. Trouble in the academic area has the potential to affect the socialization process in the classroom. High achieving students, sometimes with parent urging, segregate themselves from lower performing students. All this is troubling because the scope of academics that lead to a profile of competence are narrowly defined (i.e. reading and mathematics).

Other factors begin to differentiate students in the social realm that is a hidden curriculum in the school. Students become aware early that there are classes of haves and have nots. Wealth, or poverty, can determine acceptance in the power structure of the school and, therefore, affect the perceived control students have over their environment and life. Individuals appear to gravitate, if they can, to social and work contexts where they have some control over their surroundings. Students in public schools have little choice until they reach the age when compulsory attendance ends. Far too many make the decision to leave a system in which they feel unsuccessful, and in which they see no hope of becoming fulfilled as individuals.

One choice that appears to ameliorate this problem of social acceptance and competence is the arena of school activities. The National Federation of State High School Associations (2005) argues the importance of school activities to the overall effectiveness of schooling. Student participation in school activities is purported to positively impact the education, health, socialization and behavior of students and may predict success in later life. School activities are positive in nature, promote positive behaviors in school (i.e. attendance, academic achievement) and limit the time available for students to be involved in at-risk behaviors. Participating in school activities promotes healthy living and nutrition. A wider range of competencies are identified for school activities to determine success, i.e. music, speech, theater, athletics, when compared to core academic subjects.

Schools, as a system, offer little choice to the students, which the literature relates to the concept of self-determination. Self-determination is a critical factor in determining the strength of persistence to graduation for students. How important is this concept? According to the work of Dunn and Dunn (1993) in their construct of learning styles, choice is a critical factor in the learning process, especially when dealing with students who are identified in their model as non-conforming students. At one school where I was principal, approximately 25% of the student body in grades 9–12 were identified as having strong or extremely strong preferences for non-conforming. This would suggest that teachers' interactions with students are extremely important to the harmony of the classroom and their ability to support students in the learning process.

The authors were surprised at how closely the responses of the students interviewed mirrored the scope of the problems defined in the literature. These students had social, family and school issues. They did not find high school socially or educationally relevant. The school was not responsive to their problems nor had it, in several cases, even made the students aware of how to get help at school. From the interviews, the authors felt that each student had found hope, mainly by taking control of his/her life, setting goals and finding a place that was supportive of her/him. Only one of the students left us with the impression that he/she was on the edge and could go either way depending on how difficult circumstances became. The authors were also surprised at how little help it might have taken at a crucial moment to keep these students on track in a regular school setting.

CONCLUSION

What can we conclude from this sampling of the literature regarding disengaged students and the student interviews? Do kids hate school? These authors believe, in most cases, that students do not really hate school, and the students interviewed agreed. Students, for whatever reason, and there are many, are forced to make many life-altering, complex decisions for which they lack the knowledge, skills and dispositions. Yet, they must make them and, in many cases, they roll the dice and hope for the best. Students do not always believe dropping out is the right decision at the time. This places a heavy burden on adults in the society, regardless of what role they play, to provide supports that have the depth and breadth and the requisite financial support to address the issue of disengaged students in school. High school reform initiatives, such as Breaking Ranks (National Association of Secondary School Principals, 1996), hold promise for improvement. However, the nature and scope of the problem demands a national commitment to improve the quality of life for all families so as to ensure all students have access to appropriate and relevant education opportunities and supports at the right time and place.

Education is only one of five major institutions in a developed society. Each institution affects the others, and, unless each institution assumes responsibility for the effects of its actions, little will be accomplished. To address this problem, leadership, must come from education. Government has shown an inability to reach a consensus that does not carry political implications and expensive initiatives. Religious groups' or churches' impact is generally localized, and they are not organized in a way to lead a broad-based initiative of this nature. The family is not a unit capable of making national impact, and, in many ways, is part of the problem. The economy, as represented by the business and financial community, is a contributing factor to the conditions that produce disengaged students. When large corporations layoff or dismiss large numbers of employees, or pay low wages with few benefits, situational and generational poverty persist, affecting the children in these families. Only education has the heart of the child purely as its focus. However, education tends to be loosely connected, as are other institutions, and must organize itself systemically to provide national leadership, which is effective and efficient. It is time for education to provide leadership for education issues and stop deferring to others. Only a response that mobilizes all major institutions in society, in a coordinated response to address this issue, will enable us to realize the noble desire of *No Child Left Behind*!

REFERENCES

Astone, N. M., & McLanahan, S. S. (1991). Family structure, parental practices and high school completion. *American Sociological Review*, 56(6): 309–320.

Beekman, N. (1987). *The Dropout's Perspective on Leaving School*. Highlights: An ERIC/CAP Digest. Retrieved May 26, 2006 from www.thememoryhole.org/edu/eric

Bennett, A., Bridglall, B. L., Cauce, A. M., Everson, H. T., Gordon, E. W., Lee, C. D., Mendoza-Denton, R., Renzulli, J. S., & Stewart, J. K. (2004). *All Students Reaching the Top: Strategies for Closing Academic Achievement Gaps*. Naperville, IL: Learning Point Associates.

Bhanpuri, H., & Reynolds, G. M. (2003). *Understanding and Addressing the Issue of High School Dropout Age*. Retrieved May 26, 2006 from Learning Point Associates Web site: www.learningpt.org

Bridgeland, J. M., DiIulio, Jr., J. J., & Morison, K. B. (2006). *The Silent Epidemic: Perspectives of High School Dropouts*. A report by Civic Enterprises in association with Peter D. Hart Research Associates for the Bill and Melinda Gates Foundation.

Dunn, R. (1990). Teaching underachievers through their learning style strengths. *The Association for the Advancement of International Education, 16*(2).

Dunn, R., & Dunn, K. (1993). *Teaching Students through their Individual Learning Styles: A practical approach.* Boston, MA: Allyn and Bacon.

Ensminger, M. E., & Slusarcick, A. L. (1992). Paths to high school graduation or dropout: A longitudinal study of a first-grade cohort. *Sociology of Education,* 65: 95–113.

Fry, R. (2005). *The Higher Drop-out Rate of Foreign-born Teenagers: The Role of Schooling Abroad.* Retrieved May 26, 2006 from Pew Hispanic Center Web site: http://www.pewhispanic.org

Marzano, R. J. (2004). *Building Background Knowledge for Academic Achievement: Research on what Works in Schools.* Alexandria, VA: Association for Supervision and Curriculum Development.

Morse, A. B., Christenson, S. L., & Lehr, C. A. (2004). *School Completion and Student Engagement: Information and Strategies for Parents.* National Association of School Psychologists.

National Association of Secondary School Principals. (1996). *Breaking Ranks: Changing an American institution.* A report of the National Association of Secondary School Principals in partnership with the Carnegie Foundation on the high school of the 21st century. Reston, VA: Author.

National Center for Educational Statistics. (1988). *High School and Beyond.* Retrieved March 6, 2007 from National Center for Education Statistics Web site: http://nces.ed.gov/surveys/hsb

National Federation of High Schools. (2005). *The Case for High School Activities.* Retrieved May 26, 2006 from National Federation of High Schools Web site: http://www.nfhs.org

O'Connor, C. (1997). *Researchers Studying why Some students Stay in High School.* Retrieved May 26, 2006 from www.record.wustl.edu

Payne, R. K. (1996). *A Framework for Understanding Poverty.* Highlands, TX.: aha! Process, Inc.

Pew Hispanic Study. (2006). *The Changing Landscape of American Public Education: New Students, New Schools.* Retrieved March 6, 2007 from Pew Hispanic Center Web site: http://pewhispanic.org

Report to Congress. (1999). Retrieved May 26, 2006 from http://www.ncjrs.gov/html/ojjdp/ojjdp99 report_to_congress

Roderick, M. (1995). *Grade Retention and School Dropout: Policy Debate and Research Questions.* Phi Delta Kappa, Research Bulletin.

Vallerand, R. J., Guay, F. F., & Michelle, S. (1997). Self-determination and persistence in a real-life setting: Toward a motivational model of high school dropout. *Journal of Personality and Social Psychology,* 72(5): 1161–1176.

SUGGESTED READINGS

Dunn, R., & Dunn, K. (1993). *Teaching Students through their Individual Learning Styles: A Practical Approach*. Boston, MA: Allyn and Bacon.

Kozol, J. (1992). *Savage Inequalities: Children in America's Schools*. NY: Harper Perennial.

Marzano, R. J. (2004). *Building Background Knowledge for Academic Achievement: Research on what Works in Schools*. Alexandria, VA: Association for Supervision and Curriculum Development.

Payne, R. K. (2005). *A Framework for Understanding Poverty*. Highlands, Texas: aha! Process, Inc..

MULTIPLE CHOICE QUESTIONS:

1. Dunn and Dunn attribute at-risk characteristics that influence a student's decision to drop out of school to which of the following?

   a. negative behaviors prior to first grade

   b. aggressive behavior in older children

   c. match or mismatch of instruction to the student's learning styles

2. Which behavior, according to Ensminger and Slusarcick, negatively affects a student's chances of graduating?

   a. lack of parental involvement in early grades

   b. aggressive behavior in young children

   c. truancy

3. Which of the following statements is true regarding external motivation as discussed by Vallerand et al.?

   a. external motivation, in most circumstances, leads to long-term positive behaviors

   b. external motivation is generally viewed as producing negative behaviors

   c. external motivation has no effect on producing negative or positive behaviors

4. According to Vallerand et al., citing the work of Deci and Ryan, which of the following statements are true regarding amotivation?

   a. behaviors and consequences are not connected by the individual

   b. behaviors and consequences are connected by the individual

   c. behaviors, only, are connected by the individual

5. Social context, as discussed by Vallerand et al., best relates to the following statement.

   a. social context does not affect the level of motivation demonstrated by student behavior

   b. social context only affects interpersonal relationships between parents and students

   c. social context influences the student's perception of his/her competence and autonomy, and, therefore, his/her level of motivation

6. According to Payne, which of the following factors influences a student's ability to learn?

   a. poverty

   b. external motivation

   c. lack of mobility in the classroom

7. Which of the following would be an appropriate policy level response to the problem of dropouts?

   a. develop one policy response that each school implements in a consistent and efficient manner in order to facilitate assessment and accountability

   b. develop a policy response focused solely on teacher quality

   c. develop a policy response that allows schools flexibility in responding to issues regarding drop-outs

8. In general, according to Vallerand, et al., which of the following statements is true regarding the parent's role in addressing the drop-out issue?

   a. the more disengaged a student becomes, the more controlling is the parent

   b. the more disengaged a student becomes, the less controlling is the parent

   c. disengagement by the student and the control of the parent were found to be non-interacting variables

9. According to the Gates Foundation Study, reasons given for high school drop-outs included

   a. family problems, being bullied and need for independence

   b. aggressive behavior by the student and others and low grades

   c. lack of interest in coursework, poor attendance and need to work

10. According to Strube and Davis, as reported by O'Conner, which factors contribute to the successful completion of high school?

   a. the student's sense of empowerment to overcome barriers and his/her attitudes

   b. the school environment and socio-economic factors

   c. the two-parent family structure and parenting practices

Drop-outs or Push-outs? The Unintended Consequences of School Practices

KAREN S. SCOTT

SPRINGFIELD, MISSOURI PUBLIC SCHOOLS

INTRODUCTION

With all the school reform efforts of recent years, why have educators been unable to make significant gains in reducing drop-outs and increasing the graduation rate? Despite increased accountability and public criticism, the problem persists. The stakes are high for schools, which face increased scrutiny due to accountability, No Child Left Behind, and increased public criticism by none other than Bill Gates. The stakes are high for society. Businesses have a vested interest in the assurance of a well-educated workforce to sustain economic growth and development. Government officials at all levels are increasingly aware of added costs to welfare and criminal justice systems, as well as decreased tax revenues that result from higher drop-out rates.

On a more human level, the personal stakes for students and their families have also taken on new urgency. In an increasingly competitive, technological, global marketplace, the high school diploma represents the minimal requirement for today's job market. Research indicates a bleak future for high school drop-outs, with significantly decreased earning potential, increased dependence on public welfare programs, increased levels of incarceration and mental health problems, and shorter life spans (National Dropout Prevention Center/Network, 2006).

Perhaps the solution rests, in part, on a different approach. Historically, researchers have focused on characteristics common among students who drop out of school. Low socio-economic status, family problems, and the host of personal problems common to many dropouts focus on deficits or deficiencies within the students or their lives outside the school. These are referred to as factors that pull students out of school and most are beyond the control or influence of schools.

A second body of research utilized for this paper explored factors within the school setting that create barriers for students and have the effect of pushing certain students out of school (Jordan, Lara, & McPartland, 1999; Lee and Burkam, 2003). This research reveals policies and practices common to high schools across the nation that have the unintended consequence of contributing to students deciding to leave school. Some of the policies may have been adopted for valid reasons and may have been effective for previous generations, but are outdated for current students.

Today's schools are attempting to educate students from far more diverse backgrounds and abilities than schools of the past. The minds of today's students are different, as a result of different experiences (Jensen, 2006). Different minds require different learning environments and instructional styles. Today's students have grown up in a society that provides them with more information, freedom, choices, and responsibility than any previous generation, so the authoritarian approach of many school practices simply does not resonate with these students. Too often they voice their frustration and discontent by walking away before earning a diploma.

In addition to the existing body of research, this paper draws upon interviews conducted over a period of four years with more than two hundred students who dropped out of high school in a suburban school district in the Midwest. Students were interviewed about their school experiences and provided compelling personal stories that were consistent with findings cited in research from other schools across the country.

An exploration of push-out factors within the school setting identifies areas of change within the authority and control of educators and point the way for the full-scale systemic reform needed to make today's schools a better match for the students they serve. This paper attempts to provide an honest analysis of problems within school structures by drawing upon related research and the perspective of students who failed or were failed by the current educational traditions.

MIDDLE CLASS VALUES

One broad obstacle within the school setting for many students from poor families is the cultural disconnect that exists between the middle class values upon which school is based and the culture of poverty. Data on school drop-outs consistently reveals significantly higher rates of drop-outs among students from low socio-economic status. Researchers have identified cultural differences that explain many of the struggles common for students from poor backgrounds in the middle class world of school (Beegle, 2003; Payne, 2001).

While educators have traditionally viewed students who fail to display the appropriate behaviors as disrespectful and uncooperative, the reality is that many simply do not understand the middle class cultural norms and expectations essential for success in school (Duttweiler, 1995; Payne, 2001). Such norms include the use of appropriate language for the school setting, which is very different from the accepted language in the homes and neighborhoods of many students. Ruby Payne (2002) refers to the lack of a formal register among students from poverty, and stresses this as a key element for success in school. Students who lack a formal register are viewed as disrespectful in the middle class setting of school.

Failure to understand middle class norms for expected behaviors in the structured setting of classrooms results in a similar mistaken perception of many students. A prime example of this can be seen in students who are tardy to class. Those who understand the middle class norms for entering a formal setting after procedures are underway know that they have to enter quietly, creating as little disruption as possible. Students from the culture of poverty, where relationships and entertainment are valued, often enter with great fanfare, greeting and giving "high five's" or other familiar greeting to friends as they casually make their way to their assigned seats. The middle class norms of most teachers judge such an entrance as disrespectful and disruptive.

Even more serious is the cultural difference in whether or not education is valued. Those in the middle class view education as essential to future success, while many in the lower economic status do not know anyone who has ever benefited from education. Most students from poverty do not know "success stories" of people like them or from neighborhoods like theirs whose lives were enhanced by education, nor do they see a connection between school and their own future success (Beegle, 2003). They lack the "buy in" to the benefits of education but know all too well the negative experiences and adversarial view of schools shared by family and friends who themselves have experienced frustration and failure. These stories are reinforced by their own negative experiences resulting from unacceptable behaviors due to their lack of knowledge about middle class norms. Thus, they have no reason for persisting through the frustration of school or delaying the gratification of other more enticing daily activities when the promised reward of a diploma has no personal value.

Students from poverty also struggle with the basic concept of cause and effect—another expectation in the middle class world of school (Payne, 2001). The often chaotic, unpredictable lives of children living in poverty provide no basis for the development of a basic understanding of cause and effect. In the culture of poverty, life circumstances are viewed as random or the result of luck. Students from poverty view their experiences in school as unpredictable, random, and beyond their control (Beegle, 2003). Lacking the most basic understanding of cause and effect, they fail to see connections between their behaviors and the resulting consequences. As a result, they don't "learn from their mistakes," which is clearly a middle class expectation of discipline. They fail to see the connection between their lack of studying or effort and poor academic records. Instead, they view themselves as unlucky and lacking in some mysterious, personal attribute necessary for success in school. Eventually, like many others who are unlucky, they give up on the entire enterprise of school and move on to other pursuits where they are more successful or lucky.

Similarly, the written culture, characteristic of middle class and basic to all classrooms, varies from the oral culture which is characteristic of poverty (Beegle, 2003). Middle class, written culture places value upon abstract thinking and gaining information from printed sources. Organizational skills for keeping up with papers, books, calendars, and schedules are required for success in written cultures. Such structures are neither taught nor demonstrated in oral cultures. Imagine the difficulty of navigating through school without these essential skills!

The unintended consequences of these cultural differences are that students are confused and mistakenly judged as being deliberately uncooperative. The students themselves sense that they are out of place or lacking "something" that is needed for success in school. However, unless the expected skills and behaviors are articulated and explicitly taught, many students never realise what is needed or expected and continue to behave in unacceptable ways. They come to see themselves as outsiders and view themselves as lacking in some unknown, personal attribute needed for school success, or as just unlucky. "I just don't have what it takes," one student articulated when speaking of his struggles in school. Attributing their lack of success to luck or personal shortcomings, they determine that school is not the place for them.

UNWRITTEN RULES OF SCHOOL

Closely related to the middle class cultural norms are a host of unwritten rules for success in school. "There is a certain amount of tacit knowledge that is neither taught nor made explicit by teachers but is necessary for students to do well in the school environment" (Duttweiler, 1995, p. 38). Parents who were successful in school understand the hidden rules and teach them to their children in preparation for school. For many at-risk students, however, the unwritten rules remain a mystery. Their parents never understood the hidden rules, so they are unable to teach them to their children.

The unwritten rules include appropriate behaviors in the classroom, including simple things such as how to sit at the desk and show attention, interest, and deference to the teacher. There are unwritten rules about how to talk and how not to talk to the teacher, even when disagreeing, and especially when being disciplined. Most struggling students do not know the unwritten rules about studying. Unless other skills are specifically taught, the only study strategy they know is to read the chapter.

Appropriate ways of asking for help or expressing frustration are also a mystery to many struggling students who assume that comments such as, "This is stupid," are signals of needing help, rather than expressing disdain for the subject (often the interpretation of the teacher.) They are genuinely confused about what is expected of them when tests are returned, especially if they received a poor score. Most simply throw the test away and are puzzled by the "good" students who appear to waste everyone's time by asking the teacher about items to which they gave incorrect answers.

Void of knowledge about the unwritten rules, their behaviors send the wrong signal to teachers, leading teachers to believe that the students are apathetic and unmotivated. Another unintended consequence is that students view school as a "gotcha" game, with teachers and administrators as the adversaries. Students feel teachers expect them to perform better in school but do not explain what students can do to make this happen. "They just tell you to try harder, but that doesn't help," explained one frustrated drop-out. Possessing little understanding of the specific skills needed to improve their performance, most continue to perform poorly. Experiencing repeated frustration and failure and finding limited opportunities for success, they eventually disengage.

The solution to both the cultural differences and the unwritten rules is to explicitly teach the rules, norms, and behavioral expectations in all aspects of school life. Staff development on cultural differences should be provided to heighten teachers' awareness of the need for such direct instruction. Teachers need to model appropriate behaviors and provide clear explanations of cause and effect, reinforced with specific explanations as daily events unfold. Direct teaching of the consequences of choices made by students not only helps students develop an understanding of cause and effect, but also gives them a sense of control over their school experiences. Once the mysteries of hidden expectations are removed, students begin to see that they have within themselves the ability to succeed in school. Explicit teaching is needed at every level, throughout the year, rather than the standard secondary practice of a first-day-of school review of the syllabus, never to be addressed again, except in the form of consequences.

CURRICULUM AND PEDAGOGY

Another barrier that contributes to students' disengagement is the curriculum and the way in which it is delivered. Schools are still plagued by the lock-step, one-size-fits-all curriculum, including benchmarks and mandated tests that establish rigid timeframes for learning. The message sent to students who require more learning time for mastery is often one of failure and inadequacy. These problems are more apparent at the secondary level where students who enter high school with weak academic skills face increased rigor in graduation requirements but find very few courses that assist them in gaining the needed skills. Most students who enter high school deficient in reading skills remain deficient in those skills because few high schools offer reading instruction. Likewise, Algebra I has become the gateway class for high school graduation requirements in math. Students who fail Algebra I more than once and find no courses to gain the needed skills quickly "do the math" on graduation requirements and determine that they will not achieve the needed credits.

The lack of relevance and connection to the real world of the students in many curricular offerings presents another barrier for students (Williams,1996). Brain research applied to effective teaching strategies stresses the need for relevance and connections to previous knowledge to assist students in the learning process (Jensen, 1998). Yet, in schools, subjects are taught in isolation, and students are given no practical reason for learning the information presented, other than that "it will be on the test."

Confounding the problem are the instructional style and slow pace that are outdated for the brains of today's students. Sadly, many classrooms, especially in high school, still operate much like they did fifty years ago with students sitting as passive recipients of teacher lectures. The brains of today's students are very different, requiring different instructional styles and a much faster pace. Their increased exposure to video stimulation through fast-paced computer and video games has changed the reticular activating system in their brains so that they pick up and process information very quickly. "They are easily bored and have a difficult time maintaining information" (Nunley, 2006, p. 38). The old-fashioned format of lecture and note-taking is too slow and lacking in the visual stimulation to which their brains are accustomed.

The unintended consequence is lifeless classrooms where students are bored, discouraged, and unengaged, rather than inspired learners. Students find little relevance in the isolated subjects and facts, and no purpose for learning (O'Connor & Bangham, 2000). Those with weak academic skills fail classes and find few opportunities for catching up on needed skills. Those who repeat classes fall further behind their cohort group in the pursuit of graduation requirements. Many simply disengage due to boredom and frustration with what they see as a school that is irrelevant and outdated for the way the rest of the world operates.

The solution lies in updated, lively classrooms, with relevant, motivating, integrated curricula, including relevance for those who are not college-bound (Duttweiler, 1995). To hold the attention of today's students, classrooms must operate at a much faster pace, with more visual stimulation, movement, updated technology, and the latest strategies for brain-friendly classrooms (Jensen, 1998; Tate, 2003). Students need to be given reasons for learning, as well as connections with previous information, experiences, and their personal visions for learning (O'Conner & Bangham, 2000). Additional time and appropriate courses must be offered to students with academic weaknesses to provide support and the necessary scaffolding to improve their skills to a level that allows them to experience success. Policy makers must carefully examine traditional course offerings and requirements and selectively abandon those that are no longer relevant for today's students and the world in which they live. Budgets must be increased to allow for updated technology in sufficient amounts to provide access to all students.

DISCIPLINARY POLICIES AND PRACTICES

The area of discipline provides perhaps the most glaring example of unintended negative consequences caused by traditional practices. One assumes that the purpose of discipline is to teach students to make better choices, but many policies dole out punishments that create additional barriers for students who are already struggling academically. Both students and educators see the fallacy in suspending students for being truant, but the practice persists across the country. In-school and out-of-school suspensions prevent students from attending classes, so that they miss out on instruction and fall further behind academically. Even more damaging are attendance policies that deny credit to students who have missed a certain number of days, regardless of the student's academic performance.

Being labeled as a troublemaker, which often accompanies more serious disciplinary action, creates another kind of barrier for students who no longer feel welcomed at school (Jordan et al, 1999). One group of dropouts who had numerous disciplinary actions before dropping out spoke about their experiences with frustration and expressed feelings of hurt and bewilderment in stark contrast to their tough facades. "Once you mess up, they label you as a troublemaker, and they don't want you back," reported one former student. "They don't want you in class, and they won't help you when you ask for it once you get that reputation," added another dropout.

Students who gain such reputations feel that they are under a microscope of scrutiny and do not receive the "breaks" or leniency given to other students. "Once you get in trouble, the teachers and principals just watch for you to do something wrong and then let you have it, even if it was a little thing." Another student's chin quivered as he reported, "I got suspended for doing the same thing another guy had done five minutes earlier, but he's more popular and never gets called on anything. They think I'm just bad news, so they don't want me there."

The negative spiral set in motion by disciplinary action often has the unintended consequence of failure, leading students to give up completely. Students who are excluded from class miss out on academic instruction and fall further behind. Feeling left out and unwelcome, students disengage and become more disenfranchised. They view teachers, administrators, and the system as unfair (Black, 2002). Sometimes they express their frustration by acting out inappropriately, resulting in additional disciplinary action, and repeating the cycle. Others simply choose to drop out, rather than subject themselves to more humiliation and failure.

To remedy these problems, schools should analyze all discipline policies and practices for unintended consequences and eliminate those that punish rather than teach. Discipline conferences should be restructured to emphasize teaching students to make better choices, rather than simply doling out punishment. Students need to be encouraged to analyze the situation that led to their infraction and discuss alternative choices. Students who learn anger management, coping skills, and the concepts of cause and effect will be empowered with skills, rather than disenfranchised by punishment. Teachers need workshops to improve classroom management skills and learn additional intervention strategies for un-cooperative students. Students who are repeat offenders need the option of alternative settings which would provide more intense intervention to improve both behavioral and academic skills.

ADULT STYLES OF INTERACTING WITH STUDENTS

The greatest unintended consequences can be seen in the traditional practices of adult styles of interaction with students in the school setting. The vast majority of teachers love and nurture students, encouraging them to higher levels of academic and personal growth and inspiring confidence and a love of learning. Unfortunately, there are far too many within the educational community who negate the positive influence of those good teachers because of their styles of interacting with students. These educators ascribe to the old, authoritarian style of "the teacher as authority and person-in-charge," with the expectation that students should simply do as they are instructed, without any questions. Control is gained through power plays and intimidation. They demand compliance through harsh commands and threats of punishment, with little regard for the human frailties of young people who are still struggling to navigate the social and academic demands of the school environment with immature brains and social skills. This group of educators has little patience for the newer and more effective educational style of creating learning communities through building relationships of respect and trust between the adults and students.

More common are those teachers who occasionally vent their frustrations on students whom they find irritating or annoying. Short of patience with students who admittedly may have been difficult, they lash out with sarcasm and disrespectful comments that embarrass and humiliate students (Black, 2002; DeLuca and Rosenbaum, 2000). Although such incidents may seem minor to the adults who recognize them as momentary lapses in patience, the incidents are seared into the emotional psyches of many students who were already struggling in other areas of their lives. Students can recall with amazing clarity, even after many years, experiences in which they were publicly humiliated by the disparaging comments of a teacher over things as trivial as not bringing a pencil to class, arriving late, or forgetting an assignment. One drop-out voiced the long-term damage of such an event when he told me, "From that time on, I just didn't like school and hated going. I was doing the best I could and the teacher made me feel stupid. I knew I didn't belong there." A similar incident was described in an *American School Board Journal* article, reporting the experience of another student who said, "The day my history teacher called me a 'loser with no future,' I left for good" (Black, 2002, p. 50).

The most intolerable interactions are those in which the teacher is disrespectful to the students but expects students to be respectful in return. These adults make comments to students that they would never tolerate themselves. These practices may have worked in previous generations where most children were raised in authoritarian environments. In today's world, where students are encouraged to think and advocate for themselves and where many students parent themselves and are treated as adults in other areas, such practices are unendurable.

The unintended consequence is that students come to see the adults as unfair and uncaring. The power of negative experiences of invalidating and unkind interactions overshadows other school experiences. The use of invalidating language—language that communicates that the other person is flawed or incomplete—can have a much longer-term impact than most realize (Senge, Cambron-McCabe, Lucas, Smith, Dutton, & Kleiner, 2000, p. 143). The long-term impact is that teachers are seen as unconcerned or uncaring.

Numerous studies of at-risk students reveal that few see school as a place where the adults are concerned about them or willing to provide help (Black, 2002; Gallagher, 2002; Stevenson & Ellsworth, 1993). Although most teachers decry such opinions as inaccurate, it is the perceptions of these students that influence their decisions. Students disengage when they believe teachers do not care about them, while positive relationships with teachers reduce the risk of dropping out (Duttweiler, 1995; Lee and Burkam, 2003). Those who function as adults in their homes are unwilling to tolerate the demanding, critical parent voices used by some teachers. Students damaged by negative adult interactions disengage emotionally until they are old enough to drop out physically.

The solution is to create, within schools, a constant focus on building relationships. School staff must be reminded of their powerful influence on students and encouraged to communicate respect, welcome, and value to every student. They must provide warm, personal learning environments where students feel nurtured, encouraged, and accepted. Students of all ages and backgrounds in numerous studies indicate that what they need is a teacher who cares about them (Bernard, 1996). Students need teachers with positive attitudes about marginal students and teachers who are willing to provide support for individual needs. Such support and caring relationships have a positive influence on students' learning (Louis & Smith, 1996; Lunenburg, 2000).

Larger schools need to be organized into smaller units where adults can know and develop personal relationships with students and students can find opportunities for informal interactions with adults and a sense of community that fosters identification with the school (Lee & Burkam, 2000; Weir, 1996). Finally, administrators should never underestimate the damage done by one negative teacher and should adopt zero tolerance for invalidating language. There is simply no place for burned out, intolerant teachers who caste a negative image on a profession that should set the standard for validating, encouraging relationships.

MENTAL MODELS THAT SUPPORT THESE PRACTICES

In an era of constant talk of school reform, why do such practices go unnoticed? How can those in the business of education who work so diligently to educate students not see, yet support, these practices? One possible explanation can be found in the concept of mental models, which are assumptions we carry in our heads that influence our perceptions and thinking. "Because mental models are usually tacit, existing below the level of awareness, they are often untested and unexamined" (Senge, et al., 2000, pg 67).

Accurate identification of areas in which reform is needed will occur only through conscious reflection about how we form our mental models and sincere questioning about the accuracy of the assumptions that subconsciously shape our thinking. Examples of mental models that support practices which unintentionally push students out of school include the following: "The way things had worked for me, so it should work for students today. Everyone understands what is expected of them in school. Their job is to conform. Students who don't conform must be punished. Teachers should not be expected to teach social and behavioral skills. That's the role of parents. Schools should not have to adjust to students. Students should adjust to schools." Because public schools and the practices associated with them are such deeply engrained and widely accepted cultural institutions, it is easy to see how the impact of traditional practices and policies has been overlooked by reform efforts. They have simply become an accepted way of doing business in schools, with no thought that they might be a part of the problem.

If we are to create schools that truly provide success for all students, educators and policy makers must examine long-held beliefs that may not be accurate and make necessary changes. In *Schools that Learn* (2000), Cambron-McCabe encourages a "language of critique, in which schools should explore who benefits and who is harmed by the present structure and what values are affirmed by the existing structure" (pg. 283). We must be willing to examine honestly the impact of policies and practices and challenge those that have unintended consequences. We must change our mental models to create schools that are ready to nurture and educate all students. We must focus on getting schools ready for students from vastly diverse backgrounds, with vastly diverse skill levels and needs, rather than focusing on getting students ready for school.

But first, educators must be aware of the need for such an examination. The experiences of previous drop-outs provide the evidence that such a need exists. We must challenge those within the school community to engage in deep, honest reflection about the impact of existing practices, rather than focusing on what's wrong with the students. Such a shift in focus compels schools to engage in internal examinations of systemic structures that have outlived their usefulness or that perpetuate the disenfranchisement of countless students struggling to find meaning and success in American high schools. Such an approach empowers educators to recognize ways in which they can implement systemic changes to the traditional school environment to meet the needs of today's struggling students more effectively.

It is the belief of this author that teaching is a noble profession, comprised of people with a genuine desire to enrich the lives of their students. The highly educated teachers and administrators working in schools across this country have the intelligence and creative abilities to reform schools so that nothing within the walls of the school unintentionally creates barriers for students. Once teachers become aware of the unintended consequences of these practices, true reform will begin.

REFERENCES

Beegle, D. M. (2003). Overcoming the silence of generational poverty. *Talking points*, 15(1); 11–20.

Benard, B. (1995). Fostering resiliency in urban schools. In B. Williams (Ed.), *Closing the Achievement Gap: A Vision to Guide Change in Beliefs and Practice*. Oak Brook, IL: Research for Better Schools and North Central Regional Educational Laboratory.

Black, S, (2002). Keeping kids in schools. *American School Board Journal* 189(12): 50–52.

DeLuca, S. & Rosenbaum, J. E. (2000, December 20). *Are Dropout Decisions related to Safety Concerns, Social Isolation, and Teacher Disparagement?* Paper presented at the 2000 Civil Rights Project, Harvard University

Conference Dropouts in America. Retrieved June 15, 2006 from http://www.civilrightsproject.harvard.edu/research/dropouts/deluca.pdf

Duttweiler, P.C. (1995). *Effective Strategies for Educating Students in At-risk Situations.* Clemson, SC: National Dropout Prevention Center.

Gallagher, C.J. (2002). Stories from the strays: What dropouts can teach us about school. *American Secondary Education* 30(3): 36.

Jensen, E. (1998). *Teaching with the Brain in Mind.* Alexandria, VA: Association for Curriculum and Development.

Jensen, E. (2006). *Enriching the Brain.* San Francisco, CA: Jossey-Bass.

Jordan, W. J., Lara, J., & McPartland, J. M., (1999). Rethinking the causes of high school dropout. *The prevention researcher* 63(3): 1–4.

Lee, V. E. & Burkam, D.T. (2003). Dropping out of high school: The role of school organization & structure. *American Educational Research Journal* 40: 353–393.

Louis, S. L. & Smith, B. (1996). Teacher engagement and real reform in urban schools. In B. Williams, (Ed.) *Closing the Achievement Gap.* Alexandria, VA: Association for Curriculum and Development.

Lunenburg, F.C. (2000). America's hope: Making schools work for all children. *Journal of Instructional Psychology* 27(1): 39–46.

National Dropout Prevention Center/Network. *Impact of Dropouts.* Retrieved May 8, 2006, from http://www.dropoutprevention.org/stats/quick_facts/econ_impact.htm

Nunley, K. F. (2006). *Differentiating the High School Classroom.* Thousand Oaks, CA: Corwin Press.

O'Connor, T. & Bangham, D. (2000). Overcoming absurdity. In P. Senge, N. Cambron-McCabe, T. Lucas, B. Smith, J. Dutton, & A. Kleiner, *Schools that Learn* New York: Doubleday pp.135–149.

Payne, R. K. (2001). *A Framework for Understanding Poverty.* Highlands, TX: Aha! Process, Inc.

Senge, P., Cambron-McCabe, N., Lucas, T., Smith, B., Dutton, J., & Kleiner, A. (2000). *Schools that Learn.* New York: Doubleday.

Stevenson, R. & J. Ellsworth (1993). Dropout-outs and the silencing of critical voices. In Weis, L. and Fine, M. (Eds.) *Beyond Silenced Voices: Class, Race, and Gender in United States Schools.* New York: State University of New York.

Tate, M. L. (2003). *Worksheets don't Grow Dendrites.* Thousand Oaks, CA: Corwin Press.

Weir Jr., R. M. (1996). Lessons from a middle level at-risk program. *Clearing House* 70: 48–51.

Williams, B. (1996). The nature of the achievement gap: The call for a vision to guide change. In B. Williams (Ed), *Closing the Achievement Gap.* Alexandria, VA: Association for Supervision and Curriculum Development.

SUGGESTED ACTIVITIES

1. Interview previous or current drop-outs or students considered "at-risk" about barriers they encounter within your school setting. Ask the students to share ideas about what kinds of assistance would be most helpful to them. You may be surprised at the meaningful solutions they can provide.

2. List the "hidden" or unwritten rules necessary for school success. Plan a sample lesson in which these rules are explicitly taught.

3. Examine policies and procedures at your school that have the unintended consequence of creating additional barriers for students. Discuss alternatives for change that would be more supportive of at-risk students.

SUGGESTED READINGS

Cushman, K.(2003). *Fires in the Bathroom: Advice for Teachers from High School Students*. New York: The New Press.

MULTIPLE CHOICE QUESTIONS

1. "Push-out" factors are components within

   a. the family structure of at-risk students

   b. personal lives and the environment in which students live

   c. the school structure that present barriers for students

   d. all the above

2. The middle class culture of schools present obstacles for students from other cultures because the students do not understand

   a. behavioral expectations

   b. the appropriate language

   c. the concept of cause and effect

   d. all the above

3. Which of the following is NOT true about the unwritten rules of school?

   a. They need to be explicitly taught at all grade levels

   b. Teachers make mistaken judgments about students who do not understand the rules

c. These rules are explained to students verbally but are rarely presented in writing

d. Knowledge of the rules is essential for success in school

4. Most of the curriculum in high schools is outdated for today's students in all the following ways except

    a. It is too fast-paced

    b. It lacks relevance

    c. Subjects are taught in isolation

    d. Students are given little reason for learning the information

5. Which of the following is NOT an example of an unintended consequence of school disciplinary policies and practices?

    a. Suspensions result in students' falling further behind in academic work

    b. Students are forced to learn the consequences of their misbehavior

    c. Students view school personnel as adversaries and disengage

    d. Students are labeled as troublemakers and receive less leniency than other students

6. At-risk students view teachers as unfair because the students:

    a. do not understand the expectations

    b. feel teachers are not interested in helping them when they struggle

    c. do not feel all students receive the same behavioral consequences

    d. all the above

7. Authoritarian styles of adult interactions with students:

    a. rely on intimidation and power to control students

    b. result in better discipline

    c. help students understand behavioral expectations

    d. ensure safety and a sense of belonging

8. Positive student–teacher relationships are essential for drop-out prevention because:

    a. students cannot be successful if they don't have positive relationships

    b. many students disengage when they believe teachers don't care about them

c. relationships with teachers are the only thing about school that at-risk students value

d. all the above

9. The mental models that perpetuate many "push-out" policies and practices are:

    a. long-standing board policies

    b. personal assumptions that influence our perceptions and thinking

    c. deliberately designed to present barriers for certain students

    d. the result of discrimination and elitism

10. School reform to reduce the numbers of drop-outs must include:

    a. an honest examination of current policies that unintentionally push students out

    b. deliberate efforts to build positive relationships between educators and students

    c. a shift in focus to internal examinations of systemic structures

    d. all the above

SECTION III

Arguments for Student-Centered Teaching

I also hate school sometimes because some of our teachers are complete self-superior, self-absorbed, jerks who don't like to listen to others' opinions because they are better than us because they have a plaque and have thirty years on us.

—12-YEAR OLD MISSOURI MIDDLE SCHOOL STUDENT

I think some kids hate school because they don't see that school has any relevance to their life. They think they are held without their consent so they can fill out countless boring worksheets. But I don't think that's the case in a class where they are studying information that is relevant to their lives, where they can express their personal opinion, and when they are engaged with their other classmates and with their teacher.

—FLORIDA HIGH SCHOOL TEACHER

I think students may begin disliking school when their school lessons become disconnected from their personal experience, from their own lives, and from their first-hand experience. We are lucky in early childhood because we really believe children learn when they are having fun and we believe in creating integrated learning experiences for children.

—OREGON HEAD START TEACHER

We may say that the child is naturally active, especially along social lines. Heretofore a regime of coercion has only too often reduced our schools to aimless dawdling and our pupils to selfish individualists. The contention of this paper is that wholehearted purposeful activity in a social situation as the typical unit of school procedure is the best guarantee of the utilization of the child's native capacities now too frequently wasted. Learning of all kinds and in its desirable ramifications best proceeds in proportion as wholeheartedness of purpose is present.

—WILLIAM HEARD KILPATRICK, THE PROJECT METHOD (1918)

Standardization *or* the Courage to Be: Educational Counterpoints

DON HUFFORD

NEWMAN UNIVERSITY

> "We sacrifice the genius of the pupil, the unknown possibilities of his nature, to a neat and safe uniformity."
>
> Ralph Waldo Emerson, *On Education.*

PRELIMINARIES

Sitting in an auditorium in Wichita, Kansas, I heard the peripatetic, rebellious, "pre-eminent African-American intellectual of our time,"[1] Cornell West, comment: "I hope to say something tonight that will unnerve you." This writing may have a similar disquieting effect upon some readers. But then, we are reminded by John Dewey that being unnerved may stimulate latent intellectual possibilities. Dewey (1997 [1910]) helps us understand that serious thinking begins when we intellectually wrestle with "some perplexity, confusion, or doubt" (p.12), and he recognizes that this struggle requires enduring "a condition of mental unrest and disturbance" (p. 13).

The ideas presented here are designed to disturb, perhaps perplex; to stimulate thinking—and to encourage a creative dialogue.[2] The ideas will, no doubt, have more positive resonance with "creative doubters," those educational radicals who are not cowed—or seduced—by the growing power of an educational orthodoxy that seems to prefer standardized *doing* over resilient *being*. The ideas presented here will be less palatable for those who are philosophically, politically, and pedagogically "in tune" with an educational establishment that is allowed to authoritatively define "what knowledge is of most worth."[3] In the name of effectiveness and efficiency, such a system promotes and expects teacher-transmitted knowledge in testable form.

These divergent ways of thinking (overly-generalized as traditional vs. progressive) make possible an interesting, paradoxical dialectic that has positive implications. There is always the possibility that such dialectical thinking may lead to an intellectual tension that will eventually create new ways of thinking about controversial educational issues. The tension developed by connecting the polarities of diverse educational views may release a power that is creative rather than destructive. Such creative tension generates the power to encourage new ways of open-minded thinking on both sides of the educational divide.

THE "WHAT IS" AND THE "WHAT COULD BE"

Almost forty years ago Erich Fromm (1968), the humanist psychotherapist, wrote of a social/political philosophy which was then empowering market-driven, technocratic, authoritarian, rightist conservative, neo-liberal (today's word) inspired efforts to produce a conditioned, conforming citizenry. Fromm recognized that

> The alienated bureaucratic procedure... is a one-way system: orders, suggestions, planning emanate from the top and are directed to the bottom of the pyramid. There is no room for individual initiative... our bureaucratic method does not respond to the needs, views, requirements, of an individual. (p. 99).

Fast-forward to 2006. Ask a few critically-reflective questions. Does the above pronouncement have prophetic overtones? May it be applied to the power structure that sets the agenda and makes the rules for today's educational "market place?" Do Fromm's words resonate with the expectations that push forward today's top-down use of "teacher-proof," pre-packaged materials, standardized curricula, high-stakes testing, competitive measurements, and a teach-to-the-test mentality? Question even more deeply, and we might wonder if there is a form of bureaucratic alienation that causes many of today's students to say, "I hate school," "I won't learn from you," "what's the use?" Listen again, as Dr. Fromm (1968) speaks from the past with a seemingly prophetic understanding of today's reality.

> Dehumanization in the name of efficiency is an all-too-common occurrence... aimed at standardizing services ... If we are only concerned at figures (measurement), the system may give the impression of efficiency. If we take into account what the given methods do to the human beings in the system, we may discover that they are bored, anxious, depressed, tense, etc. (p. 34–35).

De-humanizing standardization in the name of efficiency, measurable accountability, and in deference to a powerful ideology, has a way of infiltrating a nation's social system, including its schools. This is an American historical reality; it is a current actuality. The ideologically impregnated No Child Left Behind Act is a "one-way system" with "orders, suggestions, and planning emanating from the top," and is representative of the power of today's educational orthodoxy.

There are, of course, those educational heretics who challenge the orthodoxy; who provide substantive counter-arguments to a behaviorist, mechanistic, market-inspired interpretation of educational purpose and method that "has exacerbated the alienation that so many kids feel in school" (Hytten, 2006, p. 233). There are the "radical educators (who) first understand fully the dynamics of resistance on the part of learners... (who) understand the discourse of resistance (and) provide pedagogical structures that will enable students to emancipate themselves" (Freire and Macedo, 1987, p. 90). These are the stout of heart who question; those who challenge, those who resist. They are, however, fighting against a firestorm of educational power.

In spite of these emancipatory educators, the alienation that so many students experience has been deepened by the concept of a "one-size-fits-all," standardized, corporate-imitated model for educational accountability and efficiency. In considering alternatives to this orthodox model we are reminded by Susan Ohanian (1999) that "what school should be all about (is) teachers and curriculum being flexible enough to meet the needs of each student, not shoving every kid through some distant committee's phantasmic pipe dream of a necessary curriculum for tomorrow's workforce" (p. 2).[4] The "what is" of education today—a rigid, self-regenerating orthodoxy—needs to be challenged by heretical educators espousing alternative possibilities leading to the "what could be."[5]

There are dreams to be dreamed, visions to be explored, doubt to be investigated, risks to be taken. There are students to be rescued from, in Milton's poetic imagery, "the sloughs of despair" (*Pilgrim's Progress*). Not all students, of course, fit into such pessimistically expressive metaphors. But those who are beginning to wade in—or are already drowning in—alienating, academic swampland deserve the attention of educational heretics. We are reminded that "alienated individuals abandon the process of forming themselves by evading the challenges they face" (Fisk, 2006, p. 105). And so, we have growing numbers of drop-outs, and increased refusal to "buy-in" to rigid, standardizing expectations.

It is easy to re-position a theologian's words regarding social justice issues so that they apply to a managed, standardized, alienating educational experience:

> Man can refuse to listen to the claims of the other … He can try to transform him into a manageable object, a thing, a tool. But in so doing he meets the resistance of him who has a claim to be acknowledged as an ego (Tillich, 1970, p. 78).

Those students who resist the demands of a high-stakes, test-obsessed, behavior-modifying school system are responding to a sense of objectification, to being treated as an *it* rather than a *thou* (Buber, 1965). They reject enforced homogenization , and fight against "the closure of possibility through technologies such as the examination" (Bishop, 2006). Each resister has a claim to selfhood, a claim which is minimized in an environment that values *doing* over *being*, achieving over becoming, knowledge over learning, test score over personhood. Deborah Meier reminds us that "the most significant impact of the new standardization is already evident in the increased drop-out rate in state after state" (Meier, 2002, p. 196). The teacher's sense of pedagogical authenticity, even sense of self, is diminished in those classrooms that "become repositories of dominant knowledge that anesthetizes our souls, severs our connections to our consciousness, and ignores the meaningfulness of students' lived experiences" (Kincheloe, Slattery, and Steinberg, 2000, p. 299). In such situations, both the student and teacher face significant obstacles in the struggle to be acknowledged as an individual in a sea of conformity.

In an era in which we tend to equate personal educational success with impersonal measurements by test score, we would be wise to consider the prophetic words written many years ago by a Jewish theologian: "Empirical intemperance, the desire to be exact, to attend to the 'hard facts' which are subject to measurement, may defeat its own end" (Heschel, 1965, p. 9). These are words that echo with a ring of truth. They provide the reason to give serious thought to the consequences of standardizing an educational process that should be encouraging creative potential, and open the mind to innovative opportunities. We should consider a prophetic warning issued almost a century ago by a civil rights pioneer: "There is a feeling that school is a machine. You insert a child at 9 am in the morning and extract him at 4 pm, improved and standardized" (Du Bois, 1969, p. 125). A standardized education is based on a linear-directed mechanical model. In counterpoint, the growth and development of our children <u>should be</u> modeled on an organic process; open-ended, flexibly creative, and joy-producing.

COURAGEOUS JOY: AN EDUCATIONAL ALTERNATIVE

The existentialist, humanist theologian, Paul Tillich (1961) has written that "joy accompanies the self-affirmation of being" (p. 14). Too many students in America's schools today are unable to experience the joy that is "the emotional expression of the courageous 'yes' to one's own being" (Tillich, 1961, p. 14). They have been unable to live into a "yes" that validates who they are as individuals. These unreached, unvalidated students—some calling out for attention, some lost in silent resignation—struggle with school-induced emotions that are counterpoint to self-affirming joy. In response to quickly fading hope, they resist, rebel, give-up, fail, drop-out; or simply survive while succumbing to a dislike for academic expectations that tend toward de-personalization. For many students there is a sense of being objectified, of being an "it" rather than a "thou" (see Buber, 1958);

of being manipulated and indoctrinated; of being molded, rather than being encouraged and aided in the process of self-creating.

Fromm, in his book, *The Sane Society*, recognized that: "I experience myself as an I because I doubt . . . if I am ruled by an anonymous authority, I lose my sense of self, *I* become an *It*" (153). When authority provides and requires scripted content, rigid expectations and procedures, strict accountability, and mechanically-devised test preparations (teach-to-the-test), we standardize the student—and the teacher. We minimize—or eliminate—the opportunities for achieving the self-affirming joy of essential being. "Joy is what we experience in the process of growing nearer to goal of becoming ourself" (Fromm, 1979, p. 119). Many students find that becoming oneself is not easy within an educational system that too narrowly defines the parameters of "who" one may become. As Deborah Meier (2000) has reminded us, "democratic society shouldn't have one single definition of what constitutes being well-educated" (p. 128). There is a diminished sense of self when one is forced into pre-established conforming patterns.6 In standardized educational expectations.

> Student experience is reduced to the immediacy of its performance and exists as something to be measured, administered, registered, and controlled. Its distinctiveness, its disjunctions, its lived quality are all dissolved in an ideology of control and management. Teachers who structure classroom experience out of this discourse generally face enormous problems of boredom and/or disruption (Giroux, 1988, p. 91).

Many students can accommodate and adjust successfully to officially-sanctioned, authoritarian, standardized expectations—even expectations that significantly narrow the definition of "worthwhile" knowledge. They can "talk the talk, walk the walk, and take the test." Other students, however, need creative opportunities for more idiosyncratic, less formulaic expressions of the existential self. Teachers should to be encouraged and allowed to relate to this student as "an individual, as a unique expression of the universe, incomparable, irreplaceable, and of unique significance" (Tillich, 1961, p. 19). Round pegs hammered into square holes tend to rebel. "Compulsion in education means disunion, it means humiliation and rebelliousness" (Buber, 1965, p. 91). This is not to say that there should not be expectations, standards, goals. It is, however, to recognize that a one-size-fits-all educational pattern of testing accountability negates a student from being a unique expression of the universe.

Tillich has written of a concept, the *courage to be*, that holds interpretive potential to be translated from theological literature into the educational lexicon. It is the premise of this writing that an educator's interpretive understanding of the meaning and possibilities found woven into a student's developing *courage to be* can help give voice to educational goals and methods that are hopeful counterpoints to today's educational orthodoxy. As a teacher I agree with Susan Ohanian (1999): "It is my moral duty to offer a counter-argument to people who would streamline, sanitize, and standardize education" (p. ix). It is an ethical responsibility to look behind words like accountability, assessment, quantifiable, high-stakes, standards, etc., and seek the often-hidden meaning they contain.

Teachers, in translating the *courage to be* into a more joy-producing educational meaning and practice, will uncover counter-arguments to the corporate-inspired, market-driven, measurement-obsessed standardization of American education. They will "see themselves as agents of joy and conduits for transcendence, rather than merely as licensed trainers or promoters of measurable knowledge" (Suhor, 1998, p. 16). There will be reflective consideration of the pedagogical implications of Tillich's (1961) understanding that "a self which has become a matter of calculation and management has ceased to be a self; it has become a thing" (1961, p. 124). And ... there is no joy in being a "thing." The student who is unable to find an intrinsic joy in school is the one whose *courage to be* is still awaiting birth. This is the student who is inclined to join the ranks of the school resisters. We may well minimize the sources of resistance if schools of education help future teachers understand that "schooling for self and social empowerment (the *courage to be*) is <u>ethically</u> prior to a mastery of technical or social skills" (Giroux and McLaren, 1991, p. 153–154). As we prepare future teachers with *what* and *how* techniques and knowledge, we also have a responsibility to engage their minds with significant and challenging *why* questions.

There are alternatives to standardizing the student in the name of officially sanctioned, quantifiable achievements. There are ways to re-integrate the "I hate school" student back into a meaningful pedagogical relationship. One way is for the teacher to interpret, understand, and assist in the birth of the individual student's *courage to be*. This birthing process may not meet the demands of a testable, measurable outcome. But, in the effort, we at least have a way to strengthen the disaffected student's ability and desire to re-establish an emerging self-understanding.

> Schools should teach you to realize yourself... To become yourself, you've got to be given various choices and helped to look at the choices... otherwise you're not prepared for the outside world (White and Brockton, 1983, p. 21).

This process of self-realization, this exercise in thoughtful, critical existential choice, is integral to a student's *courage to be*, and "the courage to be is the courage to affirm one's own reasonable nature" (Tillich, 1961, p. 13). It "is the ethical act in which one affirms his own being in spite of those elements of his existence (including school experiences) which conflict with his essential self-affirmation" (p. 3). The "I hate school" student needs to be helped to engage in this kind of ethical act; this self-affirmation, based on growing and truthful self-understanding. This student also needs help in re-assessing his/her relationship to a "conflicting element," in this case the school, which is part of his/her existence. And he/she needs help in finding in school the joy of self-affirmation; a joy defined by Rollo May (1980) as "the emotion that goes with heightened consciousness, the mood that accompanies the experience of actualizing one's own potentialities" (p. 45).

The student whose unique potentialities are thwarted in a standardized matrix of authority-imposed conformity is the one who finds no joy in school. There is a need for educational heretics to push for more serious consideration of alternative educational philosophies which will allow more idiosyncratic joy to penetrate the increasing standardization of the school experience. Teachers, and educational authorities, need an understanding of the *courage to be*. We need to understand that joy is that inner excitement that a student feels when the self has been given permission to expand into new realms of possibility. Joy is found in the search for, and the experiencing of, the *courage to be*.

FURTHER REFLECTION ON THE *COURAGE TO BE* AS AN EDUCATIONAL POSSIBILITY

An analysis of the *courage to be* is, of course, a philosophical exercise. It is a hermeneutical process which allows the interpreter to recognize explicit implications, and to thoughtfully extract implicit meanings. These are the kinds of implications and meanings which may become existential understandings applicable to a teacher's willingness to connect to a student's lived reality. Such a thinking process can reveal counter-arguments to a standardized, pre-determined, competitive system "in which the student is to accept whatever is prescribed rather than learn to question and explore issues and ideas" (Kozol, 1994, p. 117). Interpreting the *courage to be* is the kind of "mind work" that may reveal alternative, practical pedagogical possibilities. In philosophical, reflective thinking we prepare for active participation in the real word of education—a world in which "there is no perfect way to be. We can only do our best" (Hecht, 2004, p. 164). No perfect way, perhaps; but in doing our best we, as teachers, hope to find a way *to be*—and to help students *to be*—to forge their own *becoming* as unique, independent thinking, unrepeatable human beings. Educating the student's *courage to be* is one way to provide a counterbalance to the power of the standardizing winds which are blowing through the corridors of America's schools.

Tillich (1970), in his book, *Love, Power, and Justice*, reflects again on the *courage to be*: "Each of these words is, of course, used metaphorically. But metaphorical language can be true language, pointing to something that is both revealed and hidden in the language" (p. 38). In seeking the revealed and the hidden in the phrase, *courage to be*, our search is for educational counterpoints to standardized, testable expectations and assembly-line thinking. Counterpoints are needed because in too many cases students are "turned off" by the realities associated with the "proliferation of what is called 'teacher-proof' curriculum packages . . . predetermined content and instructional packages . . .(where) knowledge is standardized and measured through predefined forms of assessment" (Giroux, 1988, p. 124). Simmering alienation bubbles to the surface when students are faced with a school culture of "infinite examination and of compulsory objectification" (Foucault, 1995, p. 189). Students are negatively impacted when

> teachers are no longer being treated as professionals. We are being treated as assembly-line workers, preparing students solely for tests. And all blame falls on us if the students don't succeed on those tests... It has been the professional hallmark of American teachers that they determine what to teach, when to teach and how to teach their subject to their unique community of students ... Assembly-line thinking may work for a factory where all the material is uniform, but a classroom of students is anything but uniform (Schrock, 2006, p. A5).

Enforced uniformity stifles creativity, and—as someone has said—if we don't create, we destroy. We may connect this thought to the creative concept of personal growth, to self-creation, to the process of *becoming* . . . to the *courage to be*. Or, conversely, to the self-destructive aspects of the alienated, resistant student. And courageous self-creation can't be standardized, can't be quantified as an "outcome" in a syllabus, or routinely tested to prove compliance. "Classrooms, rather than demanding rigid and ready personhood or categorical and completed selves, must more intentionally become places of becoming, places to practice courage" (Infinito, 2004, p. 216).

To become a place of *becoming* is to nurture the *courage to be*. It is to help students ask self-interrogating questions about "who am I?," and "who am I becoming?," and "why?" It is to recognize that such divergent questions, and the student-generated answers, are important; just as important—or more so—than are the "right" answers to convergent questions designed by an educational expert.7 In writing of a "theology of culture," Tillich (1959) reflected on authoritarian answers, providing another opportunity to reframe the theological into the secular educational:

> We must participate, but we must not be identical and we must use this double attitude to undercut the complacency of those who assume they know all the answers ... Our answers must have as many forms as there are questions and situations, individual and social (p. 208).

The *courage to be* requires an openness to possibilities, and a willingness to participate while also challenging the orthodoxy of "right" answers. "The *courage to be* means acting, loving, thinking, creating, even though one knows he does not have the final answers, and may well be wrong" (May, 1967, p. 203). Final answers may not be in the pedagogical cards, but the *courage to be* allows one, in the words of the Taoists, to "search for the answers lovingly."

High-stakes, standardized tests require final answers, right answers. The *courage to be* requires asking the right questions, and living adventurously and ethically into the answers. The *courage to be* requires creative courage, and "creative courage is the discovery of new forms, new symbols, new patterns on which a new society can be built" (May, 1980, p. viii). In recognizing this aspect of the *courage to be* we understand that discovery and newness are reflected in the incommensurarable rather than in the standardized; and it has been noted that, "teachers, like their students, have to learn to love the questions, as they come to realize that there are no final agreements or answers, no final commensurability" (Greene, 1988, p. 134). Thinking similarly, Herbert Kohl defines the quality of courage that it takes *to be*: "The ability to break patterns and pose new questions is as important as the ability to answer questions other people set for you . . . It requires courage to create bold disruptions of routines of thought and practice" (p. 144). It requires the *courage to be*.

This is the creative courage that results from, and in, self-affirmation. "In human beings courage is necessary to make *being* and *becoming* possible. An assertion of the self, a commitment, is essential if the self is to have any reality . . . decisions require courage" (May, 1980, p. 4). For a student, or a teacher, freely-made, thoughtful decisions become expressions of the *courage to be*. And this existential courage should be recognized as an important "achievement" to be pursued in American schools. We need an understanding of this meaning of "to achieve," as a countervailing force to the pernicious "achievement ideology (Shapiro, 2006)" that so permeates the culture of America's classrooms. Educating the *courage to be* is a counterpoint to the argument that a basic purpose of schools should be to prepare students to take

> standardized tests (that) tend to measure the temporary acquisition of facts and skills, including the skill of test-taking itself, more than genuine understanding. The use of a high-stakes strategy only underscores the preoccupation with these tests and, as a result, accelerates a reliance on direct instruction and endless practice tests (Kohn, 2000, p. 37).

In challenging the mindset that generates a "test preoccupation," we will listen to the words of the Lebanese poet, Kahil Gibran (1919): "The teacher . . . if he is indeed wise does not bid you enter the house of his wisdom, but rather leads you to the threshold of your own mind" (p. 64).

CONCLUSION: EDUCATION IS TO "BRING FORTH"

The English word, "education," is derived from *educere*, meaning "to bring forth," to draw out latent possibilities. It does not mean to "pour in," as seems to be the definition of "education" in teach-to-the-test classrooms. Socrates found an implicit meaning within *educere*, and used the power of metaphor to describe the teacher as a "midwife." This metaphor is a creative representation of the teacher as a caring helper, one who aids the student in giving birth to the possibilities that reside within; to the *courage to be*. Metaphorically, the student must push, the teacher must pull, in a cooperative effort to achieve a common goal, the birth of the student's still to be realized, unique potential.

The teacher/midwife will find that bringing forth a student's potential *courage to be*, is often a hard birthing process. The *courage to* be is never given birth fully formed; it is always a becoming possibility, something to build upon. The birth is especially hard for the disheartened, "I hate school" student who has been alienated by the actions of authoritarian forces.

> In alienating activity I do not really act; I am acted upon by external forces . . . In nonalienated activity I experience myself as the subject of my activity. Nonalienated activity is a process of giving birth to something (Fromm, 1976, p. 91).

The "something"—which is a counterpoint to the demands of the standardizing educational process now alienating many students (and teachers)—is the *courage to be*. It is a sense of self that allows one to learn, grow, love, experience, cooperate, and create as a unique, unrepeatable, self-affirming individual. The wise teacher, in helping students become who they have the potential to become, will consider the advice of Martin Buber (1965):

> The genuine educator does not merely consider individual functions of his pupil, as one intending to teach him only to know or be capable of certain definite (testable) functions, but his concern is always the person as a whole, both in the actuality in which he lives before you now, and in his possibilities, what he can become (p. 104).

To consider the student in terms of "what he can become" is to recognize that one size does not fit all. It is to forge a pedagogy of possibility in which students are encouraged and expected to "constitute themselves as subjects of their own experience... to develop a sense of agency in their lives" (Simon, 1992, pp. 17–18). A pedagogy of possibility is one which gives birth to the student's *courage to be*, the courage of self-affirmation, and self-determination. It is a teaching methodology that gives permission for, even encourages, the student's *courage to be* skeptical; to question, challenge, and express doubt in a state of honest perplexity.[9] And such pedagogy can only be the result of a teacher's own realized, and developing, *courage to be*.[10] We are reminded by Maxine Greene (1973) that a teacher "may liberate himself for reflective action as someone who knows who he is as a historical being, acting on his freedom, trying each day just to *be*" (p. 7). The teacher's search for "self" is important because, as we are often reminded, "we teach who we are." With this thought in mind repeat after me: "I teach because it requires that I become my most courageous self, and I am constantly inspired by students who learn the power of being whole people" (Adel, 2005, p. 149). May it be so.

A teacher who is inspired and invigorated by the presence and power of student self-affirmation is one imbued with her/his own sense of courageous *being*. This requires a willingness to be personally and professionally vulnerable, to take risks, to be a co-learner in the classroom, to be an Emersonian non-conformist when it would be easier and less painful to passively conform without complaint to the instrumentalist standards of an educational orthodoxy. And, it is the risk-taking, emotionally vulnerable, system-challenging, self-affirming teacher who models these very qualities for students. When this modeling happens, we reach out to those "I hate school" students, and slowly, even painfully, give them permission to re-integrate into a compassionate learning community that celebrates the *courage to be* a unique, unrepeatable, self-affirming individual. And... it is by way of such self-transformation that we may hope for social transformation, and a more peaceful, just world.

NOTES

1. This description was attributed to author, Henry Gates, Jr., in the June 7, 1993 issue of *Time* magazine. Many sources continue to define West as an example of a significant "public intellectual," that is, an active academic who writes, speaks, and is heard in many venues outside the halls of academia.

2. As a presentation, this paper was developed to create dialogue between members of a participating audience. As a written essay, it is hoped that the reader will engage in an intellectual dialogue with the author; question, challenge, rework ideas, rethink possibilities.

3. This is the title of an essay by Herbert Spencer, written in 1859. Spencer believed that certain "basic" knowledge is vital for the educated person to absorb. We might consider the work of E.D. Hirsch (i.e. *Cultural Literacy*) to be in a similar vein.

4. As we consider today's school-alienated youth in connection to "a necessary curriculum for tomorrow's workforce," we might want to give heed to a 1929 comment by philosopher, Alfred North Whitehead: "It will be fatal to education... to adopt a rigid curriculum... When one considers in its length and breadth

the importance of this question of the education of a nation's young, the broken lives, the defeated hopes, the national failures... it is difficult to contain within oneself a savage rage" (p. 14).

5. The concept "heretic" is used here with consideration of the meaning of the Greek word, *hairetikos*, from which the English word is derived. Based on this derivation, a heretic is one who is able to assess various options and make freely decided, thoughtful choices; choices not unduly influenced by orthodoxies or ideologies.

6. It is interesting to note that historically early teacher education programs were called Normal Schools. The word "normal" is derived from the Latin norma, meaning "to conform to as rule or a pattern." Are we reverting to this meaning of what it means to be a teacher?

7. A divergent question is one that may have no one correct answer. It may be answered in diverse ways. A correct answer to a divergent question may even change depending on time, place, and person. A convergent question has only one right answer which can easily be found in a teacher's answer book.

8. There is a comparison here to Paulo Freire's concept of "banking education," a process in which information/facts are deposited into the student, and then withdrawn at test-taking time. "Education thus becomes an act of depositing, in which the students are depositories and the teacher is the depositor ... the students patiently receive, memorize, and repeat" (Freire, 1993, p. 53).

9. Teachers, of course, have a responsibility to help students understand that as important as it is to be skeptical of knowledge-orthodoxy, they should not allow skepticism to degenerate into intellectual or spiritual cynicism.

10. In constructing this kind of creative, hope-producing teacher style, a teacher may think imaginatively on the advice of playwright and novelist, August Wilson: "Everyone has a song. Search for your song" (radio interview). After all, we teach who we are.

REFERENCES

Adel, B. (2005). Teaching to engage. *Why We Teach*. Nieto, S. (Ed.). New York: Teachers College Press.

Bishop, J. (2006). Introduction. *Educational Studies*. June.

Buber, M. (1965). *Between Man and Man*. New York: Collier Books.

Buber, M. (1958). *I and Thou*. New York: Charles Scribner's Sons.

Dewey, J. (1997). *How We Think*. Mineola, New York: Dover Publications. Originally published: Boston: D.C. Heath, 1910.

Du Bois, W.E.B. (1969) *An ABC of color*. Reprint. New York: International Publishers.

Educational Leadership, December 1998/December 1999.

Fisk, M. (2006). Why alienation matters. *Radical Philosophy Review*. Vol. 9, No. 1.

Foucault, M. (1995) *Discipline and Punish: The Birth of the Prison*, 2nd edition. New York: Vintage.

Freire, P. (1993). *Pedagogy of the Oppressed*, copyright, 1970. New York: Contiuum.

Freire, P, and Macedo, D. (1987). *Literacy: Reading the Word and the World*. New York: Bergin and Garvey.

Fromm, E. (1976). *To Have or to Be*. New York: Harper & Row, Publishers.

Fromm, E. (1968). *The Revolution of Hope: Toward a Humanized Technology*. New York: Harper & Row.

Fromm, E. (1958). *The Sane Society*, 7th printing. New York: Rinehart & Company.

Gibran, K. (1919). *The Prophet*, 20th printing. New York: Alfred A. Knopf.

Giroux, H. (1988). *Teachers as Intellectuals*. New York: Bergin & Garvey.

Giroux, H. and McLaren, P. (1991). Radical pedagogy as cultural politics. *Theory/ Pedagogy/ Politics*. Morton, D. and Zavarzadeh, M., (Eds.). Urbana: University of Illinois Press.

Greene, M. (1988). *The Dialectic of Freedom*. New York: Teachers College Press.

Greene, M. (1973). Doing a philosophy and building a world. *Teacher as Stranger: Educational Philosophy for the Modern Age*. Belmonot, CA: Wadsworth.

Hecht, J. (2004). *Doubt: A History*. New York: HarperCollins.

Heschel, A. (1965). *Who is Man?* Chicago: University of Chicago Press.

Hytten, K. (2006). Education for social justice: Provocations and challenges. *Educational Theory*. Vol. 56, No. 2.

Infinito, J. (2004). Courage as requisite for moral education. *Philosophy of Education Yearbook*. Urbana, Illinois: Philosophy of Education Society.

Kincheloe, J., P. Slattery and S. Steinberg. (2000). *Contextualizing Teaching*. New York: Longman.

Kohn, A. (2000). *The Case against Standardized Testing*. Portsmouth, NH: Heinemann.

Kozol, H. (1994). *I won't Learn from You: And Other Thoughts on Creative Maladjustment*. New York: The New Press.

May, R. (1980). *The Courage to Create*, 6th printing. New York: W.W.W. Norton & Company.

May, R. (1967). *Man for Himself*, 7th printing. New York: Signet Classics.

Meier, D. (2002). Standardization versus standards. *Phi Delta Kappan*. November.

Meier, D. (1999). The last page. *Dissent*. Spring.

Ohanian, S. (1999). *One Size Fits Few: The Folly of Educational Standards*. Portsmouth, New Hampshire: Heinemann.

Schrock, J.R. (2006, May 27). Don't make teaching an assembly-line job. *The Wichita Eagle*.

Shapiro, H.S. (2006). Losing Heart: *The Moral and Spiritual Miseducation of American Children*. Mahwah, New Jersey: Lawrence Erlbaum Associates Publishers.

Simon, R. (1992). *Teaching against the Grain: Texts for a Pedagogy of Possibility*. New York: Bergin & Garvey.

Suhor, C. (1998). Spirituality: Letting it grow in the classroom. *Educational Leadership* December.

Tillich, P. (1961). *The Courage to Be*. 6th Printing. New Haven: Yale University Press.

Tillich, P. (1970). *Love, Power, and Justice: Ontological Analysis and Ethical Applications*. New York: Oxford University Press. Originally published: 1954.

Tillich, P. (1959). *A Theology of Culture*. New York: Oxford University Press.

White, R. and R. Brockington. (1983). *Tales out of School*. London: Routledge & Kegan Paul.

Whitehead, A.N. (1967). *The Aims of Education: And other Essays*. New York: The Free Press, originally published: New York: The Macmillan Company, 1929.

Wilson, A. (2005, October 9). *New Letters on the Air* (Radio broadcast). New York and Washington, DC: Public Broadcasting Service.

SUGGESTED READINGS

Kohn, A. (2004). *What Does it Mean to be Well Educated?: And More Essays on Standards, Grading, and other Follies*. Boston: Beacon Press.

Lewis, A. (2006) Spinning the message of NCLB. Annual *Editions: Education, 2006–07*. Dubuque, IA: McGraw-Hill.

Meier, D. (2000). *Will Standards save public Schools?* Boston: Beacon Press.

Sirotnik, K., (Ed.) (2004). *Holding accountability accountable: What Ought to Matter in Public Education*. New York: Teachers College Press.

MULTIPLE CHOICE QUESTIONS

The following is an exercise in thinking, based upon ideas presented in this paper. The exercise is not designed to elicit "correct" answers, but rather to allow individual "choices" to be explained—and challenged—in group discussion. The purpose of the exercise is to encourage a dialectical learning climate in which diverse educational issues, and personal interpretations, are open-mindedly explored.

1. The meaning inherent in Abraham Heschel's phrase, "empirical intemperance," may be used as a concept to:

    a. defend the No Child Left Behind Act

    b. criticize and challenge the act

2. W.E.B. Du Bois' metaphorical language defining the school as a "machine" designed to produce "improved and standardized" students best expresses the educational philosophy of those who:

    a. basically approve of

    b. seriously question today's emphasis on high-stakes standardized tests

3. The belief that each individual student is "a unique expression of the universe, incomparable, irreplaceable, and of unique significance" is:

    a. a concept that should be stressed in teacher education programs

    b. a "fuzzy" expression that does not relate to measurable outcomes, which are so important in educational planning

4. Using the metaphor, "midwife" to describe a teacher's pedagogical role is a way to interpret the role as:

    a. transmission of knowledge

    b. drawing out a student's latent possibilities

5. The phrase, "self-affirmation of being," has a nice ring to it, but this should not be considered one of the purposes of American public education. This statement is:

    a. true

    b. false, because a student's ability to "self-affirm" should be a goal

6. For many students in K–12 classrooms there is a sense of being objectified, of being an *it* rather than a *thou* in the classroom; of being manipulated, molded, and indoctrinated. It is:

    a. reasonable

    b. totally off-the-mark, to say that this is one of the reasons why many students say "I hate school"

7. The growth and development of students in a classroom should be based on:

    a. a linear, mechanical model

    b. an organic, open-ended process

8. A teacher education program should encourage future teachers to look behind words like accountability, assessment, quantifiable, efficiency, and standards; and seek for hidden meanings and interpretations

   a. agree

   b. disagree

9. For a classroom to become a place of student *becoming* the teacher must nurture each student's *courage to be*

   a. This is a "pie in the sky" statement that has no place in a teacher education program

   b. Teachers-to-be should be encouraged to intellectually wrestle with the meaning of this statement, and with diverse interpretations of *becoming* and the *courage to be*

10. The basic, fundamental purpose of K–12 education in the United States should be to prepare students:

   a. to do

   b. to be

Dismissed Potential: Why Kids "Hate" School

Karla J. Smart-Morstad
Sara B. Triggs
Concordia College, Moorhead, MN

INTRODUCTION

Do kids "hate" school? We hope not, but we suspect there is plenty of disinterest and disengagement. We even suspect that some teachers share in this sense of disinterest and disengagement. What is it that teachers and students are missing in their classroom experiences?

Engaging in a philosophical conversation about what is meant by student *potential* may be a starting place toward making school interesting and engaging—and, ultimately, meaningfully educative. Missing from much of what occurs in school are approaches to teaching that invite, as one of our colleagues puts it, students' "hearts and souls" to be visible in their learning. The No Child Left Behind legislation mandates that students meet predetermined curriculum standards at predetermined levels. Missing from much of what occurs in school is student-centered teaching, where curriculum emerges from students' interests and abilities and allows students to move toward their potential.

Maybe kids "hate" school because their potential is often dismissed. This can happen when standardized test scores indicating students' success are valued over a clear understanding of the breadth and depth of *what more* children can achieve. If legislative mandates for curriculum and instruction rested on understandings of the philosophical nature of potential, then maybe education could be different enough to recognize and expand students' potential.

Our purpose in this paper is to reflect on the following questions: What is the nature of potential? Does meeting legislated standards equate with meeting student potential? How can educators better structure curriculum and instruction to avoid dismissing kids' potential?

HOW WE CAME TO OUR QUESTIONS AND WHY WE CARE ABOUT THEM

Recently, we worked with colleagues in a study of children's art from Namibia (Ellingson, Smart, Triggs, Danbom, Shreve & Dopp, 2005; Danbom, Smart, & Triggs, 2006). At the close of that work, we were compelled to think further about the philosophical nature of potential and the consequences of its frequent disregard in education. What became clear to us, after studying drawings made by Namibian children was that, even though they were given assigned topics, given directions, and provided with supplies to use, individual children sought freedom of expression to make a prescribed assignment their own.

Surely teachers approach students with prescribed assignments everyday. They do so with the best of intentions. They do so because they are required to address mandated curriculum standards and prove that students have adequately progressed. They do so because Piaget's (1952) stages of child development have become crystallized as "age and stage" expectations in education. What we observed with the Namibian children's drawings was that, regardless of teachers' assumptions about students and what they should know or be able to do, children attempt to exercise freedom. They seek freedom when they refine a given concept so that it becomes a source of wonder.

A recent example caused us to further consider our questions. One of our colleagues, a professor of art education, arranged for her teacher education students to conduct a lesson in a preschool classroom. In addition to reflecting on their teaching experience, the college students were required to analyze the drawings and identify what Little Warren (1992) refers to as children's stages of artistic development. The preschoolers were asked to draw a picture of their family. Caden, a five-year old child in the class, quickly roughed out a simplistic sketch with two stick figures and the outline of a house (see Figure 1). (Caden comes from a family of five.) He then proceeded to use the majority of his time, and two additional sheets of drawing paper, to draw a detailed hockey scene (see Figure 2) and a basketball court (see Figure 3). The hockey scene Caden drew is narrative. It shows a blue sheet of ice, with a net on either side, and a hockey player dressed in black scoring on a goalie clothed in red. The puck enters the net as the goalie sprawls on the ice in an attempt to block the shot. Once Caden completed the hockey scene, he turned his attention, and the remainder of his allotted time, to drawing a basketball court. The drawing is complete with orange wood flooring, a basket and backboard on either end, and a lane and free-throw line for each basket.

Figure 2: Caden's spontaneous drawing of a hockey player.

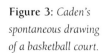

Figure 3: Caden's spontaneous drawing of a basketball court.

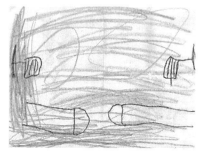

Figure 1: Caden's assigned drawing of his family.

Our colleague noted that the hockey scene appeared, developmentally, at least two levels or stages higher than the drawing Caden made for the assigned topic of family. Would Caden's potential have been overlooked, had he chosen to stay within the parameters of the assignment? The art educator's comments reveal that limiting assessment to the assigned drawing of family would have fostered inaccurate assumptions regarding Caden's potential. An assessment that allowed potential to be overlooked could have misled teachers to make inaccurate judgments about his *mind*, *self* and *potential*. But, Caden sought freedom to wonder. He continued beyond the assigned task to draw sport scenes.

When an individual student wonders, an inquiry meaningful to that child can begin. Freedom to refine, to wonder, to inquire toward meaning-making supports a child's pursuit of knowing himself and the world. Children have their own ideas. They are thoughtful, and they have something to say. Their inquiry and learning has purpose and value.

Children's avenues and tools for discovery must be larger than a classroom teacher—or a curriculum standard—can anticipate, predict, or prescribe. Learning that supports the meeting and refining of one's potential can be satisfying. When potential is approached and expanded, teachers and students have a chance to realize what phenomenologists refer to as *being* and *meaning* (Crowell, 2001). Students whose learning lets them savor *being* and *meaning* are not likely to "hate" school.

Adults, in everyday conversation, whether they are teachers in schools or parents at home, tend to make assumptions that overlook children's potential. Students' preferences for what they care to elaborate, repeat, reshape, and question, can be trivialized. To be open to children's potential is to respond to children with powerful regard. The concept of "fun" in learning remains undefined and vaguely understood as entertaining. But, when anyone—child, adolescent or adult—is striving toward and refining individual potential, there is satisfaction from fullness of engagement, discovery, creation, and sense of *being*.

WHAT IS THE NATURE OF POTENTIAL?

Potential is an aspect of mind, self and the human desire for freedom. If potential is to be afforded powerful regard, the learning activities teachers offer students must allow intellectual and creative flexibility. A child needs learning opportunities open to choice, preference, wonder, curiosity, and unique connections. Children need opportunities to explore without particular outcomes in mind. They need chances to determine the duration of their own investigation. Children need choices in learning. They need more than the either/or choices educators often set before them. Children need genuine opportunities to utilize their own discernment in considering the shape, scope, and necessary resources for knowing the world through meaningful learning. Through such learning, individuality can be made visible. While it is not possible to know a single child based on a single learning activity, it is possible to see individual expression and movement toward potential whenever the child approaches inquiry and learning with freedom.

The work children produce deserves close consideration. Looking closely at student work, without judgment or assumptions, can widen an understanding of learning and deepen an appreciation for the learner (Carini, 2001). To think of learning as *an event of being* means engagement with challenging curriculum, multiple inquiry processes; meaningful learning can then unfold.

Why is it crucial that teachers be able to see and value children's potential? Why does acknowledgement of a unique perspective matter to a child's further learning and expression? When content and learning strategies are prescribed, the learner has less ability to bring connective experience and genuine questions to the setting. The individual *self* must find an entry place and a way to move forward to make meaning. Teachers who acknowledge and respect students' individuality realize that it is not their place to bend the child's *self* to the curriculum. Rather, it is their role to recognize the power of *self* and use it as a starting point.

When educators speak of the value of individual meaning-making, yet put forward specific knowledge to be learned, and impose learning strategies, they move against the individuality of learners—and the generative and constructivist nature of the mind. *Mind* releases the *self* into the world to understand, express, and empower. Mind is different from the brain. It encompasses the totality of individual *being*. Teaching and learning that acknowledges a child's mind is different from teaching and learning that merely engages the brain. Unless learning becomes part of the child—deeply understood and comprehended from a sense of self—it remains on the surface. Surface learning reveals little about individual student potential. Surface learning is not rooted. While surface learning may be visible on checklists and objective tests, rooted learning requires a form of assessment that looks not just for the presence of particular details or the application of specific learning techniques.

When seeking freedom to reveal their own thoughts and expressions, learners exemplify Paulo Freire's (1970) position that human empowerment comes through teaching and learning that is free from oppression. Humans need learning that is fully open to the potential of the *mind* to expand the individual *self*. Freire and Myles Horton (1990) understand fullness in learning as, by necessity, requiring freedom from the "constraints of convention" (p. 53). We see that convention, represented by standards-based curriculum and standardized assessment, can present a predetermined path. Citing Spanish poet Antonio Machado's proverb—"walker there is no road, you must make the road by walking"—Freire and Horton (1990) insist that learners create their own learning (p. 6). Friere elaborates, " ... even though we need to have some outline, *I am sure that we make the road by walking. ...* The question for me is how is it possible for us, in the process of making the road, to be clear and to clarify our *own* making of the road." (Friere & Horton, p. 6–7).

DOES MEETING THE STANDARDS EQUATE WITH MEETING STUDENT POTENTIAL?

Standards-based curriculum and assessment moves away from the humanness inherent in learning. It offers an "age and stage" curriculum taught with levels of achievement defined before students begin learning. The influence of Piaget (1952), in its narrowest interpretation, supports assumptions about the capacity of individual children. Meeting standards, at standard levels of achievement is, after all, a process of *standardization*. Standardized assessment—comparing one child to the next, one classroom to the next, one district to the next—does not provide teachers with the connections necessary to develop a personally meaningful curriculum to bring mind, self and freedom to students' learning.

HOW CAN TEACHERS BETTER STRUCTURE CURRICULUM AND INSTRUCTION?

Planning should regard children as human beings able to move toward and expand their potential needs to create a meaningful, foundational relationship with each child as a growing and changing *being*. Education is a very human endeavor. Decision-making on behalf of children must value growth and learning.

If assessment of learning is to powerfully regard children's minds and selves, it must consider student work that is rooted in freedom in order to reveal potential. Curriculum, pedagogy, assessment and individual learning that moves toward potential requires wholeness. Whole learning is sensory as well as abstract. It can support a definition of learning as *an event of self moving toward potential*. Learning is intimate. Poet and philosopher Mark Doty (2002) writes, "intimacy . . . is the highest value" (p. 6). The *self* requires relationship to people and ideas; to the physical and metaphysical realms; to the past, present, and the future. For Doty, "what we want is to be brought into relation" (p. 7). Being brought into relation means connectivity. But, Doty also acknowledges that the balance requires that individuals be free. Connectivity and independence are aspects of *being*. They are fundamental to human growth and learning. From a stance that values relationship and freedom, teachers are able to use curriculum, pedagogy, and assessment to educate children toward their potential.

100

Taking time to know the child makes a child-centered curriculum possible. A child-centered curriculum is not possible when all the information gathered and assessed about a child's knowledge and understanding is quantitative, compared to pre-established ability expectations, or reduced to percentages, letter grades or numbers (Danbom, Smart & Triggs, 2006). The use of a single piece of evidence, whether a test score, reading index, or art work, cannot provide in-depth understanding about a child and what she knows and can do. Assessment involves what teachers know about children's learning and how they learn it. Ideally, assessment does not feed the dismissal of student potential.

CLOSING CONSIDERATIONS

Freedom is foundational for the development of children's potential and engagement of mind. The mind cannot function if self and potential are overlooked. The drive for standardized assessment can easily lead educators away from constructivist practices. But, if legislators and school people fully valued students' minds and voices, educators would be able to plan curriculum and use pedagogy that keeps the individual child at the center of active learning.

Constructivism, as a guide for curriculum development and teaching methodology, can help teachers welcome students' minds and selves filled with potential. Assessment practices that look for fullness can be useful to teachers in ways standardized and objective evaluations cannot. Teachers need information to assess what a child comprehends and expresses (*what is there*). They need the tools and wisdom to address *what more could be there* in the child's learning. Educators also need trust—and their own humanity—in order to recognize children as *beings* filled with potential and in need of freedom to learn. We saw in the artwork of Namibian children, and again through Caden's drawings , that individual learners can move beyond the confines of teacher directions and adult assumptions. Walkers do indeed make their own roads.

Often the best intentions of adults to shape a learning experience for children, and their instincts to apply developmental expectations to children's expressions, are limiting. Children exercise the essence of their humanity when they are allowed *being* and *meaning*. Human *being* and *meaning* can enlarge individual and relational possibilities. Expression of *being* demands space and time for the individual, a unique self to exercise the *mind* and, thus, move toward and refine potential.

Standards-based curriculum, instruction, and assessment often tells children what to learn about and how to approach learning. It can leave little regard for what else the children may want to question; how they may want to organize their knowledge; what more they are compelled to investigate; the duration of time they require; and how they will make their comprehension known.

Educators who acknowledge and respect students' individuality realize that it is not their place to bend the child's *self* to the curriculum, and that if they do so, the power of *mind* is overlooked. An example of this concept is found in Edward St. Aubyn's (2006) novel *Mother's Milk* where the protagonist reflects on what she sees as her son's " ... thrilling potential ... " (p. 158). St. Aubyn reveals an understanding of the limiting nature of adult direction and expectation when he writes of the mother's revelation that her son's " ... desire for knowledge outstripped any parental ambition" (p. 138). As in St. Aubyn's literary reference, the adults in children's lives must responsibly recognize the power of *self* as it freely inquires. They must employ that power to propel children and adolescents toward reaching and refining their potential. If as a community of learners, we embraced the complexity of the individual and the nature of learning, then maybe kids would not "hate" school.

REFERENCES

Carini, P. F. (2001). *Starting Strong: A Different Look at Children, Schools, and Standards*. New York: Teachers College Press.

Crowell, S. (2001). *Husserl, Heidegger and the Space of Meaning: Paths toward Transcendental Phenomenology*. Evanston, IL: Northwestern University Press.

Danbom, K., Smart, K., & Triggs, S. (2006). *Learning from Descriptive Review: Looking closely at Namibian Children's Art*. Manuscript submitted for publication.

Doty, M. (2002). *Still Life with Oysters and Lemon: On Objects and Intimacy*. Boston: Beacon Press.

Ellingson, S., Smart, K., Triggs, S., Danbom, K., Shreve, R., & Dopp, S. Namibian child artists and shifts in understanding for pre-K–16 education: The descriptive review process experienced and reflected upon. *The Prospect Review #23*, Spring 2005.

Freire, P. (1970). *Pedagogy of the Oppressed*. (Myra Bergman Ramos, Trans.) New York: Continuum.

Horton, M. & Freire, P. (1990). *We Make the Road by Walking: Conversations on Education and Social Change*. Philadelphia, PA: Temple University Press.

Little Warren, M. (1992). The magic of children's art. In W. Enloe & K. Sim (Eds.) *Linking through Diversity: Practical Classroom Activities for Experiencing and Understanding our Cultures* (pp. 123–136). Tucson, AZ: Zephyr Press.

Piaget, J. (1952). *The Origins of Intelligence in Children*. New York: International University Press.

St. Aubyn, E. (2006). *Mother's Milk*. New York: Open City Books.

SUGGESTED ACTIVITIES

Directions: Please use at least ten minutes for each of the following free-writings.

You are to narrate and reflect on your experiences through free-writing. Each response will require you to write rapidly to tell the story of your experience; grammar and punctuation need not be perfect in a free-writing. Your writing may serve as an early draft for later, but your immediate purpose is to tell your own stories and reflect on the meaning. The free-writing will be shared in discussion with a group of peers.

1. Share a memory from your K–12 school experiences that stands out as an example of a time when the assessment used limited your ability to show what you knew or understood. Describe the class and the curriculum topic or theme about which you had learned. What type of assessment was used? What options would have allowed you to more fully represent your understandings? What would you have liked to have been able to do?

2. Share a memory of a curriculum topic or issue that is an example of an experience you had where you elaborated an assignment to make it your own. In what curriculum area did you go beyond classroom assign-

ments because you wanted to continue your inquiry either in school or outside the school? How did you reshape the assignment to make it your own? What became of your further inquiry?

3. The authors believe that teachers must find ways to see "what more could be there" for each child in order to insure that potential is not dismissed. How can teachers assess in ways that allow them to see "what more could be there" for individual students? Share a memory of a time a classroom teacher seemed to see "what more could be there" in your learning. What did the teacher suggest, encourage or support in your inquiry that took you beyond the assigned material into the realm of individual elaboration and opportunity for rooted learning?

MULTIPLE CHOICE QUESTIONS

1. The authors believe that student potential can be limited by

    a. predetermined curriculum

    b. adherence to Piaget's developmental stages

    c. predetermined standards

    d. all of the above

2. When learning is rooted, it indicates that

    a. the child has made personal and authentic connections to the curriculum

    b. adequate yearly progress has been made

    c. learning has been engrained through drill and practice

    d. none of the above

3. The authors' concerns about strict adherence to curriculum standards include

    a. students' individual connections to curriculum can be overlooked

    b. the humanness inherent in learning can be overlooked

    c. the boundaries and parameters of standards can establish predetermined learning expectations

    d. all of the above

4. Constructivist teachers

    a. rely on predetermined curriculum to shape students' learning

    b. recognize the importance of their own specialized knowledge in the content area to inform students' learning

c. permit students to bring their own experiences and questions to the curriculum

d. make use of traditional assessment to insure students' mastery of curriculum

5. When individuals are free to wonder, ask questions, find resources and reshape an assignment

   a. their learning can be easily assessed

   b. their learning can reveal potential

   c. structured curriculum is being effectively utilized

   d. direct instruction is being effectively utilized

6. What do students need in order to move toward their own potential?

   a. freedom to elaborate assignments

   b. freedom to record their own grades

   c. freedom to shape their own inquiry and determine the amount of time they will allot to projects according to their learning needs

   d. both a. and c

7. Meaningful learning and true understanding, which can be readily applied in any situation, are the results of

   a. rote practice and memorization

   b. curriculum well coordinated with developmental stages

   c. rooted learning

   d. thorough teacher planning and instruction

8. The authors would be supportive of

   a. emerging curriculum

   b. authentic assessment

   c. inquiry

   d. all of the above

9. Child-centered curriculum is made possible when

   a. pre-established expectations for student learning have been determined

   b. when districts establish content area curriculum timelines

c. a teacher has depth of understanding about a child and what the child knows or is able to do

d. teacher understands how each individual child ranks, compared to peers, in knowledge of the topic

10. Assignments that allow students to reveal their potential

a. provide opportunities for inquiry

b. allow for freedom to elaborate or reshape a project

c. closely aligns with standards

d. both a. and b

Learner-Centered Instructional Relationships: Encouraging Students to Learn, Grow, and Like School

ADAM P. HARBAUGH
UNIVERSITY OF NORTH CAROLINA-CHARLOTTE
JEFFREY H. D. CORNELIUS-WHITE
MISSOURI STATE UNIVERSITY

This paper describes results from a recent meta-analysis (Cornelius-White, in press A) that shows how learner-centered instructional relationships (LCIR) are associated with above average school engagement, cognition, and personal and social growth. Students like and flourish in school when their teachers are learner-centered.

LCIR focus on both the learner and the learning process (McCombs & Whistler, 1997) and are defined as the measured facilitative, challenging, and flexible interactive teacher strategies that affect students' engagement, learning, and development. LCIR have roots in classical, humanistic education (Cornelius-White, 2006; Rogers, 1983), today's constructivist learner-centered model (McCombs & Whistler, 1997), and other theory and research traditions (Cornelius-White & Harbaugh, 2006).

THE META-ANALYSIS

In an effort to review and better understand the degree of relationship between positive learner-centered teacher–student relationships and comprehensive student success, Cornelius-White (in press A) synthesized 119 studies from about 1000 reviewed papers from 1948 to 2004 with 1450 findings and 355,325 students, 14,851 teachers, and 2439 schools. The research questions addressed the degree of association between all positive teacher–student relationship variables and all positive student outcomes, the associations between specific relational variables and specific student outcomes, and potential moderator analysis.

The meta-analysis design included comprehensive search mechanisms including PSYCINFO, ERIC, reference lists from other included studies, and published bibliographies. Accuracy and bias control was assessed through two-person coding of every study and an inter-rater reliability sampling (kappa coefficient of 0.85). Primary study validity assessment was conducted through two systems of grading the quality of the studies, including use of the Scientific Methods Score (Sherman et al., 1997). The synthesis satisfied all of the eight criteria with which Mackay, Barkham, Rees, & Stiles (2003) appraised 255 syntheses, where only 11% of the studies met all criteria.

The synthesized studies included male and female, Caucasian, African-American, Latino, and Filipino participants in large numbers from most areas of the US, the Philippines, Brazil, Germany, Austria, the UK, and Canada. Participants came from urban, suburban, and rural communities with low to high intellectual abilities and incomes. The median student sample for each study was 500 though the range of sample sizes was 20–81,000. Grade levels included pre K–20 though the majorities of students were in grades 1–12 and teachers' experience levels had a large range.

Coded variables included 9 independent, 18 dependent, and 39 moderators. The independent variables (relational characteristics) included empathy, warmth, genuineness, non-directivity, higher order thinking, encouraging learning/challenge, adapting to individual and social differences, and composites of these. Dependent variables (student outcomes) included the cognitive aspects of achievement batteries, grades/retention, perceived achievement, verbal achievement, math, science, social science, IQ, and creative/critical thinking and the affective/behavioral dependent variables of student participation/initiation, positive motivation, self-esteem/mental health, social connection, attendance/absences, global satisfaction, disruptive behavior, negative motivation, and drop–out prevention. Of the 39 moderator variables—16 concerned sample qualities, 19 methodological features and five publishing features. Potential moderator variables were proposed by a sample of teachers and were considered for their potential to alter the size of the relationship between the teacher relationship and student outcome variables. When studies show that differences (for example gender) on a moderator is associated with significant differences in the size of the association between relationship and student outcome, a moderating effect is said to exist. For instance, though most studies included both male and female teachers, when only female teachers were explored, it appeared that relational variables had larger effects on students than when only male teacher samples were used.

Results showed that mean correlations ($r = .31$) are above average compared to other educational innovations for cognitive, and especially affective/behavioral outcomes, but have wide variation. Fraser, Wahlberg, Welch, and Hattie (1987) in their seminal synthesis of syntheses found an overall average correlation of $r = .20$ for all educational innovations on cognitive outcomes and $r = .11$ for affective outcomes. They also advocated that, in particular, any correlation $r > .30$ "should be of much interest" (Fraser et al., 1987, p. 208). Sample and other methodological features account for some of the variability, especially in terms of the perspective used to measure the relational variables, where observers' ($r = .40$) and students' ($r = .33$) ratings of the teacher–student relationship showed larger associations between relational variables and student success variables compared to teacher perspectives ($r = .17$). In other words, students' and supervisors' views of the teacher–student relationship appear more important for predicting student outcome than teachers' own views. Another significant modifier included whether the study controlled for beginning differences in ability and achievement (aptitude and prior achievement usually correlate between $r = .50$ and $r = .75$ with subsequent achievement). When the student's starting point is controlled, the association with successful teacher–student relationship is large ($r = .46$), meaning on an average, 21% of the remaining variance in student outcomes is due to the LCIR. As mentioned, teacher gender was also a significant moderator, but less so than the two reviewed above. Regardless of teacher or student gender, learner-centered relationships show significant association with student success. Most potential modifiers, such as ethnicity, sample size, student gender, family income, grade level, or aptitude, teacher experience, year of publication, or location, did not show significant moderating effects. Learner-centered instructional relationships appear to have robust effects across a variety of settings and with a diversity of people.

SPECIFIC FINDINGS REGARDING HATING OR LIKING SCHOOL

Several affective/behavioral student outcomes assessed by the meta-analysis are relevant to the discussion of the degree to which students hate and/or like school. The corrected mean correlation between learner-centered teacher relationships and affective/behavioral student outcomes was $r = .35$, far larger than the average affect of educational elements ($r = .11$) seen in the Fraser et al. (1987) synthesis of syntheses. Cornelius-White (in press A) summarizes the specific findings:

> The highest correlations were found for participation ($r = .55$), student satisfaction ($r = .44$), dropout prevention ($r = .35$), self-efficacy/mental health ($r = .35$), positive motivation ($r = .32$), and social connection/skills ($r = .32$). Reduction of disruptive behavior ($r = .25$) and attendance ($r = .25$) showed moderate correlations. Reduction of negative motivation (effort/work avoidance) showed a negligible relationship ($r = .06$). (p. 14)

The association between learner-centered instructional relationships and student class participation is uniquely large. Over 30% of the variance in how much students participate and initiate discussions in a class are due to their relationship with the teacher. When one combines the outcomes that might be concerned solely with school engagement (attendance, class participation, student satisfaction, social connections and skills, and respect or decreased disruptive behavior), the mean correlation rises to $r = .37$ (Cornelius-White & Harbaugh, 2006). Clearly, learner-centered instructional relationships influence whether students like or hate school!

While engaging in school is important in its own right in terms of students' satisfaction and willingness to participate in activities, it also affects the economic bottom line of a school through attendance, the quality of students' peer relationships, and thus indirectly it effects achievement. For example, over 50% of the differences in international achievement are explainable by school engagement. Students in lower achieving countries have been shown to be less engaged (Boe, May, & Boruch, 2002).

IMPLICATIONS FOR SCHOOL REFORM

One of the most robust findings from all educational research is that proximal (close to the student) intervention is more potent than distal intervention (away from the student) (Fraser et al., 1987; Hattie, 1999). Cornelius-White (in press A) offers the following example: "Teacher beliefs are more distant from students than their lived behaviors, even as physical attributes of a school ($r = -.02$) is a more distant variable than students' prior achievement experiences ($r = .75$) when correlated with current achievement behavior (Fraser et al., 1987)." Because of this trend, it stands to reason that learner-centered instructional relationships, as proximal aspects of education, close to the students' experience, offer a more promising and beneficial alternative to distal reform methods such as revisions of school aims, curriculum changes, or new legislation (Cornelius-White & Brown, 2006).

While there may be many implications from existing and ongoing research on LCIR for school reform, our suggestions in this paper will be primarily intended for the structural level of the classroom. It is at this level, we argue, that some of the most meaningful changes may occur and those that may have the biggest impact on the individual student.

Recent national and state trends in accountability (i.e. high-stakes testing) have driven a number of the current reform efforts in education. While it may not be easy or convenient for teachers, administrators, and school systems to adopt assessment procedures that are in line with principles of LCIR, reform efforts in assessment should keep in mind that determining what students know and what they have learned, demands more than a few administrations of a single type of assessment instrument. Kohn (2001) warns against inaction as a result of either the belief that high-stakes testing is here to stay—which might encourage educators to work compliantly within a system with which they may not necessarily agree—or the belief that political tides will change and take high-stakes testing with them. Instead, Kohn offers suggestions to teachers, administrators, parents, and students on ways to de-emphasize the importance of "the test."

One of these ways is for stakeholders to downplay their successes with achievement on standardized tests (Kohn, 2001). By minimizing the impact of positive results of the test, Kohn suggests that standardized tests lose some of their ill-gained legitimacy. Another suggestion for teachers is to find and then do whatever is necessary and sufficient for students to be successful in the test, however that success is defined. By not spending extraneous time teaching to the test, which is what pressured teachers may feel necessary to do, teachers can utilize precious classroom time on building and benefiting from valuable LCIR. Kohn (2001) also suggests that administrators and teachers do whatever is necessary to act as a buffer between the high-stakes test and the next one below them on "the food chain of American education" (p. 349). Superintendents should protect principals; principals should protect teachers; and last but not least, teachers should protect students from the pressures of high-stakes tests.

SUGGESTIONS FOR TEACHERS AND STUDENTS

Following are several suggestions by which teachers and students can make more likely the occurrence of learner-centered instructional relationships in their classrooms (Cornelius-White, 2005, in press B; Cornelius-White & Brown, 2006; Cornelius-White & Harbaugh, 2006). These suggestions will include effective ways to create and sustain cooperative learning environments in the classroom, manage student behavior and discipline, effectively assess student learning, and reflect on instructional practices. We begin each section below with a brief justification and explanation of the ways the instructional practices are consistent with LCIR

Cooperative Learning Environments in the Classroom

Students inevitably come to each new classroom with the intellectual and emotional baggage they have been collecting from previous educational experiences. From a constructivist perspective, these prior experiences are important because they form the foundation on which students will build new knowledge and deepen understanding. As educators, we should value students' experiences in and out of the classroom. However, we cannot assume that each student is prepared emotionally or academically for a new classroom environment where they work with their classmates and teacher to make curricular and instructional choices. Educators should provide the necessary support for each student so that they can efficiently begin to make and influence choices in their own and their school communities' best interests. As part of this support mechanism, teachers can provide students opportunities to learn about themselves and their relationships within and outside the school setting.

The following suggestions are provided as a way for teachers to support students' learning and efforts in cooperative environments:

- Start off the school year with activities that promote cooperative skills. There are many team-building or trust-building activities that can provide students opportunities to develop a sense of their importance, belonging, and responsibility to their learning group. These activities should be designed to build trust, communication skills, empathy, and conflict-resolution skills within individuals and cooperative groups. Many appropriate activities can be found online or constructed by creative teachers, but teachers should anticipate the consequences of a group or individual failing to succeed at the given task. Just as in the academic domain, initial failure to achieve a goal can be motivating for the group so long as all group members understand that they are working in a safe and supportive environment. Teachers need to develop a sense of when to step in and offer support and when to allow the group to struggle. Teachers should also incorporate, throughout the school year, explicit teaching of meta-cognitive and self-regulatory learning skills. These skills are necessary and beneficial for individual and group success.

- Set unambiguous and realistic goals for the group. Regardless of who has determined the goals for the group to accomplish—whether it is the teacher, the students, or the teacher with the students—clearly defined and achievable goals should be in place to enable the group to work effectively on the problem or task. While defining the goals with the group can be an effective learner-centered instructional strategy for students, one must have some initial understanding of a topic before knowing what they want or need to know about it.

- Help the group determine individual responsibilities within the group. Once a task has been determined for or with the group, individual responsibilities for group members to achieve that task should be discussed and established. All students should be given the opportunity to develop and take various abilities and responsibilities within the group. The role of the teacher in this endeavor can vary depending on the needs of the groups; some groups may need more assistance in determining group roles whereas some may need very little and this may vary with both grade level and group cohesiveness.

- Offer continuous support and monitoring. The teacher needs to know, empathically and logistically, what is happening within each group in order to provide appropriate support. Just because a group has worked successfully in the past on multiple tasks does not mean that the teacher can leave that group alone for future tasks. With each new task, there should be academic challenges that are new to the group, even if the group dynamics are no longer new.

- Cooperative groups should learn through inquiry. Inquiry-based learning will likely be foreign to many students at most levels, even in graduate school. Teachers should, in response to the needs of the students, begin with guided inquiry-based activities and taper off their level of guidance. Inquiry skills are those independent, critical, higher-order and meta-cognitive thinking skills that we, as educators, want our students to develop.

- Supply problem-based learning environments for groups. The structure, or lack of structure, of an authentic problem may not be an ideal place to start with groups of students not ready for the independence and interdependence necessary to navigate problem-based learning. But this environment, much like the inquiry-based environment above has been shown to increase student motivation and achievement (Cornelius-White, in press A; Cornelius-White & Harbaugh, 2006.; Savoie & Hughes, 1994; Stepien & Gallagher, 1993).

Managing Student Behavior and Discipline

It may be misguided to discuss the learner-centered classroom while suggesting ways for the teacher to effectively manage student behavior and discipline, but many skeptics of LCIR may misrepresent the enacted LCIR classroom with terms such as chaos or situations where students do whatever they want, whenever they want. These misrepresentations only serve to polarize beliefs about the differences between teacher-centered and learner-centered classrooms and behaviorist and constructivist teaching. While LCIR are grounded in humanism and constructivism, they are based on successful instructional strategies drawn from a variety of theories.

Our first suggestion is that teachers should give students the primary voice in establishing and enforcing rules of the classroom. Teachers need to strive to support under-represented, quiet, and reluctant voices in the establishing of these rules. The idea here is for the classroom culture to be relevant and applicable to all students. With traditional, teacher-made sets of rules, all students may struggle to buy-in to the rules and "behavior problems" may fester throughout the school year. In a situation where the rules are created by students but where particular students are left out of the process, these overlooked students may have or cause some of the same problems as in the previous situation.

Just as all students should be an integral part of the designing of the rule structure in a classroom, discussions pertaining to the reasons why particular actions are desirable or undesirable within a school or classroom community should take place. It is the responsibility of the teacher to model empathy and care. Facilitative teacher behavior is the backbone of LCIR. Teachers should also help students develop and maintain authority on enacted empathy and care. Pro-social motives and behaviors in students at any level should be considered as natural as the antisocial motives and behaviors, which an arbitrary set of rules is designed to guard against. Just because these rules are not created by an adult, who may or may not have a pessimistic view of the nature of the student, does not ensure that students will create the rules with an optimistic view of their own motives and behaviors. Care ought to be both modeled and taught to set-up beneficial cycles of pro-social behavior so that students (and teachers!) like school.

Two themes of a learner-centered classroom are mirrored with this approach to student behavior: giving students a choice and enticing or requiring students to create and strive to achieve goals that are personally relevant to them. The goal is not necessarily to teach students exactly how you want them to behave, but to create and maintain an environment where students have a real stake in behaving appropriately, respectfully, and empathically.

Assessing Student Learning

The primary purpose of assessment is to reveal some insight into what a student knows and understands or has learned and what that student can do with that knowledge and understanding. Determining each of these aspects of a student's knowledge can be likened to putting together a puzzle with no boundaries. The entirety of the puzzle's image cannot be determined by one piece or even a few pieces. Making assumptions about the puzzle based on a limited number of pieces will affect our overall approach to putting more pieces together. If these assumptions are made naively and without basis, they may misguide future efforts at the puzzle.

Similarly with assessment, no one test can or should determine the label that we attach to students and use to inform our instructional practices, our curricular choices, and students' educational future. The description of the test has become the common understanding of the high-stakes test. High-stakes tests are not inherently ineffective or malevolent and can be one piece of a student's puzzle. After all, despite a paucity of validity studies, a student's performance on a high-stakes test will reliably reveal something about what the student knows or can do. We suggest that this "something" is less effective for LCIR as a large piece in determining what the puzzle reveals and should not warrant the high-stakes.

To encourage meaningful assessment practices, which can be time-consuming and labor-intensive for both teachers and students, we suggest designing at least some assessment instruments that serve as both evaluation (summative) and instruction (formative) tools. Assessment with these dual and complementary purposes is meaningful for students, teachers, and other stake holders. Detailed feedback on student performance should be provided to students so that they have a better understanding of what they know, in terms of the teacher's expectations, and what they need to do to improve their understanding.

So what are the alternatives to using an efficient multiple-choice test to inform teachers, administrators, parents, and students about what students know? In the current air of accountability, with standardized tests having much impact on states, districts, administrators, teachers, students, and parents, educators still have a degree of autonomy over their classrooms and the way their students show what they know, can do, and understand. We offer an answer with a small collection of alternative assessment methods consistent with current research in assessment and consistent with LCIR that can and should be used to suit the needs of individual classrooms and students:

- Portfolios – Some educators consider portfolios to be the gold standard of learner-centered, alternative assessments. Teachers should decide a priori the purpose of the portfolio, whether it is used to show student achievement or to highlight growth or both. Depending on the school's and the students' access to technology, a portfolio may also be created electronically. The use of portfolios offers students choice at many levels and can promote independent thinking and a sense of autonomy.

- Oral Presentations – In groups or individually, students can show and tell teachers and classmates what they have learned in ways that go beyond the limitations of traditional assessment methods that tend to de-contextualize the subject. Students can be given opportunities to practice their presentations within their own small group with feedback from their group members and the teacher; this can serve as instructional and as formative assessment for both the students and the teacher. In order for the assessment to also serve an instructional purpose, oral presentations can be peer reviewed by the whole class; this process ensures active participation by the class and reduces the passive nature of the audience of many presentations. Research has shown that peer review and tutoring often helps the one reviewing or tutoring more than the one receiving the feedback or help.

- Jigsaw and Mini-teach – Following closely to the previous suggestion, we recommend having students frequently take on teaching roles in the classroom. Although the jigsaws and mini- or micro-teaching opportunities are most often considered instructional strategies, we suggest also making these occasions for students to show what they have learned and where teachers might lead future instruction, i.e., summative and formative assessments, respectively. The empowerment of these approaches also build emotionally positive and instructionally effective teacher–student and student–student relationships.

- Interviews – One of the most prevalent qualitative research methods is the individual interview. Given that the learner-centered teacher has developed a quality rapport with students on an individual basis, the interview is a safe setting for students to exhibit what they have learned about a topic. Although even short interviews can be time-consuming for teachers, a well-constructed interview can likely provide more widely applicable and practical information about what a student understands and can do than any multiple-choice test.

- Rubrics – For any type of authentic, performance assessment, the use of a rubric for evaluation can be appropriate. Rubrics make the assessment more transparent, letting students know what is expected of them to meet particular standards. Teachers can also involve students in the creation of rubrics.

Reflecting on Instructional Practices

Our experiences with pre- and in-service teachers have shown that many of them have become numb to ideas surrounding reflection. Reflection has become so much of a buzz word that many educators feel necessary to include, highlight, or focus on it in their classrooms and writing. Nevertheless, reflection on instructional practices should be more to teachers than a section they must include on a submitted lesson-plan to receive full credit with their administrators or their instructors. Reflection on instructional practices should become habitual and, at the same time, deliberate. It does not necessarily require a quiet environment, a comfortable seat, or a hot cup of tea – although any or all of these amenities may help. Reflection should be focused, goal-driven thought about how things went and is often best done, at least occasionally, in the company of a colleague or supervisor. It is key to the development and maintenance of LCIR and to meeting the challenges of adjusting to this style of school that is so strongly related to when kids and adults like school.

Teachers have to make thousands of decisions per day. Many of these decisions are made in a split-second, but some may be made arbitrarily or without keeping the class or the student central to the decision. Developing LCIR to facilitate students liking school through reflection helps inform every one implicitly of these split-second decisions. One reason teachers may be resistant to reflective thinking about their instructional practices is that they already have too much to do in the classroom and cannot see the benefits of reflection. Teachers, in general, are overworked and may see reflection as one more task to add on to their long list of daily activities. What we are proposing is that reflection should be an infused facet of a teacher's educational training and instructional practices, not an add-on.

Summary

Learner-centered instructional relationships (LCIR) focus on both the learner and the learning process. In a synthesis of studies with over 350,000 students from pre-school through graduate school, LCIR were shown to have an above average empirical relationship with student success. Liking school in particular is strongly related to the quality of teacher–student instructional relationships. This paper discussed the method and results of this meta-analytic study as well as implications for school reform based on the initiation of classroom strategies, including cooperative learning environments, egalitarian classroom management, alternative assessments, and reflection. We hope educators are able to help build better instructional relationships between teachers and students to help students both like school and succeed.

References

Boe, E. E., May, H., & Boruch, R. F. (2002). *Student Task Persistence in the Third International Mathematics and Science Study: A MajorSsource ofAachievement Differences at the National, Classroom, and Student Levels.* (Research Rep. No. 2002-TIMSS1). Philadelphia: University of Pennsylvania, Graduate School of Education, Center for Research and Evaluation in Social Policy

Cornelius-White, J. H. D. (2005). "Teaching" Person-centered multicultural counseling: Experiential transcendence of resistance to increase awareness. *Journal of Humanistic Counseling Education and Development,* 44: 225–240.

Cornelius-White, J. H. D. (2006) A review and evolution of Rogers' theory of education. Manuscript submitted for publication.

Cornelius-White, J. H. D. (in press A). Learner-Centered Teacher-Student Relationships are effective: A Meta-analysis. *Review of Educational Research*.

Cornelius-White, J. H. D. (in press B). A learner's guide to person-centered education. *The Person-Centered Journal, 13*.

Cornelius-White, J. H. D. & Brown, R. D. (2006) Politicizing school reform through the person-centered approach: Mandate and advocacy. For M. Cooper, B. Malcolm, G. Proctor, & P. Sanders (Eds.). *Politicizing the Person-Centered Approach: An Agenda for Social Change.* (pp. 263–269) Ross-on-Wye: PCCS Books.

Cornelius-White, J. H. D., & Harbaugh, A. P. (2006). *Learner-centered Instruction: Building Relationships for Student Success.* Manuscript in preparation for Sage Publications.

Fraser, B. J., Wahlberg, H. J., Welch, W. W., & Hattie, J. A. (1987). Syntheses of educational productivity research. *International Journal of Educational Research* 11: 144–252.

Hattie, J. A. (1999, August 2). Influences on Student Learning. *Inaugural Lecture at the University* of Auckland, Australia.

Kohn, A. (2001). Fighting the tests: A practical guide to rescuing our schools. *Phi Delta Kappan, 82*: 348–357.

Mackay, H. C., Barkham, M., & Rees, A., & Stiles, W. B. (2003). Appraisal of published reviews of research on psychotherapy and counseling with adults 1990–1998. *Journal of Consulting and Clinical Psychology* 71(4): 652–656.

McCombs, B. L., & Whisler, J. S. (1997). *The Learner-centered classroom and school: Strategies forEenhancing Student motivation and Achievement.* San Francisco: Jossey-Bass.

Rogers, C. R. (1983). *Freedom to Learn for the 80s.* Columbus: Charles E. Merrill Publishing.

Savoie, J. M., & Hughes, A. S. (1994). Problem-based learning as classroom solution. *Educational Leadership, 52*(3): 54–57.

Sherman, L. W., Gottfredon, D., MacKenzie, D., Eck, J., Reuter, P., & Bushway, S. (1997). *Preventing Crime: What Works,Wwhat Doesn't, What's Promising* (NCJ No. 165366). A Report to the United States Congress prepared for the National Institute of Justice. College Park, MD: University of Maryland.

Stepien, W., & Gallagher, S. (1993). Problem-based learning: As authentic as it gets. *Educational Leadership, 50*(7): 25–28.

SUGGESTED ACTIVITIES

Developing LCIR to facilitate students to like school through reflection helps implicitly inform every one of the thousands of split-second decisions teachers make.

The following questions or activities are intended to give the reader an opportunity to reflect on the ideas discussed in this chapter. These activities and questions should be considered in cooperative groups, if possible.

A. Classroom Management Plan

Reflect on your own experiences as a student in a K–12 classroom and some of the rules by which you were forced to abide. What if you had a hand in creating or changing these rules? Would you have bought in to the rules more if you had helped to create them? Now thinking as a teacher, devise a plan for the beginning of the school year to work with students, having them create a system of classroom rules and procedures. Try to include more detail in this action plan than you think you will need. Share and compare your plan with your colleagues and/or classmates.

B. Selling Assessment

Many teachers and administrators view alternative assessments as inefficient. These teachers may also be unwilling to use alternative assessments in their classroom. Choose one of the following types of assessment and create a brochure describing the assessment and how it can be used in your classroom setting.

Alternative assessments:

- Portfolios

- Journals

- Oral Presentations

- Mini-teach

- Interviews

- Rubrics

Make the brochure compelling. Emphasize its strengths, especially in relation to traditional or other assessments. Really sell the assessment. Share your brochure with colleagues and/or classmates and discuss ways you can use these brochures to help teachers use these or other alternative forms of assessment.

C. Teaching is like...

Many experienced teachers can articulate an analogy for what teaching is like for them. It's important to gain this skill if you don't already have it. This exercise is a natural extension of the previous exercise. Forcing yourself to express your analogy in detail will further help you understand your own beliefs about teaching and your purpose as a teacher.

Try now to complete the sentence "Teaching is like... _____ ."

After you have made an analogy, you can further extend this exercise by considering the following.

1. Think about ways it falls short of describing your beliefs about teaching. Try to extend your chosen simile to encompass your beliefs about teaching. In other words, what else is teaching like?

2. What are some implications of your simile for your classroom? In other words, when you realize your beliefs about teaching better, what do you need to change about how you teach?

3. What aspects of your analogy are learner-centered, that is focusing on learners and the learning process more than content or teacher-directed agenda.

4. Think about how your simile of teaching may have changed over the years in light of new information, ideas, or experiences. Remember specific events or years where your ideas of what teaching is like clearly developed.

5. How do you think your analogy may change in the next year? In other words, what is your growing edge now? What values, behaviors, or projects have you been hoping to try on which may further influence your basic understanding of what teaching is?

MULTIPLE CHOICE QUESTIONS

Choose the best answer for each of the following questions.

1. Which of the following could be considered a proximal educational intervention?

    a. New school policy regarding talking in the hallways

    b. Teachers welcoming every student with a warm greeting before each class

    c. New standards-based mathematics curriculum

    d. Professional-development program in reading across the curriculum

2. Which of the following are considered promising assessment alternatives?

    a. Portfolios

    b. Oral presentations

    c. Interviews

    d. All of the above

3. Which of the following should teachers NOT do when creating cooperative learning environments?

    a. Begin the school year with activities that promote cooperative skills

    b. Set unambiguous and realistic goals for the group

    c. Allow groups to be exclusively self-monitoring

    d. Help the group determine individual responsibilities within the group

4. Which of the following statements best reflect the authors' position on teacher reflection?

    a. Reflection must be made in a quiet place, free of distractions

    b. Reflection should be focused, goal-driven thought about how things went and is often best done at least occasionally in the company of a colleague or supervisor

    c. Reflection should be done after any decision a teacher has made during the course of the school day

    d. All of the above

5. Teachers should include students in the creation of classroom rules because

    a. most students bring to the table several years of experience with school rules

    b. it is more time-efficient to have students create the rules

    c. students will be less likely to buy-in to the rules they have helped to create

    d. student-created rules are in a language students can better understand

6. In the supporting meta-analysis discussed in this chapter, the corrected mean correlation between learner-centered teacher relationships and affective/behavioral student outcomes was found to be

    a. $r = .67$

    b. $r = .35$

    c. $r = .25$

    d. $r = .11$

7. Which of the following potential modifiers considered in the meta-analysis showed significant moderating effects?

    a. ethnicity, particularly of the students

    b. social class, especially family income

    c. number of years of teacher experience

    d. observers' or supervisors' views of the teacher–student relationship

8. Teachers building LCIR should

    a. lecture most of the time

    b. discourage talking out of turn

    c. expect that students will like school if you let them do only what they want

    d. none of the above

9. Research has shown LCIR to have the greatest effect on students'

    a. participation

    b. test scores

    c. intelligence

    d. attitudes

10. A meta-analysis is a

    a. systematic review of the research

    b. quantitative synthesis

    c. secondary analysis, combining similar studies to better describe the overall effect of a given variable or set of variables

    d. all of the above

SECTION IV

Philosophical Considerations

Philosophers would do better to test their philosophic positions by first familiarizing themselves with what takes place in the educational process. A Philosophy of education, worthy of consideration, will not develop as a result of philosophers applying their philosophy to questions of education. It will develop when philosophers and educators, as well as other intelligent citizens, concern themselves with questions of education, explore their bearing on conflicting value commitments and seek some comprehensive theory of human values to guide us in the resolution of conflicts.

—Sidney Hook, The Scope of Philosophy of Education (1956)

If we are willing to conceive education as the process of forming fundamental dispositions, intellectual and emotional, toward nature and fellow men, philosophy may even be defined as the general theory of education.

—John Dewey, Democracy and Education (1916)

A "working definition" of philosophy of education: The criticism, clarification, and analysis of the language, concepts, and logic of the ends and means of education.

—Robert R. Sherman, Philosophy of Education
Course Lecture (1994)

And when we call for education, we mean real education. We believe in work. We ourselves are workers, but work is not necessarily education. Education is the development of power and ideal.

—W.E.B Du Bois, The Georgia Equal Rights Conference (1906)

John Dewey's Theory of Experience: Some Ideas as to Why Kids (might) Hate School

Eric C. Sheffield
Missouri State University

Experience and Schooling...a "Felt Problem"

I recently picked up John Dewey's classic work, *Experience and Education*, in preparation to teaching the text to twenty or so graduate students. I teach Missouri State University's Philosophy of Education course and fervently believe it essential for students doing advanced work in education to "engage" Mr. Dewey. Originally a series of Kappa Delta Pi lectures to teachers, *Experience and Education* is one of the best for just such a "Deweyan engagement"—it's brief; it's theoretical while very practical in its implications; and, it asks students to think about education much more philosophically than they have typically been asked to do.

As I yet again made my way through this rather dense defense of progressive education, I was struck, as is usually the case with Dewey's work, by its incredible clarity and its enduring timeliness—*Experience and Education* continues to speak to me loudly and clearly even now, nearly seventy years after its initial publication and nearly a decade after my own first reading of it. As I will point out later, this timeliness might be less to do with John Dewey's prophetic vision and more about our staggering sluggishness toward reasonable educational reform; or, maybe, less about John Dewey's prophetic vision and more about would-be and actual reformers being ignorant of his work—I often wonder how many of the crafters of the No Child Left Behind legislation have taken the time to engage Mr. Dewey in any meaningful way and how many of our kids hate school because the school experience does not take into account their actual lived experiences—hence, the "felt problem" of this paper.

Philosophical "Either-Oriness"

Dewey penned *Experience and Education* in defense of progressive education and in reaction to what he saw as a general "either–or" philosophical disposition among "mankind" that resulted in an "either–or" misunderstanding of progressive educational philosophy among American educators, policy makers, and politicians: "The problems [within educational philosophy, policy and practice] are not even recognized, to say nothing of being solved when it is assumed that it suffices to reject the ideas and practices of the old education and then go to the opposite extreme" (1938, p. 22). In other words, and as one of my students recently expressed it, "either–or" thinking can and often does result in throwing the proverbial baby out with the proverbial bathwater. A shift in philosophical thinking does not mean that we can or should deny those practices from the old that remain viable in the new, simply because they were part of the old. It is, I think, this habit of reaction rather than pro-action among politicians particularly and the American public more generally that has lead us through the back and forth pendulum swings of educational reforms found in the (albeit brief) history of the American public school system.

THE NECESSITY FOR A THEORY OF EXPERIENCE

In *Experience and Education*, Dewey (1938) argues that an evaluation of either the traditional or progressive philosophy of education and the problems of practice entailed in them must ultimately be understood as being rooted in a theory of experience and it is only from within such a theory that judgments as to educational value can be made:

> I assume that amid all uncertainties there is one permanent frame of reference: namely, the organic connection between education and personal experience; or, that the new philosophy of education is committed to some kind of empirical and experimental philosophy.

> The belief that all genuine education comes about through experience does not mean that all experiences are genuinely or equally educative. Experience and education cannot be directly equated to each other. For some experiences are mis-educative. Any experience is mis-educative that has the effect of arresting or distorting the growth of further experience (p. 25).

That is, on Dewey's count (and I think he is correct to say so), the judgment as to the educational value of any experience can only be made via first an understanding of human experience generally. Then and only then can we (teachers, parents, students, community members, etc.) more specifically evaluate the degree to which such experiences lead to further enriching experiences rather than to stagnation or even distortion of the student and, ultimately, her community. In a word, the value of any educational experience is directly tied to its potential and actual impact on human growth.

EXPERIENCE AS CONTINUAL

As to the specifics of his theory, Dewey talks about two components that constitute any experience: continuity and interaction. For Dewey, it is the continuous nature of experience that allows educators to discriminate those experiences that are educative from those that are mis-educative and continuity of experience is tied directly to habit formation. As he says it,

> the basic characteristic of habit is that every experience enacted and undergone modifies the one who acts and undergoes, while this modification affects, whether we wish it or not, the quality of subsequent experiences. *For it is a somewhat different person who enters into them.* The principle of habit so understood obviously goes deeper than the ordinary conception of a habit as a more or less fixed way of doing things, although it includes the latter as one of its special cases. It covers the formation of attitudes, attitudes that are emotional and intellectual; it covers our basic sensitivities and ways of meeting and responding to all the conditions which we meet in living. From this point of view, the principle of continuity of experience means that every experience both takes up something from those which have gone before and modifies in some way the quality of those which come after (emphasis mine, 1938, p. 5).

Understanding that one experience impacts future experiences seems a simple matter and yet when it comes to educating our youth in our public schools, the continuity of experience holds the keys to the kingdom—

and rarely are those keys considered carefully for their practical implications. If an educational experience provides the impetus toward further, ever expanding, experiences, then it is certainly educative. On the other hand, if an experience closes off students from future experiences, then it is anything but educational and is, in fact, mis-educative because it retards rather than promotes human growth. And, on Dewey's count, the problems associated with traditional, lecture, rote memorization, "regurgitative" student experiences are a direct result of not thinking thoroughly through the continuous nature of human experience and its relationship to educational practice and educational growth. Again, I think Mr. Dewey (1938) says it best:

> It is a great mistake to suppose, even tacitly, that the traditional schoolroom was not a place in which pupils had experiences. Yet this is tacitly assumed when progressive education as a plan of learning by experience is placed in sharp opposition to the old. The proper line of attack is that the experiences which were had, by pupils and teachers alike, were largely of a wrong kind. How many students for example, were rendered callous to ideas, and how many lost the impetus to learn because of the way in which learning was experienced by them? How many acquired special skills by means of automatic drill so that their power of judgment and capacity to act intelligently in new situations was limited? How many came to associate books with dull drudgery, so that they were "conditioned" to all but flashy reading matter? It is not enough to insist upon the necessity of experience, nor even of activity in experience. Everything depends upon the quality of the experience which is had (p. 26).

As an example that might be more familiar to a broader audience—an audience outside of education per se', Dewey (1938) writes:

> We speak of spoiling a child and of the spoilt child. The effect of over-indulging a child is a continuing one. It sets up an attitude which operates as an automatic demand that persons and objects cater to his desires and caprices in the future. It makes him seek the kind of situation that will enable him to do what he feels like doing at the time. It renders him averse to and comparatively incompetent in situations which require effort and perseverance in overcoming obstacles. There is no paradox in the fact that the principle of the continuity of experience may operate so as to leave a person arrested on a low plane of development, in a way which limits later capacity for growth.

> On the other hand, if an experience arouses curiosity, strengthens initiative, and sets up desires and purposes that are sufficiently intense to carry a person over dead places in the future, continuity works in a very different way. Every experience is a moving force. Its value can be judged only on the ground of what it moves toward and into (pp. 37–38).

This notion of continuity completely shifts the role of the teacher from the traditional deliverer of knowledge to someone with a much different task. Educationally speaking, it does not mean simply turning education over to the immature student; in fact, it makes the role of the teacher and the policies under which a school operates, much more guidance-oriented, complicated, communicative, personal, and social:

> The greater maturity of experience which should belong to the adult as educator puts him in a position to evaluate each experience of the young in a way in which the one having the less mature experience cannot do. It is then the business of the educator to see in what direction an experience is heading. There is no point in his being more mature if, instead of using his greater insight to help organize the conditions of the experience of the immature, he throws away his insight. Failure to take the moving force of an experience into account so as to judge and direct it on the ground of what it is moving into means disloyalty to the principle of expe-

rience itself. The disloyalty operates in two directions. The educator is false to the understanding that he should have obtained from his own past experience. He is also unfaithful to the fact that all human experience is ultimately social: that it involves contact and communication (Dewey, 1938, p. 38).

EXPERIENCE AS INTERACTIVE

The second Deweyan component of individual experiential situations specifically and human experience generally is that of interaction. Certainly, and Dewey is vehemently clear on this, it seems obvious if not downright trite to talk about human experience as anything but interactive; however, in our "either–or" philosophical leanings (and, historically speaking, coming out of the old philosophical fight over the mythic mind/matter dualism) it is crucial to understand and then emphasize the interactive nature of human experience because it is most often the case that one or the other (yet another "either–or"), the objective or the subjective, is taken as primary to the detriment of the other and that can certainly lead to mis-educative experiences.

At the outset of *Experience and Education*, Dewey writes on this matter that "the history of educational theory is marked by opposition between the idea that education is development from within and that it is formation from without; that it is based upon natural endowments and that education is a process of overcoming natural inclination and substituting in its place habits acquired under external pressure." So, as a way to emphasize the equal import of both the objective and subjective, he speaks of experience as an interaction between the individual, the subjective self and the objective, common sense, physical facts of human existence:

> the word 'interaction,' expresses the second chief principle for interpreting an experience in its educational function and force. It assigns equal rights to both factors in experience—objective and internal conditions. Any normal experience is an interplay of these two sets of conditions. Taken together, or in their interaction, they form what we call a *situation* (Dewey, 1938, p. 42; emphasis his).

That is, we humans live in a world where we are surrounded by things that and people who we interact with. It is in this stream of interactive situations, one leading to another, and to another that we find the secret to teaching and learning as a matter of subjective and objective reconstruction or individual and social growth. And, maybe, the key to why kids hate or at least are bored, disengaged, and/or ambivalent with school.

SCHOOL AS PREPARATION FOR THE "REAL WORLD"

I recently received, via my ten-year old son, a note home from the fifth grade teachers of his school. It seems that they had somehow not been following their own self-imposed mandate of pounding home the importance of "responsibility." (Clearly, the fifth grade team of teachers had decided that responsibility becomes—as if by magic—*really* important for fifth-graders.) To solve that shortcoming, they were instituting a new policy on turning "work" in late. The policy itself is not so important for the present discussion, but the underlying assumption about education certainly is because it clearly indicates the value educators typically assign to "experience." The explanation as to why they were instituting the new policy now, two-thirds of the way through the school year, was that if they did not emphasize the importance of deadlines, they would not be preparing our children for the "real world."

I must admit to being sick and tired of hearing teachers of all levels and all subject areas say that what they are doing when they teach, is preparing students for the "real world" or for their imagined "futures." First of all, I think it is a pat answer that is relied on when no substantial reason can be given for school policies/practices; second of all, the answer makes some kind of strange experiential claim that our students are somehow not living in the real world or that they don't need guidance to succeed, be happy, or solve problems in the here and now. Not surprisingly, Dewey (1938) has a few choice words on this issue himself:

> Now preparation is a treacherous idea. In a certain sense every experience should do something to prepare a person for later experiences of a deeper and more expansive quality. That is the very meaning of growth, continuity, reconstruction of experience. But it is a mistake to suppose that the mere acquisition of a certain amount of arithmetic, geography, history, etc., which is taught and studied because it may be useful at some time in the future, has this (preparatory) effect and it is a mistake to suppose that acquisition of skills in reading and figuring will automatically constitute preparation for their right and effective use under conditions *very unlike those in which they were acquired.*

> Almost everyone has had occasion to look back upon his school days and wonder what has become of the knowledge he was supposed to have amassed during his years of schooling, and why it is that the technical skills he acquired have to be learned over again in changed form in order to stand him in good stead. Indeed, he is lucky who does not find that in order to make progress, in order to go ahead intellectually, he does not have to unlearn much of what he learned in school. What, then, is the true meaning of preparation in the educational scheme? In the first place, it means that a person, young or old, gets out of his present experience all that there is in it for him at the time in which he has it. The ideal of using the present simply to get ready for the future contradicts itself. It omits, and even shuts out, the very conditions by which a person can be prepared for his future. We always live at the time we live and not at some other time, and only extracting at each present time the full meaning of each present experience are we prepared for doing the same thing in the future. This is the only preparation which in the long run amounts to anything (pp. 47–48; emphasis mine).

Amen, Brother Dewey, Amen.

NO CHILD LEFT BEHIND, STANDARDIZED TESTING, AND EXPERIENCE: STAGNATION OF GROWTH

To judge the educational value of any educational "experience" is to evaluate the degree to which that experience matches student-as-human experience in its interaction of the subjective self and the objective world—or more simply, does the experience reflect the understanding that human experience is an interaction between self, the world, and other selves? Secondly, the particular educational practice or situation must be evaluated on the degree to which it causes a student to become more open to further growth experiences; that is, does the experience promote "growth" or does it, instead, promote stagnation?

The hallmark of No Child Left Behind (NCLB) is that assessment is approached via a single paper-pencil, bubble-in-the-answers, standardized test that all students will take. That testing regimen is then used to evaluate the success or failure of the school, school district, and entire state. Actions based on a school's overall score become increasingly punitive ultimately providing the option of closing a school down and allowing parents to choose a different school for their children to attend (one that is not failing—assuming that there is one); by 2014, it is expected that all students can and will make acceptable annual yearly progress on said examinations because it is believed by educational policy makers that threatening individuals (B.F Skinner would certainly agree) will produce better students and better schools.

I often suggest to my students that if Mr. Dewey crawled out of his grave to visit us, he would be certainly wagging his experiential index finger at us wondering why we had not listened to him a century earlier. In the case of standardized testing and particularly the way we currently use it, it is rather simple to judge the experiential and therefore, the educational value of the practice—there is very little value to be found. Mr. Dewey was alive when standardized testing came into existence. He suggested that such testing could be a crucial tool for a teacher to have at her disposal when constructing experiences that might provide educational growth. Imagine, as Dewey did, a test that would show individual weaknesses in particular subject areas; and imagine, a teacher discussing those weaknesses with a student such that the teacher and student might plan future experiences with the aim of improving on those individual weaknesses—an incredible "tool" to have at one's disposal; one that could help the teacher-as-guide get to know a student's "place" in the educational experience as a means to construct future experiences that promote growth.

Alas, the testing called for by NCLB is not a tool for constructing future educational experiences; in fact, it is not a tool at all—unless, that is, you consider a whipping post a tool. NCLB testing is the major means by which educational experiences are stopped in their tracks. Again, we must turn to our evaluative, experiential questions: does the testing experience incorporate the understanding that human experience consists of the interaction between the subjective, objective, and social? In the case of high-stakes testing, it is the objective that is over-emphasized to the elimination of the subjective and social. The testing process goes something like this: prepare for the test via mostly memorizing facts, and drilling skills. Take the test alone, and then have your scores reported as a school wide matter, never taken up with individual teachers (who have very little training/understanding of how the tests might be interpreted anyway), and never visit the test again to make decisions on an individual basis as to how to proceed with future educational experiences. This form of "education" assumes that mostly the opposite of what Dewey believed is true of education—knowledge is static and has no social or subjective quality; it is the aggregate or the system rather than the individual that is important in an educational experience (a point Phil Cusick makes in his piece); and, the standardized test itself is the goal of learning rather than individual and community "growth."

On the essential question of whether the high-stakes testing experience is an educational situation that encourages or discourages student growth, how can it accomplish anything other than stagnation of growth? Knowledge and skills are evaluated apart from the real value they have for lived experience. And, the only educational value tests might have as a tool to construct real experiences that might lead to strengthening individual weaknesses—experiences that might, in fact, develop desired habits of growth—are ignored by not using individual test scores by individual teachers and students to construct such future experiences. Finally, what about this notion that when we enter into and leave a single experience, we are changed in some way? The habits that I think are important (openness to further growth experiences; openness to participation; openness to social interaction; openness to seeing newness of thought as helpful to navigating through lived experience; openness to knowledge-creation based on problems in experience; etc.) are simply stopped in their tracks and these testing situations have the affect of closing students to the inspiring possibilities that knowledge holds. As to the impact the testing regimen has on the guiding question for this paper, is it any wonder students may not like school when the end game (doing well on a standardized test) is so far removed from their real, individual and social, experiences?

No Child Left Behind, Character Education, and Experience: Misdirection of Growth

NCLB contains numerous "smaller" dictates (aside from testing) including some interesting rules relative to what counts as science, which approach to reading instruction should be used, what rights the Boy Scouts have when it comes to using public property, what individual students can and cannot do to keep personal information from military recruiters, and the requirement to teach character education, among others. The character education requirement brings to mind a concern Dewey had about the direction growth might take—a concern many opponents of Dewey (1938) had with his notion that growth should be a deciding factor in whether or not an experience was truly educative:

> The objection made is that growth might take many different directions: a man, for example, who starts out on a career of burglary may grow in that direction, and by practice may grow into a highly expert burglar. Hence it is argued that "growth" is not enough; we must also specify the direction in which growth takes place, the end towards which it tends. Before, however, we decide that the objection is conclusive we must analyze the case a little further.

> That a man may grow in efficiency as a burglar, as a gangster, or as a corrupt politician, cannot be doubted. But from the standpoint of growth as education and education as growth the question is whether growth in this direction promotes or retards growth in general. Does this form of growth create conditions for further growth, or does it set up conditions that shut off the person who is grown in this particular direction from the occasions, stimuli, and opportunities for continuing growth in new directions? What is the effect of growth in a special direction upon the attitudes and habits which alone open up avenues for development in other lines? I shall leave you to answer these questions, saying simply that when and *only* when development in a particular line conduces to continuing growth does it answer to the criterion of education as growing (p. 36; emphasis his).

In other words, judging the direction of growth is a large part of what it means to judge growth value in general. More concretely, becoming a better burglar as a directional matter is not the same as providing for continuing growth; becoming a better burglar, in fact, closes off further growth in other more morally acceptable behavior. The improvement in skills (burglary or otherwise) does not necessarily equate to experiential growth because growth in certain directions actually contracts rather than expands future growth possibilities—it is not growth at all. So, when it comes particularly to moral or "character education," the direction of growth will greatly determine its educational value more generally in answering the essential question, does the experience lead to further growth experiences?

Certainly moral training has been at the historic heart of public education in our country and is often the driving force behind changes in educational practice. As such, it is crucial to examine how NCLB mandated character education programs are playing out—and it is maybe the most frightening of all NCLB program mandates when it comes to educational experiences understood as growth experiences. In the school district that my children attend, character education is being promoted via a program entitled "Character Cash." Yes, that's right, good character in return for cash! Now, this school district has not reduced character instruction to being paid in U.S. dollars as it is being done elsewhere (some school districts in our area actually pay students to attend school and/or to take and perform well on our state standardized test). However, the Character Cash program certainly has a token if not actual economic basis: each student begins each day with 15 character cash dollars and throughout the course of each day, students have the opportunity to add character cash (by, of course, acting with character) or to lose character cash (by behaving without character). The end-game of all this cash-grab is an interesting one indeed: each student who has at least 1500 character cash dollars at the end of the school year can redeem that cash to "pay" for a field trip to Dolly Parton's *Dixie Stampede* theater in Branson, Missouri. The last I checked, my son is not going to make it—a point of pride for me.

Ignoring any questions as to what types of behavior are considered of good character (NCLB actually provides a list of those to be promoted), and there are certainly some very important discussions to be had on that question, there remain some horrendous implications when we take Dewey's notion of direction in growth. The last ethics course I took, granted, it has been awhile, never once equated good moral character with the collection of wealth. Maybe I am wrong, but I consider ethical character to be all about *not* doing something for wealth, but, in fact, acting with character because it has important individual and social implications for our lives. Not only are we teaching that character and cash are intimately and positively intertwined, we are teaching that those with the most cash certainly must have the most character. We should probably not be surprised to hear older generations complain that, "kids these days just don't know right from wrong."

As to how this kind of education might be impacting student perceptions of schooling, imagine our kids' confusion upon coming home from school to find that telling the truth, caring for one another, being responsible, and standing up for what one believes are not virtues that will necessarily make one monetarily rich—a horrible disconnection between experience in school and lived experience. It is a glaring example to students that their life experiences do not match their school experiences (are, in fact, antithetical to their life experiences). This kind of experiential disconnection leads to growth of a distorted nature: children entering a school's character education program, come out of it certainly changed; however, changed in a rather tragic new understanding of how ethics "works" in our shared experiences. It is also an example where "growth" on its face (more "ethical" behavior) will actually limit growth by limiting our students' perceptions of what ethical behavior might truly entail and leads students to understand that what they learn in school has precious little to do with their lived experiences.

TEACHER EDUCATION PROGRAMS: THE ENTRENCHMENT OF NON-EXPERIENTIAL MODES OF TEACHING

To stand on high in the ivory tower of academia and scream to the heavens that kids might hate school because of federal legislation such as NCLB (such as I have done thus far in this discussion) means missing one of the most egregious aspects of our question—colleges and universities who "produce" our nation's teachers. Early on in this discussion I mentioned Dewey's timeliness, and I would add, his timelessness. How is it that someone as respected as Dewey, as insightful as Dewey, as clear and concise as Dewey, and as "ancient" (in my students' opinion) as Dewey could be so completely ignored by politicians and policy makers? Simply put, most of them are not trained educators. George Counts (1932) suggested, again over seventy years ago, that it is teachers who we should look to as agents of social change because it is teachers who can construct growth experiences for both individuals and society generally:

> That the teachers should deliberately reach for power and then make the most of their conquest is my firm conviction. To the extent that they are permitted to fashion the curriculum and the procedures of the school they will definitely and positively influence the social attitudes, ideals, and behavior of the coming generation. In doing this they should resort to no subterfuge or false modesty. They should say neither that they are merely teaching the truth nor that they are unwilling to wield power in their own right. The first position is false and the second is a confession of incompetence. It is my observation that the men and women who have affected the course of human events are those who have not hesitated to use the power that has come to them. Representing as they do, not the interests of the moment or of any special class, but rather the common and abiding interests of the people, teachers are under heavy social obligation to protect and further those interests. In this they occupy a relatively unique position in society. Also since the profession should embrace scientists and scholars of the highest rank, as well as teachers working at all levels of the educational system, it has at its dis-

posal, as no other group, the knowledge and wisdom of the ages. It is scarcely thinkable that these men and women would ever act as selfishly or bungle as badly as have the so-called "practical" men of our generation—the politicians, the financiers, the industrialists. If all of these facts are taken into account, instead of shunning power, the profession should rather seek power and then strive to use that power fully and wisely and in the interests of the great masses of the people (pp. 32–34).

However, if you are familiar with teacher education programs you will know that we spend precious little time asking future teachers to engage with people like John Dewey or George Counts. Maybe we should not be surprised that politicians are unfamiliar with Dewey's understanding that to teach well means to understand the essence of human experience; but, we should feel great shame that our future teachers have very little experience with such issues. Instead of taking up important conceptual discussions that might drive reasonable practice, our students are increasingly given their bag of methodological tricks sans any discussion of the value of those "tricks" in promoting real human/social growth. In fact, courses that would ask our future teachers to engage in philosophical discussions such as these in colleges of education are being replaced or eliminated to make room for more "methods" course work; and the closer you look at these "methods," the more you find a disconnection between experience and education.

Why might our kids hate school? In short, and as suggested throughout this paper, because our politicians, our policy makers, and, most importantly, our future teachers do not understand the nature and value of human experience because they have not engaged in important philosophical questions concerning the human condition. Without this kind of engagement, particularly on the part of teachers, we should not be surprised to find that educational experiences (in both general policy and particular practice) have been and continue to be built on something other than a sound understanding of human experience and are, therefore, disconnected from the experiences of our students. In the end, Mr. Dewey would probably be, and rightly so, shaking his finger most vehemently in our faces—we who teach our future teachers.

REFERENCES

Counts, George S. (1978 [1932]). *Dare the School Build a New Social Order?* Carbondale, Illinois: Southern Illinois University Press.

Dewey, John. (1938). *Experience and Education.* New York: Simon and Schuster.

SUGGESTED READINGS/ACTIVITIES

Read *Experience and Education*. Discuss/write about whether Dewey's understanding of human experience matches your own experience. How? How not?

Visit a local school and observe some "teaching." Discuss/write about how that teaching is either educative or mis-educative under Dewey's understanding.

Construct a lesson/unit plan that takes into account Dewey's understanding of experience.

MULTIPLE CHOICE QUESTIONS

1. According to Dewey, humans often fall into the trap of what kind of thinking?

   a. sloppy

   b. either–or

   c. mis-educative

   d. sophisticated

2. Dewey claims that in order to understand progressive versus traditional education, one must first have a theory of

   a. metaphysics

   b. reality

   c. experience

   d. pedagogy

3. The two components of experience that Dewey explains are

   a. interaction and subjectivity

   b. interaction and objectivity

   c. educative and mis-educative

   d. interaction and continuity

4. Continuity is the idea that

   a. one experience is disconnected from other experiences

   b. one experience directly impacts other experiences

   c. experiences are subjective

   d. experiences are objective

5. Interaction, for Dewey, consists of

   a. the objective and the subjective

   b. character education

   c. preparation for life

   d. dialogue between teacher and student

6. The evaluation of an experience as educative or mis-educative should be based on

    a. how it matches curriculum frameworks

    b. whether students enjoy themselves

    c. how objective it is

    d. the degree to which it promotes further growth

7. According to Dewey and the author, seeing education as merely preparation for future life is

    a. a sound philosophical perspective

    b. an unreasonable aim for educators

    c. untenable when experience is understood as interactive and continuous

    d. the most important goal for educators

8. According to the author, John Dewey would

    a. support NCLB

    b. not understand the intricacies of NCLB

    c. run for senate

    d. find NCLB experientially unsound

9. The Character Cash program, according to the article, is

    a. antithetical to Dewey's notion of educative experiences

    b. is supported by Dewey's notion of experience

    c. promotes ethical growth

    d. stagnates ethical growth

10. Every student who has 1500 character cash dollars will win a trip to

    a. Disneyland

    b. Six Flags

    c. The Dixie Stampede

    d. Washington D.C.

Inspiration from the Ancients: Quintilian on the Art of Teaching

Pauline Nugent

Missouri State University

After some twenty years in the classroom as a teacher of Rhetoric, Quintilian retired to write his memoirs: *The Institute of Oratory* or How to Succeed in an Academic Career. A Spaniard by birth, this 1st century A.D. author spent most of his professional life in Rome and became the first public school teacher to be paid by the State. His blueprint for a profitable and enjoyable pedagogical career bears many remarkable resemblances to what educational experts of the 21st century advocate for positive results in today's classroom. Even a cursory reading of Quintilian's masterpiece, the *Institute of Oratory*—or, indeed, the 4th century *Confessions* of Augustine— offers abundant evidence of the far-reaching influence a teacher can exert on the learning environment of the classroom. Among multiple matters of a pedagogical nature, Quintilian discussed such modern topics as teacher training, individual differences, student motivation, passion for learning, respect for students, lifelong learning, and intellectual Enjoyment. Handling these classical writings "by day and by night" as Horace advises in his Ars *Poetica* (Fairclough, 1932), we discover principles of pedagogy that worked very well in the ancient world and are no less effective today (p. 472). A salutary review of ancient literature may help refocus and replenish the psychic energies of today's *paedagogi, magistri, grammatici*—energies, alas, too frequently diffused by debates over merit formulae, normative standards for tenure and promotion, and the perennial salary salvos—all of which, though necessary, can deplete the inner resources essential for effective and dynamic teaching.

This paper ponders a few pedagogical principles, gleaned from reflective practitioners in the ancient world— Quintilian and Augustine, *inter alios*—in an attempt to appreciate anew what the classical authors considered the art of teaching. Having mastered the "what" and the "how" of solid classroom instruction—namely, the course content and effective methods for disseminating this fascinating subject—it is hoped that both neophyte and veteran will reach far beyond these basic essentials and evoke the inner qualities of mind and spirit that transform lifeless content into an exhilarating and dynamic pursuit of learning. Only such emotive experiences can impact our audiences and convince them of the enduring value of learning, perchance even happily launching them on the exciting adventure of a lifetime. Of necessity, I shall limit myself to those Principles of Pedagogy that have brought solace and inspiration to me and to myriads of teachers over the centuries, with the hope that perhaps you, the reader, may likewise resonate with their wisdom.

Principle One: Here Quintilian (Butler, 1996) underscores the bright hopes that sustain the teachers' efforts:

> There is absolutely no foundation for the complaint that but few people have the power to take
> in the knowledge that is imparted to them, and that the majority are so slow of understanding
> that education is a waste of time and labor. On the contrary you will find that most are quick

to reason and ready to learn. Reasoning comes as naturally to a human being as flying to birds, speed to horses and ferocity to beasts of prey: our minds are endowed by nature with such activity and sagacity that the soul is believed to proceed from heaven. Those who are dull and un-teachable are as abnormal as prodigious births and monstrosities and are but few in number (p. 19–20).

This Principle is a salutary reminder that it is the duty, and the privilege, of the teacher to enliven the content and engage the students' minds in ways suitable to their age and disposition. Ours, then, is the noble task of discovering the source of inquiry and motivation in each of our students. Undoubtedly there will be various degrees of accomplishments, but, as Quintilian (Butler, 1996) states in the *Institutes of Oratory* "that there are any who gain nothing from education, I absolutely deny" (p. 21). This claim by the expert challenges us to understand our students well, to discover the magic key to each student's interest and to use it wisely to open the doors of their minds, lest time and treasure be expended on education to no avail.

Principle Two: In the second Principle, Quintilian (Butler, 1996) emphasizes the awesome and onerous task of the teacher, namely, to insure that the students develop a deep love of learning and to see to it that none is turned off by an unfavorable classroom experience. "We must take care that the student, who is not yet old enough to love his studies, does not come to hate them and dread the bitterness which s/he once tasted, even when the years of infancy are left behind" (p. 29). This is, indeed, a solemn statement of tutorial responsibility that ought to be engraved over the entrance to every classroom. It sums up our basic duties as professional teachers. How we accomplish this sacred trust may imply a variety of approaches, but *that* we accomplish it is the *sine qua non* of instruction. It is at the heart of good teaching. As the well-known educators, Banner and Cannon (1997) state, it represents the innate ability of the teacher to "animate inert knowledge with qualities of our own personality and spirit that affect, or ought to affect, our students" (p. 2). This is the true challenge of pedagogy. Our task is to find a meaningful way of engaging each and every individual student in the learning process. Not only is this our challenge as teachers, it is truly the essence of our duty! Without this connection of teacher with content and with student, no true learning can occur. Hence, the critical need for complete control of one's subject matter and the relaxed ease of methodology on the part of the teacher, so that when in the classroom, the teacher may devote all the necessary psychical energies to engaging the student in the learning process. Again, Banner and Cannon (1997) affirm the fact that the basic elements of teaching are truly qualities we summon from within ourselves: "These are ingredients of our own humanity, to which contents and methods are adjunct" (p. 2). These qualities adhere in our individual personhood and are as specific to us as our own name or our DNA. Schools of education do not teach us these qualities, nor, indeed, can they, for these are not qualities that can be learned. Instead, they are attitudes of our being that we cultivate daily—aspects of our character that make us who we are—aids that we call forth from within ourselves and engage to empower our students. Before we can be successful teachers, we must identify these character traits for ourselves, cultivate them in creative and reflective moments, and then use them to assist, encourage and support our students. Once again our modern educators share their words of wisdom: "While pedagogical expertise and technical knowledge are essential to it, ultimately teaching is a creative act; it makes something fresh from existing knowledge in spontaneous, improvised efforts of mind and spirit, disciplined by education and experience" (Banner and Cannon, 1997, p. 3). Thus, teaching yields astonishing results. What works today may well not succeed in the classroom of tomorrow. Hence, there is a need for the teacher to be continually creative and alert to the everyday challenges of the profession. Teaching is as individualized a profession as each teacher is unique, and the sum total of one's efforts yields wonderment and awe. This is the heart of teaching, the goal of every truly committed professional. It is interesting to note that the Latin word for school is *ludus*, the same term that means "game" or "play". Hence, Quintilian (Butler, 1996) admonishes the teacher:

> Let the student's studies be made amusement: he must be questioned and praised and taught
> to rejoice when he has done well; sometimes too when he refuses instruction, it should be

given to someone else to excite his envy; at times also he must be engaged in competition and should be allowed to believe himself successful more often than not, while he should be encouraged to do his best by such rewards as may appeal to his tender years (p. 30–31).

Elsewhere the master reminds us that the love of literature and the value of reading are not confined to our school-days but end only with our life, noting that: "The study of literature is a necessity of childhood and the delight of old age, the sweet companion of our privacy and the sole branch of study which has more substance than display" (Butler, 1996, p. 65). Thus he re-emphasizes the far-reaching effects of a teacher's influence, for good or ill.

Principle Three: In this Principle, Quintilian (Butler, 1996) underscores the importance of elementary education, a topic to which he frequently returns. Indeed, so insistent is he on this pride of place for early education that he repeatedly insists on the importance of pre-school and primary level training. He even mentions how hard it is to get rid of faults once they have become second nature and relates the story of the famous piper Timotheus who reportedly charged a double fee to students who had previously studied under another master, by contrast with those who came to him untaught, citing by way of explanation that the work of un-teaching something is harder than that of teaching it in the first place.

> Would Philip of Macedon have wished that his son Alexander should be taught the rudiments of letters by Aristotle, the greatest philosopher of the age, or would he later have undertaken the task, if he had not thought that even the earliest instruction is best given by the most perfect teacher and has real reference to the whole of education (p. 31–33)?

Here Quintilian asks us to imagine that the student placed under our tutelage is Alexander, and that he deserves no less attention than that famous scion—although, the master is quick to add that everybody's child deserves equal attention. This dictum of unswerving impartiality is a *sine qua non* for general classroom protocol. Coupled with a deep sense of reverence and respect for students is the need to individualize their instruction. Students learn differently and are variously motivated. It is the task of the teacher to discern what treatment must be applied to the mind of each of his students. Thus, Quintilian (Butler, 1996) continues:

> Some are slack, unless urged on, others are impatient of control; some are amenable to fear, while others are paralyzed by it; in some cases the mind requires continual application to form it, in others this result is best obtained by rapid concentration (p. 57).

Hence, the Herculean task of teachers requires absolute expertise in both methodology and content so that their full attention in the classroom is focused on students' individual needs. While urging students to perform to their maximum potential, Quintilian (Butler, 1996) wisely prescribes relaxation, "because study depends on the good will of the student, a quality that cannot be secured by compulsion" (p. 57). But while Quintilian enthusiastically approves and warmly encourages play for the young, he is equally emphatic about outlawing physical punishment, a practice which, unfortunately is still occasionally in vogue in the 21st century. Quintilian (Butler, 1996) calls this treatment a "disgraceful form of punishment, fit only for slaves, and a definite insult" (p. 59–61). Moreover, he claims that if a student is so insensible to instruction that reproof is useless, he will merely become hardened to blows, rather than improved by this harsh and shameful treatment. Rather than dwell on the horrifying effects of corporal abuse, Quintilian (Butler, 1996) contents himself with stating "that children are helpless and easily victimized, and therefore no one should be given unlimited power over them" (p. 61). It is unfortunately only too evident that this *caveat* from Quintilian still needs to be emphasized in the enlightened, technologically savvy society of the 21st century. His sense of respect and reverence for his students is a salutary lesson for today's pedagogical classroom.

Quintilian devotes the Second Book of his *Institute of Oratory* (Butler, 1996) to a treatment of the character and behavior of the teacher who is seen both as a role model for his students and as their friend. This notion of friendship with students is a visible witness to the inner qualities of the teacher that sustain, encourage and support the students in the challenges and vicissitudes of the classroom routine.

Principle Four: The main focus of the Second Book of the Art of Oratory is a discussion of the need for moral and ethical qualities in the teacher. Quintilian (Butler, 1996) stresses the importance of good example and the prerequisite for every teacher to be a person of sterling, upright character. He says:

> Our first task is to inquire whether the teacher is of good character.... We must spare no effort to insure that the wholesomeness of the teacher's character should preserve those of tenderer years from corruption, while its authority should keep the bolder spirits from breaking out into license. Nor is it sufficient that he should merely set an example of the highest personal self-control; he must also be able to govern the behavior of his students by the strictness of his discipline (p. 211–213).

At this point Quintilian (Butler, 1996) suggests that the teacher adopt a parental attitude toward his students—no doubt the source of our expression: *in loco parentis*—regarding himself as the representative of the parents who have entrusted their children to him. He continues:

> Let him be free from vice himself and refuse to tolerate it in others. Let him be strict, but not austere, genial but not too familiar: for austerity will make him unpopular, while familiarity will breed contempt. Let his discourse continually turn on what is good and honorable; the more he admonishes, the less he will have to punish. He must control his temper without, however, closing his eyes to faults that require correction; his instruction must be free from affectation, his industry great, his demand on his class continuous, but not extravagant. He must be ready to answer questions and pose them unasked to those who sit in silence. In praising the recitations of his students he must be neither grudging nor over-generous: the former quality will give them distaste for work, while the latter will produce a complacent self-satisfaction. In correcting faulty he must avoid sarcasm and above all abuse: for teachers whose rebukes seem to imply positive dislike discourage industry. He should declaim daily himself, and what is more, without stint, that his class may take his utterances home with them. For however many models for imitation he may give them from the authors they are reading, it will still be found that fuller nourishment is provided by the living voice, as we call it, more especially when it proceeds from the teacher himself, who, if his students are rightly instructed, should be the object of their affection and respect. And it is scarcely possible to say how much more readily we imitate those whom we like (p. 213).

This lengthy and useful checklist covers all the necessary bases for a successful, safe and productive classroom experience. Quintilian's instruction is surely timely and apropos for our own day and time. We find here an echo of that compassionate attention to students mentioned recently by a Columbine survivor attending the White House Conference on School Violence. Perhaps there is instruction here even for our Government officials in their dealings with young pages! Quintilian (Butler, 1996) may even be saying something to 21st century distance-learning advocates about the persuasive power of the personal presence of a dynamic and caring instructor, insisting, as he does, on the "fuller nourishment ...provided by the living voice" (p. 215). Later on in his writing we find him insisting on an attentive and quiet hearing from the class, on orderliness—a problem then as now—and especially on the need to avoid not only the actual charge of corruption but even the merest suspicion of it.

Quintilian includes many other miscellaneous topics relevant to a Conference on Education, particularly his views on such contemporary issues as general education, public versus private or home schooling, second language learning, the perennial argument on nature versus nurture, as well as specific advice about how to teach the rudimentary subjects of reading, writing, spelling. With reference to general education, Quintilian envisions it as essential instruction and preparation for good citizenship. Regarding public versus private schooling, he clearly favors the former as providing both the necessary impetus for students to vie with each other and excel in their studies. Moreover, public education provides concomitant training in social behavior that provides the students with essential life management skills. In the area of second language learning, Quintilian advises beginning with the less familiar tongue, claiming that the everyday language can be readily mastered, with or without much schooling. As for the argument of nature versus nurture, the master clearly defines nature as the essential foundation, "the raw material for education; the one forms, the other is formed" (Butler, 1996, p. 349).

Thus, in the 1st century of our era, Quintilian treats, in large part, the same topics that engage the energies of many modern educators. Not only does he bear witness to the enduring qualities and needs of humanity, but he also reminds us that the art of teaching/learning "can only be attained by hard work and assiduity of study, by a variety of exercises and repeated trial, the highest prudence and unfailing alacrity of judgment" (Butler, 1996, p. 297). Here he repeats the ancient adage of the Greek tragedian Aeschylus, *pathei mathos*, (we learn the hard way). Acknowledging that the teacher's task covers a large and spacious territory, is extremely varied and develops some new aspects almost every day, Quintilian (Butler, 1996) also concludes very wisely, indeed, "that the last word on the subject will never have been said" (p. 297). Reflecting on his own situation as he puts the finishing touches on his masterpiece, he expresses the sentiments of many a modern professor, recently retired from the active ranks, and proves once again that the ancient world has much wisdom to offer our modern society:

> As for myself I have long since retired from the task of teaching in the schools and of speaking in the courts, thinking it the most honorable conclusion to retire while my services were still in request, and all I ask is to be allowed to console my leisure by doing such research and composing such instructions as will, I hope, prove useful to young people of ability, and are, at any rate, a pleasure to myself (Butler, 1996, p. 289).

REFERENCES

Banner. J.M. & Cannon. H. (1997). *The Elements of Teaching*. New Haven: Yale University Press.

Butler. H. E. (1996). *Loeb Classical Library: Quintilian. Institutio Oratoria* (H. E. Butler, Trans.). London: Harvard University Press.

Fairclough. H. Rushton. (1932). *Loeb Classical Library: Horace. Satires, Epistles and Ars Poetica*. London: Heinemann, Ltd.

SUGGESTED READINGS

Marrou, H. (1982). *A History of Education in Antiquity*. Madison, WI: University of Wisconsin Press.

MULTIPLE CHOICE QUESTIONS

1. A famous educator from the ancient Roman world was

    a. Homer

    b. Vergil

    c. Quintilian

    d. Augustine

2. The author of the *Ars Poetica* was

    a. Horace

    b. Quintilian

    c. Homer

    d. Augustine

3. Ancient educators faced many of the same problems that we encounter in school today, except:

    a. low teacher salaries

    b. student motivation

    c. truancy

    d. merit pay

4. Pedagogical topics discussed in Roman times included

    a. life-long learning

    b. individual differences

    c. teacher training

    d. all of the above

5. According to the modern educators, Banner and Cannon, it is not possible to be truly successful teachers unless we:

    a. know our students well

    b. know our subject matter thoroughly

c. master the methodology

d. develop interior qualities of our own personhood to engage students in learning

6. While expertise in pedagogy and technical knowledge are essential, teaching is ultimately an art, not merely a science. This statement is

a. totally true

b. mostly true

c. totally false

d. mostly false

7. The Latin word for school is *ludus*, which means

a. learning

b. homework

c. a game

d. punishment

8. Ancient educators thought that reading was an activity for

a. elementary school

b. life

c. home training

d. advanced study

9. To impress teachers with the need for excellence in elementary teaching, Quintilian asks teachers to imagine that they are instructing

a. Alexander

b. Aristotle

c. Philip of Macedon

d. Socrates

10. Ancient educators discussed all of the following issues of the 21st century, except

   a. general education

   b. home-schooling versus public education

   c. second language learning

   d. distance learning

I Just Don't See the Point! Purpose and Attitudes Toward School

STEFAN BROIDY

WITTENBERG UNIVERSITY

We worry when children tell us that they hate school. We *should* worry, because students' attitudes toward school have a number of important consequences and correlations. Kids who are disengaged from school are "more likely than their peers to use and abuse drugs and alcohol, fall prey to depression, experiment with early sex, and commit acts of crime and delinquency" (Steinberg, 1996). Conversely, positive school attitudes are associated with protective effects for students who are at risk (Kennedy & Bennett, 2006). There is evidence that attitudes toward school, independent of proficiency in academic skills and student background, predict the likelihood of participation in higher education (Australian Council for Educational Research, n.d.). Levels of connectedness (how well a student perceives him/herself as accepted and supported) with school are good predictors of risky practices such as sexual intercourse (Bersamin, Walker, Fisher, & Grube, 2006).

Moreover, years of research in human development have made it clear that attitudes toward school both affect and are affected by levels of self-efficacy—which in turn is a key element of school accomplishment. Hating school also often entails active opposition to what goes on in there, which makes school failure in both academic and other institutional senses more likely.

It makes sense, then, to ask why kids hate school. I want to propose an answer that, while attending to only one of many factors that make for a comprehensive response to that question, seems to me both crucial and widely ignored.

There are some preliminaries to considering my argument, and I hope the reader will indulge my consideration of them.

First, how can we tell if a child actually hates school? Some answers seem obvious: in the year and season in which I write, there has been an outbreak of violent and sometimes fatal school attacks, several of them by students. And, as often occurs, this rash of violence has inspired other planned attacks that were thwarted at various stages, in various parts of the country. Surely these episodes are evidence that some students hate school!

But closer inspection suggests that even this kind of "evidence" can be ambiguous. What, exactly, did these students "hate;" and is all hatred of school of the sort that might provoke such violence? It seems important to ask, "Why do kids hate school?" But sorting out possible answers depends first on asking a clear question. Before I attempt to provide one sort of answer that seems important to me—to one version of the question—some efforts at clarification should help the reader place my argument in its proper role in the continuing investigation of the relationship among student attitudes toward school, contributing factors to those attitudes, and the effects of those attitudes on school "outcomes."

HATRED AND ITS ROTTEN RELATIVES

There is really not much evidence that many kids hate school, when we're talking about what we might term "pure hatred." In contrast to what many children and adults mean when they tell us that they "hate school," pure hatred seems to include features that make it an opposite of such phenomena as disengagement, boredom, and anomie—terms that describe accurately what many students past and present associate with their experiences in hating school.

Two such distinguishing features are energy and purpose. While disengagement, boredom, and anomie are characterized in part by a lack of interest, pure hatred is energizing and focusing. Robert Frost (1991), in his poem "Vindictive" illustrates these points:

> The best way to hate is the worst.
> Tis to find what the hated need,
> Never mind of what actual worth,
> And wipe that out of the earth.

Similarly, pure hatred does not separate or isolate the individual from what is hated, as do the three related terms above. On the contrary, it is recognizable in part through the obsessive connection it makes with its object. "Hate traps us by binding us too tightly to our adversary," says Milan Kundera (1991) in *Immortality*. Often hate, in this sense, dies only when its object does.

Finally, as a number of writers have observed, pure hatred is constituted in part by fear mixed, paradoxically, with love. As long ago as the 13th Century, Thomas Aquinas observed in his *Summa Theologica* that "Love must precede hatred, and nothing is hated save through being contrary to a suitable thing which is loved. And hence it is that every hatred is caused by love" (*Shopcote, 1990, pt.2. 2nd pt, qu. 29, art. 2*). Fear created when what is valued and cherished betrays or proves false is a driving constituent of pure hatred. Unlike contempt, therefore, pure hatred appears as a heart-felt rather than as a reasoned phenomenon.

It may be that some of the violent attacks on schools that students have perpetrated were driven by pure hatred of school (though we have yet to explore the ambiguities of 'school,' in this context). In light of the above analysis, if pure hatred has driven students to such acts, it also illustrates the significance of school for such students, and the emotional involvement of such students with school (along with the bitterness of seeing such investment come to nothing). But it seems more likely that when many kids say they hate school, they mean to communicate other feelings than pure hatred, or other evaluations of their situation. Besides the four senses of "hating school" mentioned earlier, likely candidates include frustration with, opposition to, impatience with, or disappointment in school. These all represent dissatisfaction, sometimes strongly felt; but not pure hatred.

Unfortunately, the research literature that purports to report on "student attitudes toward school" is often equivocal, failing to distinguish among the many senses in which one may "hate school." Later, I will focus on a particular set of senses of "hating school," in arguing for an often overlooked, but important correlate and possible cause of negative student attitudes toward school. For now, it is necessary to review the research findings, however unclear, on this topic. We must keep in mind, however, that this review ignores ambiguities in its key terms. Not only is it sometimes left unclear what sense of "hate" is being discussed, but it is often left unclear whether that hatred is directed at school as an institution, a particular school institution, the academic, social, or physical climate of a school, school policies and procedures, the school staff or particular members of the staff (or the pedagogy they encounter with staff), the student's academic performance, or merely the obligation to attend school.

Nevertheless, my point in skimming the surface of this body of research is to point out that many factors do contribute to students' general dissatisfaction with features of school and schooling. There are many reasons "why kids hate school."

Reasons for Hating (in Some Sense) School (in Some Sense)

The range of factors that are to significant degrees correlated with hating school is very broad. Some of these are what might be termed "institutional" factors. For instance, there is some evidence that small schools positively affect student attitudes toward school and toward particular school subjects. This holds true particularly for low SES and minority students (Cotton, 1996). Large schools, by contrast, are associated with higher levels of negative student attitudes. A number of studies have found a school calendar that includes a long summer break, is correlated more strongly with negative student attitudes toward school than calendars that do away with such a break (Cooper, Valentine, Charlton & Melson, 2003).

Relationships play a strong role in student attitudes toward school. Interpersonal relations between child and parent carry over to school attitudes. Improving children's and parents' interpersonal skills has been shown to increase liking for school (Hon & Yeung, 2005). Similarly, the relationships students form with their teachers, with classmates, and with those who administer school policies affect students' attitudes toward school.

Other "school climate" factors can play a role. A 2000 FBI report on 18 school shootings found similar problems in the schools involved: tolerance of disrespectful behavior, inequitable discipline, "inflexible" school culture, and staff favoritism of some students (cited in *Avalon High School*, 2005). A recent poll by Public Agenda found that thirty percent of black students said that teachers spend more time trying to keep order in class than teaching (Feller, 2006). Positive attitudes toward school, on the other hand, have been linked to factors such as personal relationships of care between teachers and students, incentives and rewards, and consistent and fair discipline (Ferreira, 1995).

Success or failure in the tasks schools set for themselves affects attitudes toward school. Continuing difficulty with academics, for instance, including difficulties with high-stakes decision points such as required graduation tests or grade level advancement, strongly affects student attitudes. Moreover the generalized oppositional and autonomy-seeking attitudes of young adolescents, which some developmentalists associate with identity-seeking, but which are also connected to kids' growing intellectual and physical competence, lead many to take critical stances toward school.

Racism and cultural conflicts, too, can affect student attitudes toward school, especially where these are continuing problems (Tyson, 2002).

Especially relevant to the point I hope to make later are studies that report negative student attitudes connected to dissatisfaction with schools meeting student goal aspirations. A 2005 National Governors Association survey entitled "Rate Your Future," for instance, found that more than one-third of high school students said that their schools were not "properly preparing them in many areas critical for their future success," like critical thinking, analyzing problems, and communicating well (NGA press release, 2005).

Of course, these factors, and probably many others, often overlap and accumulate in individual cases, feeding off one another and amplifying the effects of each. Consider this actual case, for instance:

"Davey" is a small, skinny, active Caucasian boy whose family moved from rural Southeast Ohio hill country to the impoverished inner core of a medium-sized Ohio city. He's a 6th grader, and it certainly looks as though he hates school. He says as much, constantly, to anyone who will listen. He fights constantly, losing spectacularly most of the time. Often, he is attacked or ridiculed by classmates during school, even in his classes. He harasses classmates and teachers at his middle school, trying to trip or shove most people who pass him. He ignores or complains about teachers' directions, refusing actively or passively to do most class activities. He has failed several of his classes. Most of all, he loudly and frequently tells teachers and students he'd rather be anywhere than at school. He says this so often that some of the teachers have taken to calling him "Anywhere," when discussing him (sometimes in his presence).

Davey's older half-sister was killed last year at her paper-delivery job, by a drunken driver. School officials suspect that family members have been responding to Davey's erratic behavior after his sister's death with physical and psychological abuse.

Davey's behaviour and attitude could be that of dozens of kids at his school. To what should we attribute his negative attitude toward school? Clearly, many factors play a role.

Having noted all these contributors (and undoubtedly overlooking others equally important), and their individual and collective effects on students' attitudes toward school, I would like to focus on a factor that may seem, by comparison, quite esoteric—far removed from the on-the-ground forces that I've described so far.

I want to talk about the role that educational *purpose* has in affecting students' attitudes toward their schooling and their schools. I believe what by some accounts is a rising level of student dissatisfaction with school has been greatly affected by schools' failure to commit to, communicate, and teach toward long-term, even ideal educational ends. This failure has made teaching and learning, and living in schools, seem a fragmented and even pointless existence—even in the face of a coherent standards-based learning environment and very high-stakes testing. I believe this failure has contributed to the dissolution of schools and classrooms as communities and to the loosening of ties between schools and families—features that in turn contribute to negative attitudes toward school. And I believe this failure contributes directly to that dissatisfaction, by distancing student learning from students' own hopes for their lives.

More positively, I want to argue that a purpose-driven school can support the resilience of children like Davey. Without such an environment for at least part of his life, what can support any effort of his to learn, academically, socially, or otherwise? And, why shouldn't he wish to be "anywhere but here"—even if he has absolutely no idea what situation would be more desirable for him?

PERILS OF PURPOSE IN A SEARCH FOR PURPOSE

I should make clear at the outset that I am not making what would be an outrageous claim that schools do not operate with purposes in mind. Purpose, in some sense, is integral to almost everything that is done in American schools. In academics, teachers not only design lesson-based objectives that address unit goals that in turn address the goals of courses; they also align their lessons, units, courses, and programs of study with local and state standards, benchmarks, and indicators. On the administrative level, not just academics but also administrative policies of every sort are tied to aims that might range from creating safe learning environments, to efficient building and district procedures, to addressing particular issues of popular concern such as reducing the drop-out rate.

But all of this is insufficient. Moreover, some of it is, in practice, doing harm.

The fundamental problem with the role of educational purposes in American schools today is—to hopefully re-invigorate an old saw—that because of the way schools and school people use purposes, they can't see the forest for the trees. They have moved away from the valuable localized principle that for most learning tasks, students learn better when they can "place" the task in its context of previous and prospective learning, to an obsession with sequence, completeness, and "alignment" of every learning task. Academics has become a logical exercise designed backwards from maps of complete disciplinary knowledge to the individual lessons that build to that complete picture (cf. Popham, 2004). Add to that the sometimes complementary, sometimes antithetical influence of NCLB's focus on particular areas of learning, driven by high-stakes assessments that threaten teachers' jobs and schools' continued existence, and we may begin to understand why schools' attention has been increasingly focused on the details of particular sets of knowledge and skills.

But because of this focus on a selected set of academic purposes, what schools have lost is a vision of what transcends legislated goals of annual yearly progress and systems of disciplinary knowledge. And in forgetting the larger purposes through which the value of what's learned may be determined, and by which the progress and success of schooling may be judged, schools have isolated their students from deep, lasting, and life-focusing purposes that can sustain and even stimulate their efforts to learn even in the face of obstacles, failures, and disasters.

Consider standards-based education (SBE) that has resulted in the development of remarkably coherent and all-encompassing approaches to schooling. It is not only that SBE has unified school knowledge in every school discipline area and provided for—even mandated—curricular and pedagogical planning and practice in every school, at all levels. SBE has also driven the development of forms of teacher education and administrative structure and procedure, to serve the curriculum. What has been forgotten is what justifies the system itself.

No Child Left Behind has been the most powerful engine of change in American education in generations. Its provisions for attention to traditionally marginalized students, its leveraging of parent choice, and its accountability demands have effectively changed the ways schools operate and teachers teach. Supported by political powers from nearly every constituency, massively (if inadequately, according to a number of lawsuits) funded, it rolls on without reference to the larger ends in view that it should have begun with. These remain, at best, implicit.

What have been ignored are the ultimate aims to which we must commit ourselves to, in undertaking the huge effort of educating. When I speak of purposes in this sense, I mean to speak of them at a level that is at once beyond the range of what is actually and finally attainable; and in the form of a personal commitment to a vision.

Many writers, in different ways, have discussed educational purposes of this sort. Most recently, Neil Postman, in his book *The End of Education* (1996) has called these transcendent aims "gods" and their setting as "narratives." These aims represent the ultimate reasons for learning, and for teaching, too. He writes,

> This kind of reason is somewhat abstract, not always present in one's consciousness, not at all
> easy to describe. And yet for all that, without it schooling does not work. For school to make
> sense, the young, their parents, and their teachers must have a god to serve, or even better sev-

eral gods. If they have none, school is pointless....To put it simply, there is no surer way to bring an end to schooling than for it to have no end (p. 4).

Postman does not mean to speak of these sorts of aims as "reasons" in the sense that educators now limit themselves to in justifying teaching decisions. Speaking of this sort of aim, he says "it must not be confused with a reason for being in a classroom, for listening to a teacher, for taking an examination, for doing homework, for putting up with school even if you are not motivated" (Postman, 1995, p. 4). Educators are very quick to provide reasons of this more localized aim. They refer students to such things as the next designated content to learn as part of SBE; to what it will take to help the school to achieve an Adequate Yearly Progress; to what it will take for students to move to the next grade level or the next school level; or to pass the state graduation test and prepare for college. These proximal sorts of reasons for engaging and for persevering in learning are certainly on the minds of educators, and on the minds of some students and parents. But they are self-referring—they talk about matters inside a system; they often fail to penetrate into the personal visions of students, or help students to create such visions.

In the end, a system of schooling is arbitrary if it is not directed by aims to which it is instrumental. It cannot be justified, evaluated, or its progress gauged, without such a reference. And arbitrary activity does not inspire commitment; it discourages it.

Donald Arnstine, in *Democracy and the Arts of Schooling* (1995), called these over arching aims "ideals":

> Ideals are what people strive for. Standards are what they try to meet....Education can succeed only if teachers know what they're teaching *for*. Their immediate aims and objectives are shaped by their values, but their long-range goals are guided by ideals. Their activities are *regulated* by standards...(p. 22, last italics mine).

Aims of this sort provide us with direction, when we have envisioned them and are committed to them. It doesn't matter if they represent literally unattainable outcomes or ever-shifting targets. Building, maintaining, and extending a democratic society, whether in Deweyan, Freireian, or any other conception, is one such ideal or god. Developing what is truly human potential in individuals and human communities is another and ancient ideal. Providing for individual and societal survival and prospering, in an ever-changing world, is yet another such ideal—and one that may well be implicit in such initiatives as NCLB. Developing autonomous individuals who can direct their own lives as they wish is yet another ideal, as is the newer (but with ancient roots) "god" of shepherding the earth.

Most Americans can recognize and honor all of these, when they are articulated. But in the absence of any sustained discussion and consensus-building, anywhere in education, of such ideals, most public use of them is in a gut-level opposition to particular educational initiatives. We *feel* that some plan is taking education "in the wrong direction," but we don't know how to talk about why. It is not surprising that almost every educational initiative, including NCLB, eventually is subject to damaging opposition in this country.

And it is also no wonder that kids in school often feel cut off from any real meaning to their studies. If schools and educators either feel no commitment to, or can't articulate a commitment to overarching educational ideals, the work they assign will appear to their students finally as useless as breaking rocks on a chain gang.

Students can occasionally articulate a desire for such ideals or gods. The survey findings I mentioned earlier, in which many students expressed their dissatisfaction with school by complaining that schools weren't preparing them well in areas crucial to their future success, may reveal a partially articulated commitment to one of several possible ideals. Parents, too, often form public positions that seem to rest on educational ideals. I am sympathetic to parents who agitate for inclusion of "intelligent design" arguments into science classes. Their view rests on logical category mistakes, confusing empirical questions with metaphysical ones on several levels (and the expression of their views is sometimes directed by political agendas); but what draws me to these parents is what seems to be their obvious search for meaningfulness in what is learned—a connection of empirical knowledge and acquired skill to aims and purposes that encompass and ennoble that learning.

This search for connection to educational ideals is more easily observed in educational settings where students are more like free agents. In higher education, for instance, researchers have noticed that many students come to college with commitments to partly conscious long-term aims—often centering on their material success. Their college experiences often cause them to strive to fully articulate their commitments, and subject them to critique. Freshmen often complain bitterly about general education requirements, even at liberal arts institutions like my own, when they judge those requirements against an ideal of material success for themselves. One study noted that students often pick ill-fitting majors for themselves, get discouraged, and either drop out or stumble toward other majors (Leppel, 2005). What makes their choices "ill-fitting" tends to be an incomplete understanding of the ideals they navigate by; and good fit awaits a clear and conscious match of ideal and major.

There is some evidence that when students independently arrive at commitments to educational ideals, it provides a firm foundation for persevering and succeeding in school. For instance, one recent study (Schallert, Reed & Turner, 2006) was inspired by previous research that connected school success to positive attitudes even in the face of setbacks to long-term aims. The authors wrote that "We were very interested in discovering what it was about those in the resilient group that allowed them to recover their emotional footing, recommit to their goals for the class, and invest even more effort to their studies. As we discuss,...an important part of the answer was that these students' aspirations...had been more explicitly stated and more highly valued than those of students in the nonresilient group."

Postman (1995), quoting Nietzche, put it this way: "He who has a *why* to live can bear with almost any *how*" (p. 4).

As I see it, though there are many reasons why kids hate school, in any of the senses discussed earlier, an important factor in such an attitude is a lack of Purpose. This is not only an important reason, but one that schools and educators seem not to recognize. It also seems to me that schools can help students change their attitudes, or at least persevere in the face of them, by dedicating themselves to, continually communicating, seeking consensus on, and—most importantly—teaching toward the educational ideals that can make students see their learning as something ultimately precious to them. This will certainly entail a painful self-examination and public search for consensus among schools and school people. And it is long overdue.

REFERENCES

Aquinas, T. (1990). *Summa theological*. Fr.L. Shapcote, (Trans.). Chicago: Encyclopedia Britannica.

Arnstine, D. (1995). *Democracy and the Arts of Schooling*. Albany, N.Y.: State University of New York Press.

Australian Council for Educational Research. (no date). Attitudes, Intention, and Participation, Longitudinal, of Australian Youth, research report #41. ERIC Document Reproduction Services, ED486069.

Avalon High School Students. (2002). Listening to student voices. St. Paul, Minnesota, July, 2005. Retrieved October 9, 2006, from http://www.eduationevolving.org/pdf/Listening_to_Student_Voices.pdf.

Bersamin, M.M., Walker, S., Fisher, D., & Grube, J.W. (2006). Correlates of oral sex and vaginal intercourse in early and middle adolescence. *Journal of Research on Adolescence* (16/1): 59–68.

Cotton, K., (1996, May). School size, school, climate, and student performance. Northwest Regional Education Laboratory Close Up #20. Retreived from http://www.nwrel.org/Scpd/Sirs/10/co20.htm, October 1, 2006.

Feller, B. (2006, May 30). Black, Hispanic pupils see school as tough. Retrieved From http://www.publicagenda.org, September 1, 2006.

Ferreira, M.M. (1995). The caring of a suburban middle school. ERIC Document Reproduction Services, ED 385011.

Frost, Robert. (1991). The Vindictives. In L. Untermeyer (Ed.), *New Enlarged Anthology of Robert Frost's Poems*. New York: Pocket Books.

Hon, R.Y. H., & Yeung, A.S. (2005, November). Low achievers' parent–child relations and liking of school. ERIC Reproduction Services, ED490059.

Kennedy A., & Bennett, L. (2006). Urban adolescent mothers exposed to community, family, and partner violence: Is cumulative violence exposure a barrier to school performance and participation? *Journal of Interpersonal Violence* (21/6): 750–773.

Kundera, M. (1991). *Immortality*. New York: Harper Collins.

Leppel, K. (2005, June). College persistence and student attitudes toward financial success. Retrieved from http://findarticles.com/p/artiles/mi_m0FCR/is_2_3a, October 8, 2006.

National Governors Association. (2005, April 19). Governors seek input from 10,000 high school students. Retrieved from www.nga.org, October 10, 2006.

Popham, J. (2004). Standards-based education: Two wrongs don't make a right. In S. Mathison & E.W. Ross (Eds.), *Defending Public Schools Volume Four: The Nature and Limits of Standards-Based Reform and Assessment* (pp. 15–26) Westport, Connecticut: Praeger.

Postman, N. (1995). *The End of Education: Redefining the Value of School*. New York: Vintage Books.

Schallert, D., Reed, J.H., & Turner, J.E. (2004). The interplay of aspirations, enjoyment, and work habits in academic endeavors: Why is it so hard to keep long-term commitments? *Teachers College Record* [electronic version]. (106/9): 1715–28. Retrieved from http://www.tcrecord.org, ID #11667, July 24, 2006.

Tyson, K. (2002). Weighing in: Elementary age students and the debate in attitudes toward school among black students. *Social Forces* (80/4): 1157–89.

Valentine, J.C., Charlton, K., & Melson, A. (2003). The effects of modified school calendars on student achievement and on school and community attitudes. *Review of Educational Research* (73/1): 1–52.

Multiple Choice Questions

1. Students' attitudes toward school are strongly correlated to

    a. the chances that "at-risk" students will have success in school

    b. the chances that students will engage in practices that put their health at risk

    c. the level of confidence students have that they will succeed in school tasks

    d. all of the above

2. A clear and relevant investigation of student attitudes toward school includes

    a. surveying students by means of asking them the degree to which they hate or love school

    b. beginning by making clear what we mean by "attitude" and "school"

    c. cataloguing incidents of school violence in the student population, over time

3. Research suggests that students hate school when

    a. problems in relationships at home spill over to school

    b. disrespectful behavior is tolerated by school personnel

    c. there are cultural conflicts between students and the dominant school culture

    d. a. and c

    e. There are probably many reasons: a., b., and c., above, are among them

4. The usual range of "purposes" that underlie schools' policies and practices

    a. are not, ordinarily, consciously tied to long-range "ideals" for educating

    b. are usually justified by school personnel in terms of their legal necessity

    c. are always clearly communicated to students, since this is legally required

5. "Ideals" are purposes that

    a. are really just pie-in-the-sky wishes

    b. can provide over-all and long-term direction for the particular decisions we make in education

    c. are important but not difficult to accomplish

    d. most people are clearly aware that they have, and that most people usually refer to in justifying their views on particular educational issues

6. When students make commitments to long-term educational ideals

    a. some research suggests that they are more likely to drop out of school

    b. some research suggests that college students change majors more often

    c. some research suggests that students persevere in school, even in the face of setbacks and frustrations

    d. a. and b

7. Most Americans

    a. have no educational ideals that guide their decisions about educational issues

    b. see value in a number of educational ideals, but give priority to one

    c. don't usually articulate their commitment to an educational ideal, except in the context of expressing opposition to a proposal that works against the ideal

    d. b. and c

8. It would be fair to say that, in the U.S.,

    a. educational ideals are not often the basis for public discussion of important educational issues

    b. there has been, in recent decades, little attempt to build toward a consensus on the educational ideals that should guide American educational decisionmaking

    c. schools rarely attempt to instill a vision of an educational ideal in their students

    d. all of the above

9. An educational ideal, as opposed to a reason for doing something in education,

    a. is an accurate account of what will occur, rather than what might

    b. is a morally defensible justification for acting, rather than one that benefits the one who acts

    c. represents a vision of an ultimate outcome of educating that provides a continuing reference point for educational choices

10. It would be fair to say that the conclusion of the main argument in this article is that

    a. It is important for students, educators, and citizens to have a clear vision of what education is ultimately for

    b. It is important for Americans to seek a measure of consensus on what education is ultimately for

    c. The lack of a clear and well articulated commitment to an educational ideal is among the more important reasons why students don't like school

    d. all of the above

SECTION V

Subject-Matter Considerations

I like every subject but art…one time I was trying to make a shape that wasn't too small and wasn't too fat and wasn't too skinny and wasn't too small; but, for the first three writings my teacher said, "no, no, no." And I tried my best on those first three writings. I'd get rid of art.

—7-YEAR OLD BOYS AND GIRLS CLUB STUDENT

The learning part's ok…some of my classes aren't too hard. I really hate math because I am really bad at it. But I really like band. That's like the best subject. We just get to do a lot of cool things together in band.

—16-YEAR OLD MISSOURI HIGH SCHOOL STUDENT

I like science. Most of the time we read out of the book and take quizzes. We haven't done much science yet this year. We've done social studies because social studies and science are during the same hour…sometimes it switches from social studies to science. There's lots of cool experiments in there (the text) and I'm just like, oh, I can't wait to try these and we don't get to do them.

—12-YEAR OLD MISSOURI STUDENT

The solution I am urging, is to eradicate the fatal disconnection of subjects which kills the vitality of our modern curriculum. There is only one subject-matter for education, and that is Life in all its manifestations Instead of this single unity, we offer children—Algebra, from which nothing follows; Geometry, from which nothing follows; Science, from which nothing follows; History, from which nothing follows; a Couple of Languages, never mastered; and lastly, most dreary of all, Literature, represented by plays of Shakespeare, with philological notes and short analyses of plot and character to be in substance committed to memory. Can such a list be said to represent Life, as it is known in the midst of the living of it?

—ALFRED NORTH WHITEHEAD, *THE AIMS OF EDUCATION* (1929)

What's Wrong with American Education, and Can it be Fixed?

Thomas Deering

Augusta State University

INTRODUCTION

The five-or six-year-old child enters kindergarten a virtual sponge, soaking up as much information as the teacher and the school environment has to offer. But this quest to discover and to understand doesn't begin when the child enters the school house door. No, parents can attest to their child crawling into closets, behind sofas and chairs, making a plaything out of almost everything. The very young love to learn by using almost anything they can get their hands on—crayons, sticks, blocks, pots and pans! They watch and they listen and they touch all, so that they can *know*. This inborn inquisitiveness is revealed simply but forcefully in the single most famous child question of all—"Why?"

What happens to that natural inquisitiveness after just a few short years in school? It seems that by the time children have completed four or five years of school, that flame of curiosity has been extinguished, or at least doused. Yes, parents must be held accountable for not motivating their children. And yes, the blatant anti-intellectualism and rampant materialism that permeates our culture defy the idea of an education for education's sake. No one would deny that the child's life outside the school impacts his motivation inside the school. But schools are a powerful institution that help shape young lives. Schools help acculturate and socialize young children, and it is in schools that they learn much of the academic content and skills needed to succeed in life. Teachers have a unique power and opportunity to sink a hook into a child—to shape and inspire a child's life. Teachers and schools cannot point fingers without examining their own actions. When children lose interest in learning, teachers and schools must bear some of the responsibility. It is too easy, unfair, and most importantly, counter-productive to argue that parents, the media, and our culture are to blame, and that schools are the only bright spot on an otherwise bleak landscape.

What is going on in schools to dampen children's desire to know, explore, question, and learn? Quite simply, American schools offer a curriculum most students find meaningless, the lessons are taught in a boring way, and students are assessed in a manner that is not helpful in measuring what students know and can do.

A MEANINGLESS CURRICULUM AND POOR TEACHING

Does the current curriculum of the average American school teach students to be life-long learners, or do students learn to feed back trivia and drivel? Much of the American curriculum is mindless memorization. In a world with easy access to technology and an almost limitless access to data, we still have students memorizing the states, their capitals, our presidents, and the world's longest river. Such lessons are neither good geography nor good history. Simple memorization of trivial information is not the only problem with the curriculum and teaching in American schools. So much of the content itself is of questionable worth for the majority of students.

Is it any wonder that students are turned off from biology when teachers try to claim that all high school students must dissect a fetal pig, or engage in some similar hands-on lesson? Without question many students enjoy "digging around in a pig," but the lack of science knowledge and appreciation for science exhibited by American students is evidence that these lessons are either taught poorly or that the lessons themselves are not capturing students' interest. All too often teachers teach what interests them, not what interests students. Let's not assume that which interests teachers is important and that which interests students isn't. There can be a happy meeting of the two, if teachers are willing to think of, and willing to think as, their students. Rutherford and Ahlgren (1990) asserted that "the present curricula in science and mathematics are overstuffed and undernourished" (p. viii). The standards upon which they were commenting in 1990 are the same standards in place today. No one should be surprised that in international studies, American students consistently lag far behind their international cohorts in science (Walberg, 2004). This is a fact that is of concern to Walberg and should be to all science educators. An examination of the Web site of the National Science Teachers Association is clear evidence of Walberg's concern (http://www.nsta.org/standards). The standards are full of terms such as analyze, synthesize, data, research, inquiry, and problem solving. These are all well and good, but they are not unique to science and fail to say why or how they will explain science or why science is important to learn. There is nothing in the standards that will sink a hook in students so that the teacher can reel them in to loving or at least appreciating science.

American schools do little better in art and music. The arts are taught as performance courses instead of appreciation courses. The appreciation of beauty is the unique strength of the arts. Those standards that aren't performance-dominated tend to be simple learning of content similar to any other discipline. The teaching of content is important in all disciplines, but it should rarely be the end goal. This is especially true in the arts, which should be engaging and moving. In fact, students would be better served if the arts were taught with less content, less emphasis on performance and more emphasis on appreciation. The National Council for the Arts has almost 100 standards for dance, music, theatre, and visual arts. The following is a small sample of music and visual arts standards. (http://artsedge.kennedy-center.org/teach/standards.cfm):

Grades 5–8

Music

Content Standard: 4: Composing and arranging music within specified guidelines
Content Standard: 5: Reading and notating music

Visual Arts

Content Standard: 3: Choosing and evaluating a range of subject matter, symbols, and ideas
Content Standard: 4: Understanding the visual arts in relation to history and cultures

Grades 9–12

Music

Content Standard: 1: Singing, alone and with others, a varied repertoire of music
Content Standard: 4: Composing and arranging music within specified guidelines

Visual Arts

Content Standard: 1: Understanding and applying media, techniques, and processes
Content Standard: 4: Understanding the visual arts in relation to history and cultures

In general, these standards aren't ill-conceived. Some represent very good intentions and include discipline content that arts specialists believe to be important. However, the misplaced emphasis on content and performance leaves the many students without artistic talent feeling left out. It fails to give them what they need to have a life- long appreciation of art or music. What these standards and art programs lack is any teaching of an understanding and appreciation of beauty, which is the special nature of the arts. The arts can open a student's mind, heart, and soul in a deeply moving emotional way that other disciplines cannot.

An important question is what do we do with students who have little talent in art or music, or who don't view the arts as a content to be learned as if it were a government course? What does their class look like? How much time and effort is given to these students? Talented or not, a student can appreciate the beauty in a Van Gogh painting, or Tchaikovsky's Swan Lake ballet. A young person can be enchanted by Pavarotti as he hits a high "C" for which he is so rightfully admired. Students can be moved by lessons where the appreciation of beauty is the goal. Unfortunately, the recognition and admiration of beauty isn't what we teach for in most art or music courses. Instead, if appreciation is taught at all, music teachers are still playing a brief piece of music and asking students to identify the composer or to name the piece, and art teachers are asking students to identify the artist and name the period in which a masterpiece was painted or sculpted. Unfortunately, little or nothing is taught about the power of art or music. The arts have the power to move students in a way other subjects do not. The arts can touch our very soul, but not as they are currently taught. The awe produced by being captured by the arts is lost in America's schools, and so are our students. To be overly impressed by a computer that can produce a picture to rival the Mona Lisa or a computer program that can play a symphony that is indistinguishable from a philharmonic loses sight of what true beauty is and what it means in our lives. Beauty is all around us in the natural world. Students should be in awe of a sunrise over the ocean, or a sunset behind a mountain. They should marvel at the Grand Canyon, and be inspired by a star lit night. What students are missing in their arts curriculum is the realization that we as humans are capable of producing beauty able to enchant us. Composers, artists, historical periods in art or music, compositions—they might all have a place in the curriculum. They are, however, icing on the cake. Let's not confuse facts with the cake.

The teaching of literature suffers from the same problems as the teaching of science—poor teaching and meaningless curriculum. A recent study reported by the Educational Testing Service (2007) finds that between 1984 and 2004, reading scores for the 13–17 year old group have remained flat and the achievement gap is wide and stable. Are American students unable to learn to read or is reading instruction boring? The answer, of course, is that what we do in reading and literature classes lacks meaning for many students. It is, in fact, boring. Students are unable to discriminate the very best from the merely very good in literature if they spend time reading the works of second-tier authors.

The very best literature deals with time-honored questions and issues in a way that is groundbreaking and creative, thought-provoking and challenging. Rather than assigning *The Bell Jar, The Great Gatsby*, or *Catch 22*, English teachers should have students study *Oliver Twist, A Tale of Two Cities* and *Anna Karenina*. It can be said that Angelou, Hemingway, Vonnegut, or Morrison are very good authors and their works have a place in American schools. However, as a literate society we cannot pretend that they are comparable to Dickens, Shakespeare, Plato, or Chaucer. The fact is that if students were reading, studying, becoming immersed in the very best literature, they wouldn't have time for the merely very good. Students should read those authors who have been tested by time. They need to read those who have wrestled with the questions that have perplexed humans from the very earliest days. It is lessons on these which will give the readers the greatest insight into the mind of Shakespeare, Aristotle, Rousseau, Tolstoy, Aquinas, Chaucer, and others considered the greatest writers of the Western world. Lessons that will get at the heart of what these authors have to say will primarily involve an analysis of the issues and questions the author is dealing with. The lesson will revolve around conversations of the essence of the author's intent, not the presentation of factual data of the piece.

Less time should be spent on the "story line" and more on what makes the piece worth reading. What are the timeless and human questions that the author is wrestling with? The works students read and the lessons taught should treat issues of good and bad, right and wrong, beauty, freedom, the nature of human conflict and other similar questions. Instead, literature is taught in the same shallow way as art and music. The minutia of the story gets in the way of the purpose for the story. Educators are unwilling to accept the fact that students are speaking loudly and clearly about what they think of literature and reading instructions. Educators are blaming the messenger—the student—when it would be so much easier and more productive to look in the mirror.

Social studies instruction is equally dreary and the curriculum as irrelevant for students. A careful reading of the National Council for the Social Studies Web site (http://www.socialstudies.org/standards/) includes a list of standards that is long on facts and memorization and short on meaningful ideas. Instead of asking students to memorize lists of facts, we should be teaching the significance of those facts on the lists. If while teaching the geography of the Southeast United States, a teacher engaged students with issues such as the culture, social patterns, economic influence of the region, the main geographic features, and the history of the region, the names of states and cities would be natural components of the lessons and would have meaning to the students. They would come alive for the students. The students wouldn't just memorize, they would learn.

We must add mathematics to our list of weaknesses in the American school curriculum. When math is taught as a series of formulas and theorems without helping the students to understand what those formulas and theorems mean, then they are divorced from the appreciation of the importance and the majesty of math. Math is all around us and students need to know the simple, intricate, and yet undeniable truth of math's role in our lives. Without that message from teachers, the subject loses its meaning and interest to most students.

If you scan the Web site of the National Council of Teachers of Mathematics (http://www.nctm.org/standards/) you will see the same pattern of memorization and questionable content that is on the Web sites for the arts, science, literature and the social studies. Mathematics is important, many of the mathematic standards are valuable, and they contain some worthwhile content. However, as in the typical arts, literature, science, and social studies curriculum, there is much in the mathematics standards that is simply unimportant to most students and is certainly taught for the wrong reason and in the wrong way.

Students can sometimes "get something" from a weak curriculum, but that usually requires a gifted teacher. Unfortunately, the teaching of math is poor. A sad fact is that little time is spent in the average math class, teaching math. The typical math class begins with a review of the homework from the night before. It ends with a significant block of time spent working on homework assigned today. So, the amount of time actually spent teaching new material is surprisingly little. This is a poor teaching strategy of dubious value that takes away time from the actual teaching of what should be important content, yet, it is a fixture in math classes. It seems obvious that more time teaching and less time correcting homework or working on homework in class will lead to more learning.

As previously mentioned, teaching math as a series of formulas and theorems to be memorized misses what math is all about. Plugging in numbers to "get the right answer" keeps math a mystery instead of a subject to be understood and enjoyed. Of equal importance with how math is taught is what kind of math is taught. Memorizing a process and finding the correct answer seems to be the bottom-line approach to math. Without question, finding the correct answer is the bottom line for math. But, students must be taught to understand the mathematical process, not simply memorize formulas and theorems and plug in numbers. Both teaching methods will produce the correct answer, but only the first will produce an understanding of math.

A serious problem in the teaching of math is that math teachers don't make a good case for learning math. Telling students they need to know *this* math so that they can do *that* math is senseless and breeds contempt for the subject. A recent study reported that among 29 OECD countries supplying data on student proficiency in math, the United States ranked 24th (Walberg, 2004). Are American students unable to learn math? No, the answer must lie elsewhere. Teachers must find a way to show students a reason for learning math. If they can't convince students that math is worth knowing, American students will continue to lag behind their international colleagues.

The intent here is not to blame these specific disciplines or teachers. Instead, these disciplines serve as examples of the entire curriculum in American education. The American curriculum (and to the extent that National Standards drive state standards, there is an American curriculum) and current teaching methods don't help students become thinking, discerning adults. American schools produce shallow individuals who have very little in-depth knowledge. American students become adults who are unable to recall those mindless lists they were required to memorize, and lack any knowledge or understanding that is essential for citizens of a democracy. Every state in the Union has given the schools a mandate to educate students to be informed citizens who will be able to participate in our electoral process. Yet, anyone who has spent much time with high school, university students, or young adults is struck by how little these individuals know about candidates and issues. The Nation's next generation of leaders, these 18—25 year olds, have the lowest voter turn-out rate of any age group in the country. Whether it is from a lack of knowledge or apathy, this trend is not good for America.

ASSESSMENT

Where should one begin when discussing assessment? Is it an evil that should be eliminated? No! Do assessments give the teacher, school administrator, parent, employer, or university admissions office an accurate picture of a student's ability, what he or she has learned, or what he or she can do? Generally not. Unfortunately, prospective teachers are being prepared to continue the established practices of measuring student success, of perpetuating the modes of evaluation and grading to which they have been accustomed through their years in primary and secondary grades, in their college careers, and in their teacher education courses. Student work and student progress must be examined, and the student must receive some response regarding the quality or appropriateness of his or her work or progress. This takes the form of a grade or some other written, oral, or symbolic indicator. The belief is that through such examinations and responses, a measure of success can be determined—the success of the teacher in conveying ideas or lessons to the student, the student's success in comprehending the lessons, or both. The contention here is that, that which is of most importance in an educational endeavor is often not measurable; that that which is measurable becomes the curriculum, even if it is of questionable worth; that success in teaching and in learning is oftentimes not apparent until years after the fact; and that the method of evaluation currently being foisted upon the teaching profession by "educational scientists" is based upon a misguided understanding of the educational process. The concern here is that the over-emphasis on assessment and evaluation of student work is a by-product of the demand that teachers be held accountable for student learning without holding students accountable for their own learning, and has little relationship to what students know and can do. This emphasis encourages teachers to grade, measure, and evaluate voraciously—complete with classroom charts, gold stars, computer grading systems, and loaded grade books. Unfortunately, "educational scientists" are unable to accept that the entire assessment and evaluation effort is unscientific. To compound this problem, teachers have little understanding of what should be taught or assessed. So what can be done to make the assessment component of the educational process better?

A necessary first step: all educators must realize that no matter what they do to assess a student, it is not scientific. An objective assessment of what students have learned is next to impossible, and most types of assessment measure what is tested, not always what is taught or known. Moreover, most assessments fail to measure what is most important.

Let's first look at standardized tests. The claim is generally made that assessment instruments are objective, accurate, and measure that which is important. This argument is based usually upon the fact that such tests are checked for validity and reliability. As stated above, the fallacy of such claims is that standardized tests objectively measure what is tested, but not necessarily what is taught or known. But, the greatest fault to the claim of objectivity is the subjectivity of what is objectively measured. What is objective about the claim that all students must know that the world's longest river is the Nile? Has there been a consensus reached that all students should know the names of all fifty states and their capitals? If so, does that make it objective? The measurement of test items can be objective, but the decision to assess material is almost always subjective. Furthermore, what standardized tests assess is oftentimes not what is taught. Even when a curriculum that is taught is aligned with some standardized test, there is little evidence to support the notion that that particular material is taught with the same emphasis that it is assessed. And, once again, even if the material is taught with the same emphasis that it is assessed, there is little to show that standardized tests measure that which is important.

The danger of believing that standardized tests are scientific leads to the trap of believing that they can accurately discriminate between students. Can an admissions officer feel confident that a student with an ACT score of 34 is a better gamble for the university than a student with an ACT score of 18? Yes, and their professional judgment will probably be proven accurate. The problem is that believing an assessment is scientifically accurate, objective, and has been checked for validity and reliability has led the educational establishment to be convinced that a student with an ACT score of 30 is a better gamble than a student with an ACT score of 29. In fact the ACT claims, "The ACT® test assesses high school students' general educational development and their *ability to complete college-level work*" (Emphasis mine) (http://www.act.org/aap/). Moreover, the ACT is advertised as "America's Most Widely Accepted College Entrance Exam" (ibid.). It is true that the ACT and other standardized tests state that their tests give only a general assessment and that scores are not to be used as the sole criteria for college admission. It is also true that the developers of these tests can't be held accountable for the misuse of their product. However, the claim to scientific validity has led educators at all levels to take the ACT and other standardized tests too seriously and place too much importance on them. A quick glance at college admissions standards across the country will support this statement. While the ACT, SAT, and other standardized tests can give a fairly accurate big, general picture of a student's academic abilities, the close-ups—the specifics of the student's ability and success—are out of focus. Educators should understand that standardized tests can be helpful, but that they are not the answer to assessing students.

If standardized tests are not the answer to an educator's assessment needs, can we at least trust teacher-made assessments? Certainly the teacher knows what was taught and the emphasis it was given, and so he or she must know how accurately the assessment instrument measures the material? In fact, this is not necessarily the case. Teacher assessments are not very accurate in measuring what students know. It is true that teachers know what was taught, but not how well it was taught. Checking for understanding and teaching for mastery are ideas that for the most part have been discarded by far too many teachers, and not surprisingly, are not emphasized in many teacher education programs. Likewise, what a teacher tests is not always what was taught or learned. A small slip of the tongue during a lesson, a misspelled word on an assignment, a poorly-worded test question, or a point taken away or not awarded on a subjective assignment or test can all have devastating effects on a teacher's assessment of a student. In many classes, particularly in the lower grades and even in upper grades math courses, homework is often graded in class by the student or a classmate. Students grading their own work or that of a friend can lead to inaccurate grades being recorded. This inaccuracy can be either by mistake or design, but in both cases it leads to unreliable scores being used to figure a student's grade. Even relatively small errors can have a significant impact on a final grade. It is the rare teacher—I have never met this person—who would say the above never happens. Yet, student performance on assessments of all kinds is taken to be totally the responsibility of the student. Teachers have convinced themselves that what, how, why, and when they assess students is accurate and valid.

To underscore the inaccuracy of assessments, let's examine the careers of two high school students. Each student took 25 units—a completely arbitrary number—of Carnegie credits. They took the same 25 units, and were in the exact same classes at the same time with the same teachers throughout their high school careers. One student averaged a 90% in every course—this grading scale was selected for ease of description —and had a perfect 4.0 GPA. The other student had 24 "A's" averaging 98% and one "B" with an average of 89%. This student's GPA was 3.96. In the present scenario, the student having the higher GPA might very well be the class valedictorian, while the second student at best would be the class salutatorian. Does anyone want to make the claim that the first student was more successful in learning than the second student? You can state that there is a significant difference between a 98% and a 90%, but how many want to claim that there is a meaningful difference between 90% and 89%?

A silly assignment, taught in a boring fashion with a trivial assessment, leads to the time in school being wasted. Little of importance is gained by having students answer multiple choice, fill-in-the-blank, or matching questions. Even the push for authentic assessment is flawed. Jones (2002) analyzed the problems of "authentic" assessment, stressing that little of importance is gained through such assessment, and that teachers must be careful not to place too much importance on it. Long conversations with students which are in-depth and on important topics can tell a teacher more than any other assessment devised. It is through conversations that teachers can understand the student's thought process: where they took off for the sky and where they failed to make the connection. It is through conversations that students can see how teachers think. This approach will help students understand how teachers approach their work and their discipline. Instead, assessments are used as a summative tool to measure and to judge what a student knows or can do. Teachers claim that they don't have time to use student assessment as a formative tool to guide their teaching. But, if teachers don't use student work to evaluate their own work and the progress students are making, valuable time can be wasted before they discover that students haven't followed their teaching, and the students aren't where the teacher wants them to be. This is not to say that other forms of teaching and assessing can't be used or that there isn't a place for them. It is simply a warning to stop thinking that teaching, learning, and assessing are scientific in nature. We as educators are dealing with humans in schools, not rats in a maze.

SUGGESTIONS AND CONCLUSIONS

Many will read this piece as a criticism of teachers and the educational establishment for all the problems in our nation's schools and in our students' relative lack of success in schools. Teachers and the educational system are not to blame for the problems in America's schools, but teachers and schools are a part of the problem. The problems cannot be corrected until that truth is faced. It is true that educators don't always decide what the curriculum is, but they do have a say, and they have an even greater say in *how* they teach. Yes, state and national officials mandate that students be assessed—this was true long before NCLB. Teachers, however, have been assessing students since the beginning of the teaching learning process, in fact, even before schools when learning was an informal process. Assessment in and of itself is not the problem. The problem is much bigger. How, what, and why we assess is tied to the curriculum and the teaching process. They are three strands of the same problem that can't be worked on individually. It is the interchange and connection between these three strands—curriculum, teaching methods, and assessment—that has played such a major role in shaping contemporary American education. The time is ripe now to consider serious change in the Nation's schools, and without question, educators must be intimately involved in this change process.

How that change can come about is both simple and complex. First, educators need to stop complaining about NCLB, family, environment, and social factors. These are realities which are not under their control. Second, educators must focus on educating students instead of covering material. Students must be presented the most meaningful curriculum professional educators can develop. It must be taught in an engaging way and assessed in a fashion that measures what they have learned. In a school with these three components present, students would know what was "taught," why they were taught it, and would understand and value what they learned. This isn't accomplished through magic like lead being turned into gold. Good teaching is hard work. It begins with a solid teacher education program including significant field experience, years of practice, and continual professional development. Third, America as a nation has to answer some fundamental questions about what it wants from schools. These questions seem obvious and many took them for settled long ago. The reality is that these questions are neither obvious nor settled. In 1988 Hirsch wrote that "Americans have hesitated to make a decision about the specific knowledge that children need to learn in school" (p. 19). This is a call to action that is as true today as it was when Hirsch first produced a storm of outrage almost 20 years ago. There has to be a consensus about the purpose of the nation's schools. What is the purpose of an education? What does it mean to be educated and, how does an educated person differ from an uneducated or under-educated person? How do we decide what is worth knowing and what is less worthy of serious study? What are the possibilities and limitations of schools? These and other essential questions need to be asked and answered. Again, to quote Hirsch, "There is a pressing need for clarity about our educational priorities (p. 25)." America continues to ignore his warning today. Until America takes notice, the nation's teachers will continue to teach in a boring fashion a curriculum many students will find meaningless, and students will be assessed in a manner that will help neither them nor their teachers measure their level of success in school.

The answer to these and similar questions is the real issue, and the lack of a national consensus will hamper the implementation of the required changes for America's schools. What is clear to the author is that society needs to decide the purpose of schooling. America is no longer the country it was in the 1830s when the common school movement was established. The America of the 19th and 21st centuries is different in diversity of all kinds—race, national origin, religion, culture, and more. This is no longer a country of shopkeepers, small businesses, and farmers. America is no longer isolated from Europe and Asia by oceans. Originally, the American common school was designed to provide all students that which is *common* to all. Content and the use of that content has changed. What has stayed the same according to Adler (1983) is that basic education must:

"1) give the young an introduction to the world of learning; 2) give them all the skills of learning; and 3) give them the incentives and the stimulation to continue learning without end after schooling is ended" (p 9).

Once a student possesses these skills and dispositions, and an appreciation of learning, he or she is ready for life. In short, education is a process of self-improvement for a better life as a human being. Throughout the years Adler has been attacked as an elitist and as being out of touch with the realities of American society. However, his proposal is strikingly similar to the findings of Murnane and Levy (1996). Students need to be life-long learners with a set of skills and a knowledge base to build upon.

We can continue to argue about specific content that all students must learn, but the development of life-long learners must be a given. Hirsch, Adler, Murnane, Levy, and a host of others would say that the consequences of inaction are dire for America. Our students are not learning as much as they should, they participate in the political process at an alarmingly low rate, and America's high school graduation rates lag behind those of other developed countries. In a time when the world is shrinking, and the world economy is becoming interdependent, our schools are not measuring up. America's on-time graduation rates for 2001 were dismal (Swanson, 2004).

Blacks 50%

Hispanics 53%

White 75%

Asian 77%

In 2003 America's graduation rate compared to other developed countries was equally disappointing (Organization for Economic Co-Operation, 2005). While the United States estimated that the graduation rate was 77%, Germany, Greece, Ireland, Japan, and Switzerland all reported estimates of 90%. These results illustrate how inadequate our schools are in educating our Nation's youth, and how precarious the United States' position is in a global marketplace.

To bring about the needed changes in American education, teachers and administrators alike must stop following and begin leading the educational reform movement. Before that is possible, educators themselves must be more fully educated and better prepared as professionals. Only then can they demand their rightful place in the education decision making process. Most politicians have the best of intentions when it comes to education policy, but good intentions are not sufficient. They are in over their heads and make political decisions rather than educationally sound ones. Oftentimes they have no idea of the consequences of the laws they pass nor a sound understanding of contemporary schools or the educational process. Educators need to play a role in shaping politicians' positions so that they have the greatest positive effect on our schools. The bureaucrats in charge of implementing these mandates and laws lack an understanding and commitment to the teaching/learning process. This is a small piece of their job, and they need educators' guidance to perform their responsibility in the most effective and least intrusive manner. Government at the state and national levels is now intimately involved in education policy. Educators cannot leave such an important component of American life as education to well-meaning, but ill-informed politicians. Educators must recapture the momentum and become involved in policy making. Only then can America have the schools it needs and our children deserve.

References

ACT. (2007). http://www.act.org/aap/.

Adler, M. J. (1983). *Paideia Problems and Possibilities*. New York: MacMillan Publishing Company.

Artsedge: standards. (2007). http://artsedge.kennedy-center.org/teach/standards.cfm:

Educational Testing Service, (2007). www.ets.org/research/pic.

Hirsch, E. D. Jr. (1988). *Cultural Literacy*. New York: Vintage Books.

___ (1996). *The Schools we Need*. New York: Doubleday.

Jones, S. P. (2002). Authentic assessment: What is it and why it must be critiqued. In Thomas E. Deering (ed.), *Teacher Education*. Meerut, India: ANU Books.

Murnane, R. J. and Levy, F. (1996). *Teaching the New Basic Skills*. New York: The Free Press.

National Council for the Social Studies. (2007). http://www.socialstudies.org/standards/.

National Council of Teachers of Mathematics. (2007). http://www.nctm.org/standards/.

National Science Teachers Association. (2007). http://www.nsta.org/standards.

Organization for Economic Co-operation and Development. (2005). *Education at a Glance*. OECD Indicators.

Rutherfor, F. J. and Ahlgren, A. (1990). *Science for All Americans*. New York: Oxford University Press.

Swanson, C. B. (2004). Sketching a portrait of public high school graduation: Who graduates? Who doesn't. In *Dropouts in America: Confronting the Graduation Rate Crisis*. Cambridge, MA: Harvard Education Press.

Walberg, H. J. (2004). Examinations for educational productivity. In Williamson Evers and Herbert J. Walberg (eds.), *Testing Student Learning, Evaluating Teacher Effectiveness*. Stanford, CA: Hoover Institution Press, Stanford University.

Multiple Choice Questions

1. According to the author, the strength of a standardized test is

   a. they are objective, hence accurate

   b. they are reliable and valid

   c. their scientific basis is beyond question

   d. none of the above

2. Teacher made tests are better than any other type of assessment because

    a. the teacher knows exactly what was taught and how

    b. the teacher knows his/her students and what they should learn

    c. both a. and b

    d. none of the above

3. American schools have a high school graduation rate that is

    a. significantly higher than most developed countries

    b. about the same as other developed countries

    c. lower than most developed countries

    d. somewhat higher than other developed countries

4. These questions represent

    a. what the author says we should be testing in schools

    b. are examples what we shouldn't be testing in schools

    c. both a. and b

    d. how teachers assess students is irrelevant

5. The purpose of American education must be to

    a. prepare students for college

    b. prepare students for a career

    c. prepare students to be life-long learners

    d. help students be happy with themselves

6. One of the greatest mistakes teachers can make is

    a. to under-estimate the importance of standardized tests

    b. to over-estimate the importance of standardized tests

    c. to expect students to become engaged in deep meaningful conversations in the classroom

    d. to use publisher prepared tests

7. According to the author which of the following is the most important for students to memorize?

    a. state names and capitals

    b. the composer of certain pieces of classical music

    c. that Shakespeare is considered the greatest author in the English language

    d. both c. and d

8. What is the author's position about government mandates for American education?

    a. as elected officials responsible for the Nation's schools their opinions are generally in the best interest of students

    b. although they have good intentions, they are often times mistaken about what is and should be happening in America's schools

    c. it doesn't matter because teachers have no say over what elected officials do

    d. too many officials are critics of America's schools and support efforts to undermine what educators are doing

9. The way to help students learn and enjoy school is to

    a. have teachers teach students to understand and appreciate a discipline instead of simply covering the material

    b. use more hands-on activities

    c. help students understand the assessment process so they will do better on tests

    d. all of the above

10. The problems in America's schools are primarily the result of

    a. teaching strategies that are so controversial the public doesn't support them

    b. lack of adequate funding

    c. the tension between teachers and administrators

    d. none of the above

Why Kids Hate Special Education: The Unfulfilled Promises of the IDEA

JERRY WHITWORTH

TEXAS WOMAN'S UNIVERSITY

In 1975 what was considered to be a landmark piece of legislation was passed by the U.S. Congress. It was known at the time as P.L. 94-142, the Education for All Handicapped Children Act. Proponents hailed the law as the savior for every student with a disability and promised that it would make the school experience rewarding and successful for everyone. Opponents condemned it as a catastrophe for school districts and claimed that it would destroy school budgets and lower the quality of education in our schools. History has shown that neither side was completely right or completely wrong. The reality of P.L. 94-142, now known as the IDEA, is that while it has accomplished some remarkable things, its potential has fallen short of its promise.

Emerging from the Civil Rights movement of the 1960s, the IDEA was envisioned as a law that would transform schools into places of achievement and success for all children, especially those with special needs. It was a response to decades of acknowledged discrimination, exclusion and inadequate instruction in our schools for students with disabilities. In fact, the original law's first words, its preamble as it were, proclaimed that "All children are entitled to a free, appropriate public education." In this sense, the law has as its guiding vision schools that lead to high levels of achievement for everyone. The IDEA proposes doing this by carefully identifying the individual strengths and needs of each student with a disability and then carefully and collaboratively developing an individual plan to meet the unique needs of that student. This individualized education program, or IEP, is developed by a team of educators and other professionals and includes parents/guardians and the student. The intent of the IEP team is to determine the goals, objectives, services and resources necessary for the student to be successful in school and in life. The team is required to specify how progress toward objectives will be assessed and monitored.

The IDEA also recognizes the importance of quality teachers on the achievement of students with disabilities. The law provides funding for recruiting, retaining and preparing quality special education personnel and requires each state to develop and implement a Comprehensive System of Personnel Development for special education. Funds are also distributed under the IDEA for research and adoption of promising practices in instruction and services for students with disabilities.

Over the past thirty-one years, the IDEA has transformed special education services in our nation's schools, but has that transformation really accomplished what we want it to and what it was meant to accomplish? Has it, in fact, led to better outcomes for all students, not just students with disabilities? And, if it has, why do so many people, teachers, administrators, parents, and the students themselves, dislike "special education" so much? Is special education really "special" or is it just another bureaucratic nightmare for teachers and administrators?

Does it really do anything to help kids? The answers to these questions, like the law itself, are quite complex. Like for many great and noble ideas, reality has a way of introducing unforeseen barriers and uncontrollable variables that can force even the best of intentions over the cliff of frustration and anguish.

A LITTLE HISTORY

For much of our history, educational services to children with disabilities have been either non-existent or inappropriate and inadequate. For many centuries there was no attempt to educate these children, since it was widely believed that they were incapable of learning. Most early records refer to individuals with disabilities in ways that make it difficult to determine whether those referred to were mentally retarded, mentally ill, or deaf and unable to communicate. In many societies, a father could determine whether he wanted to keep a newborn infant. If he didn't, the infant might be thrown off a cliff, left in the wilderness, or by a roadside. Such practices were usually justified by the common belief that such individuals were possessed by demons or evil spirits and that the actions were not taken against the child, but against the demons. At the very least, if infants who were different did manage to survive, they could expect a life in which they were ignored and abused by the rest of society.

As the middle ages approached, this situation was still the norm with rare exceptions. Occasionally, for instance, members of the nobility would employ private tutors for their child. This was most often done for children with hearing impairments. For the most part, though, children who had disabilities were not allowed to attend school or to engage in any type of formal learning experience. Slowly, though, the picture began to change. During the latter part of the 16th century, a Spanish monk, Pedro Ponce de Leon, was successful in teaching a small group of pupils who were deaf to speak, read, and write. This major breakthrough led to a reversal of the official position of the Catholic church that individuals who were deaf and could not speak could not think and were, therefore, uneducable, a position originally put forth by Aristotle.

Another development during this time was Itard's work with Victor, the wild boy of Alveryon. Jean Marc Gaspard Itard was a young French physician who was assigned the task of trying to civilize Victor, a young 12-year old boy found wandering in the woods near the small French village of Alveryon in the late 1700s. He evidently had lived in the woods among wild animals most of his life. Victor was totally uncivilized and was considered a "hopeless idiot" by virtually everyone who met him. He had no language, other than animal-like grunts and noises, and no social skills at all. However, Itard was convinced that he could teach Victor language, thereby taking away his disability.

Itard, generally acknowledged today as the "Father" of special education, eventually abandoned the project, considering it a failure. However, many of the techniques he developed to teach Victor are still in use today and formed the beginning of education for people with disabilities. Edouard Sequin, Itard's student, emigrated to the United States in 1848 and brought Itard's teaching methods to this country. The methods Itard, Sequin, and their successors developed were revolutionary for their time and are still used today. These methods include:

1. Individualized teaching built around the child's characteristics rather than a prescribed curriculum;

2. An emphasis on stimulating the child's senses to make the child more aware of educational stimuli;

168

3. A carefully sequenced series of educational tasks that start with fundamental or basic skills the child is capable of performing and moving gradually to more complex skills;

4. Careful arrangement of the child's environment so that the structure of the environment and the student's experience with it allow for a natural learning experience.

These early pioneers began to generate the idea that people with disabilities were capable of much more than society had assumed, and might even be able to lead somewhat "normal" lives.

In the United States the development of educational services to children with disabilities paralleled that of Europe, although it was about fifty years later. The first institutions were "asylums" for the sensory impaired. A difference in the United States was that these institutions were usually funded and supported by state governments. In fact, it was regarded as a sign of a state's maturity and sophistication to have institutions for individuals with sensory impairments.

The introduction of public education for students with disabilities began toward the close of the 19th century with mentally retardated children being the first to receive services in the public schools. Such classes were attempted in New York, Cleveland, and Providence, Rhode Island before 1900, but they tended to be classes for "problem children" and probably included more non-retarded children than children with disabilities.

Early in the 20th century, several cities tried gathering groups of students who had been previously unschooled and who for the most part were mentally retarded. The schools were interested in returning these students to "normalcy," meaning normal learning ability, but for the most part they were not successful. With compulsory school laws being passed in this country, came the problem of providing education for all children, even those with disabilities. Since children with sensory impairments (hearing, vision) were generally served in institutions, this meant mainly children with mental retardation.

However, many of these classes included students having behavior problems with low academic performance. There was little attempt to determine the cause of students' low school performance, or to differentiate in identification or programming. Indeed, little attempt was made to understand various disabilities and their impact on learning, and what knowledge did exist was often inaccurate and discriminated against the poor and minorities. As a result, special education often became a "dumping ground" for students who could not be educated successfully in the general education setting. Those who had difficulty learning there were simple banned from the school.

The battle to win an appropriate education for students with disabilities culminated in the passage of the Education for All Handicapped Children Act in 1975. It was actually a civil rights battle that mirrored the battle in the 1950s and 60s by African-Americans to win equal educational opportunities. In the early 1970s parents and professionals challenged a number of state laws that had limited the rights of people with disabilities. These actions were primarily based on the Fourteenth Amendment to the U.S. Constitution which states, *All persons born or naturalized in the United States, and subject to the jurisdiction thereof, are citizens of the United States and of the State wherein they reside. No State shall make or enforce any law which shall abridge the privileges or immunities of citizens of the United States; nor shall any State deprive any person of life, liberty, or property, without due process of law; nor deny to any person within its jurisdiction the equal protection of the laws.*

The fact that many states were denying the right of an appropriate education to some of its citizens (those with disabilities) while providing it to others was argued to be unequal protection of the law. The courts began to agree with this argument, ordering state after state to remedy the situation. The eventual outcome was the 1975 law guaranteeing a "free and appropriate public education" to all children. This law, which today is known as the Individuals with Disabilities Education Act or IDEA, has had a major impact on public schools and is the main mechanism directing and guiding how schools educate students with disabilities. It has, in many ways, been a highly controversial and debated law and has spawned a considerable number of court cases to further define and clarify its provisions and requirements.

Yet, while the IDEA included a number of provisions to protect the right of students with disabilities to educational opportunities, the way those opportunities were provided left much to be desired. To understand this, we must take a look at the historical development of our public system of education.

In 1858 Samuel Cartwright coined the term "dreptomania" to describe the condition that caused slaves to run away from their masters. The institution of slavery was considered to be right and acceptable, so, if a slave ran away, the reasoning went, there must be something wrong with the slave. This illustrates society's tendency to assume that when a person does not fit into an institution of society, then the problem must be with the person, not with the institution. This can be seen in our public school system.

Our present system of education acquired its structure around the turn of the twentieth century. In the midst of the industrial revolution, our country was undergoing tremendous changes. Industrialists, concerned about the supply of educated workers for their factories, helped design the modern public school. That is why many of the school buildings built during the first part of this century look very similar to factories built at the same time. The similarities didn't end there, either. The structure of the school resembled factory assembly lines, with rows of desks occupied by obedient students, working their way quietly through a rigid, lock-step curriculum. This produced the type of workers that the factory owners needed, and it was, after all, an efficient way of educating children.

One of the problems with this system is that, although the needs of business and industry have changed substantially over the intervening decades, the structure of our public schools has not changed a great deal. We still see many schools operating according to a factory model with students in neat rows working on the same thing, in the same way, at the same time, with very little interaction with one another—schools with little tolerance for diversity.

In much the same way as a factory assembly line is set up to standardize parts and assembly, so our schools operate according to a prescribed structure. The majority of students do all right in this system—many of them even excel. But, when a student comes along who does not do well, the assumption is that the problem is the student's. We tend to believe that our system of education is correct and appropriate. Seldom does it occur to us to change the system. We determine that it is the student who must change. So, in much the way a nonstandard unit is pulled off an assembly line, we "pull-out" these students who don't "fit" in with our system. Our intention is to "fix" them and then return them to the general education system.

This is referred to as the child pathology perspective of education in which the pathology is assumed to be within the child, rather than the system. This perspective has a number of drawbacks:

- It places unnecessary limits on students.

- It often operates on a "watered-down" curriculum.

- It rejects those who need help the most.

- It results in low self-esteem on the part of students.

- It sets unnecessarily low expectations.

- It can be seen as punitive.

- It develops disaffected learners.

- It creates drop-outs from school and from society.

A growing dissatisfaction with this system and a growing realization that there must be a better way of educating eventually led many educators, parents, and advocates to the door of inclusion, which today is perhaps the most controversial and debated aspect of services to students with disabilities.

THE IDEAL VS. THE REALITY IN SPECIAL EDUCATION

Although the IDEA was designed to correct some very real and very serious problems, the implementation of the law itself has been problematic. Skrtic (1991) pointed out over a decade ago that there is an ever widening chasm between the original purpose of special education and its actual practice. And, as Sailor and Roger (2005) noted, special education has evolved over the last three decades into a system that often has only loose connections to the general education system. The National Education Association (2006) observed that the promise made in 1975 remains largely unfulfilled. Finn, Rotherham and Hokanson (2001) concluded that the IDEA has been enveloped by an orientation to civil rights that has more to do with addressing discrimination than it does with teaching students what they need to learn. In a survey of more than 130 aspiring and practicing principals, Roberson, Schweinle, and Styron (2003) found, as perceived by principals, that special education rates as one of the most critical issues facing schools today.

Fully half of the students served by schools in special education services are diagnosed as learning disabled. Yet, Edgar (2005) has noted that the current condition of schools regarding students with learning disabilities is worse that it was 20 years ago. According to Edgar, a fatal mistake resulted when "we accepted legal remedies for our problems" (p. 171). He goes on to note that those people who are in the trenches, the teachers, administrators, and other professionals, are not trusted to make good decisions. Instead, bureaucrats have developed detailed procedures for schools to follow with students even when those procedures result in inappropriate services.

Gloeckler listed five areas in which the IDEA must be changed in order to fulfill its promises to the youth and children of our nation.

- Reduce paperwork;

- Focus on program quality, not process;

- Base accountability on performance;

- Streamline discipline without denying students an education; and

- Provide full funding sooner, not later.

There are multiple reasons why special education has not fulfilled its promises and why many children, and teachers, end up hating special education. Some of these are systemic, some are inherent in the nature of the

171

field itself, and some are of our own making. The responsibility is shared by everyone, by special and general education teachers, by administrators, by government officials, by university professors and by parents. Unfortunately, it is the students themselves who end up bearing the impact of these problems.

Underfunded Mandate

When the federal special education law now known as the IDEA was first debated on by Congress, much of the discussion centered on its high anticipated cost. School boards and school administrators warned that it had the potential to bankrupt school districts. To address this concern, the law's proponents inserted special wording in the act. The wording promised that the federal government would pay the "excess costs" of services provided as a result of the law. And, when the legislation first began to be implemented, the federal government kept its promise. Funding was more than adequate. In fact, in the first few years of the law it was sometimes difficult to spend all of the money schools were given. And, the more children we put into special education, the more money we received. Rules and regulations for identifying and placing students were lax and oversight was inconsistent. There became an incentive, therefore, to identify and place more and more students into special education programs.

Today, however, the situation has drastically changed. The funding has slowed to a trickle, but the rules and regulations have increased exponentially. Teachers now face a disturbing and frustrating mix of too many regulations and too little resources. Pardini (2002) noted that our nation's special education system is the most heavily regulated and under-funded of all federal education mandates. Even though the federal government originally promised to pay the "excess costs" of providing the services mandated under the IDEA, it has never paid for more than 20% of those costs. Pardini concluded,

> "Indeed, there is widespread recognition that, to be meaningful, special education policies must respond to classroom conditions that limit teachers' effectiveness – in particular problems such as inadequate training, unmanageable costs, and too much paperwork" (p. 1).

With this in mind the NEA (2006) has called for full funding of the IDEA, which, in reality, only amounts to part of the actual cost of providing special education services. As the NEA points out, not to do so "creates a burden on local communities and denies full opportunity to all students—with and without disabilities." However, this is not likely to occur in our lifetimes and the issue of inadequate resources is one which will continue to plague both teachers and administers alike and remain a barrier to appropriate services to students with special needs.

Teacher Preparation

It has long been a struggle to determine how to appropriately prepare professionals to teach students with special needs. This problem has been further compounded by inadequate resources, state mandates and regulations, lack of understanding, and market-driven forces. Brownell, Sindlar, Bishop, Langley, and Seo (2005) have identified this as one of the biggest challenges to special education today:

> Special education is facing the daunting challenge of increasing the supply of teachers while simultaneously upgrading its quality. Shortages of fully qualified teachers have plagued special education for two decades, and schools also have struggled to find qualified math, science and ESL teachers. Shortages in all of these fields are likely to worsen as the teaching workforce ages and as statewide initiatives (such as reduction in class size) fuel increased demand. The quality of the teaching workforce also has come under scrutiny, as schools across the country are

initiating standards-based reforms in which teacher competence is linked to student performance on high-stakes assessments (p. 103).

In many states special education teachers are certified as all-level, generic special education. This means that they are certified to teach children with all types of disabilities, at all levels of severity, and from age three through to grade 12. With the complexity of disabilities and needs represented by the field of special education, this is a most unrealistic approach. It is also complicated by the fact that most states place a limit on the number of hours of coursework a university can require of its students. Those pursuing special education certification are often held to the same credit hour limit as someone seeking certification in a much narrower field and grade level. What this often results in are teachers who are inadequately prepared to teach children who often have very severe and complex educational needs.

There is also a move toward getting teachers into classrooms much quicker. This movement has spawned a host of alternative certification programs, some of which short-circuit the preparation of special education teachers even more. The over-reliance on testing as the be-all and end-all of teacher quality has also served to further erode the quality of preparation special education teachers receive. The push to put more adult bodies in classrooms often tends, too, to force preparation programs to admit marginal candidates into their programs.

Teacher Issues

Once teachers have completed their preparation and been placed in classrooms, there are still other issues that create barriers to effectively teach students with special needs. Barbour (2005) noted the demands that the No Child Left Behind Act has placed on special education, often to the detriment of services to students. According to Barbour, the growth of federal and state education mandates are resulting in a "Perfect Storm" that is producing some unique challenges to the survival of special education.

In addition to the lack of funding, the time and paperwork requirements of special education have not only lowered the quality of education to students, but have sent many special educators fleeing the profession. The Council for Exceptional Children reports that 68 percent of special education teachers spend fewer than two hours per week in individual instruction with each of their students and 83 percent spend half a day to one and half days per week in IEP meetings. This is further compounded by issues of dealing with parents and with issues brought about by many of the provisions of the IDEA such as the due process provision that sometimes results in lengthy and exhausting hearings with parents over services to their children. The time and stress involved in such activities take their toll on the special education teacher, reducing the time, energy and attention they have to give to students with very unique and demanding needs.

Kilgore, Griffin, Otis-Wilborn, and Winn ((2003) found in their teacher survey that beginning special education teachers reported a number of contextual factors that caused problems for them while doing their jobs. Among these factors were insufficient resources, student behavior and collaboration with general education. Respondents felt segregated from the general education community and the administrative staff. Richards and Sze (2004) have also pointed out the "marginalization" of special education teachers who are often excluded from the mainstream of the normative setting. This often results in segregation and isolation of the special educator and a lack of access to support, advice, encouragement and new ideas. They believe this is a leading factor in many special education teachers leaving the field.

This often makes it difficult to attract and retain qualified special education teachers in many schools, particularly in those schools that need them the most. The Center for the Future of Teaching and Learning (2004) reported a severe shortage of credentialed special education teachers in California, and this situation is mirrored throughout the country. Prater (2005) has commented on the shortage of teachers in rural areas of the country which is further compounded by the effects of the No Child Left Behind Act as it commingles with the IDEA. The U.S. Department of Education (2006) noted that many school districts are reporting a serious shortage in special education personnel.

There are many initiatives to attract new special education teachers into the profession, but in many ways these initiatives seem pointless without addressing the problem of retention. It seems to do little good to focus so much effort and resources on preparing and hiring qualified special education personnel only to have them leave within a few short years. The U.S. Department of Education (2006) reports that a large number of special education vacancies will result due to special education teachers switching to teaching general education, changing careers altogether, or retiring. The U.S. Department of Education found that of five teacher quality factors in special education the strongest was teacher experience. And, yet, our most experienced special education teachers are leaving the classroom. Whitaker (2005) noted that the literature has identified five factors that impact the retention of teachers in their first year of teaching.

1. An inability to transfer learning from theory into practice,

2. A lack of preparation for many of the difficulties and demands of teaching,

3. Reluctance to ask questions or seek help,

4. The difficulty of the teaching assignment and the inadequate resources provided,

5. Unrealistic expectations and the associated loss of a sense of efficacy.

In the light of these factors, those issues that are forcing qualified special education teachers out of the classroom, such as excessive regulations, lack of mentoring, and isolation must be addressed if we are to have an adequate supply of well-qualified professionals to teach students with special needs.

Contention in the Field

Another factor that interferes with the education of students with special needs is the lack of agreement and focus within the field of special education itself. Special education is constantly changing and shifting and, while many extremely valuable and useful insights into teaching and learning have emerged from the field, there is also significant disagreement on many issues. Perhaps the most volatile issue is the one revolving around the imperative of inclusion. The inclusion issue highlights a leading source of dissension in the special education field. It is essentially a disagreement regarding philosophy and centers on what should be the purpose of special education.

On one side are those who say that the purpose of special education is an egalitarian one and that it should be a vehicle for achieving a more inclusive, tolerant society. This approach is sometimes referred to as the value-driven philosophy because it rests on promoting what is seen as noble and just, emphasizing altruistic values. Proponents of this approach see the promotion of their value system as the most important objective of special education. Inclusion is the leading way this philosophy is implemented. While educational outcomes and achievement are important, they are secondary to the fulfillment of inclusionary principles and practices.

On the other side of the debate are those who believe that the only way value and success can be seen is in the data. Students must achieve and make appropriate academic progress in order for their program to be effective. Where that program is provided and what is provided is secondary to the evidence. Research validated practices and methods are the cornerstone of this philosophy. If it can't be proven to work, then it shouldn't be used in the classroom, say the proponents of this approach.

This debate and controversy also spills out into other areas of special education, including curriculum, strategies, and administrative policies. The field of special education often seems overflowing with fad curriculums, approaches, methods, and programs. Special education personnel tend to use whatever fits their own comfort level and personal philosophy rather than those things that have demonstrated success in improving student learning. The result of all of this is often confusion and inconsistency in the field of special education and lack of appropriate outcomes for students with disabilities. Until teachers, administrators, and researchers can speak with one voice on what is important and effective in special education the field will remain splintered and disorganized.

THE STUDENT IN THE CLASSROOM: WHERE THE RUBBER MEETS THE ROAD

What does all of this mean in the classroom for the student with special needs? How have all of these issues affected the education students receive? Has special education fulfilled its promises to our children? While the IDEA has provided greater access, improved quality, expanded services, and changed attitudes, there are still a number of barriers to insuring that special education is a success for all our students.

First, we still have a system that discriminates against students based on culture and ethnicity. Ferri and Connor (2005) noted that the first part of this century saw two milestones, the 50th anniversary of the Brown v. Board of Education decision and the 30th anniversary of the IDEA. Both laws were designed to improve access and educational opportunities for previously excluded groups of children. Yet, Ferri and Connor conclude that, in many ways, both of these efforts have resulted in unfulfilled promises. In spite of laws, regulation, policies and improved educational methods, our special education classes and programs still tend to be overpopulated by students of color. We have yet to eliminate from special education the vestiges and effects of discrimination.

For all students, special education remains a stigmatizing system that can have an adverse effect on student achievement. Kniverton (2004) found that the perceptions of teachers, parents, and "significant others" has a definite impact on how successful students with special needs are in the classroom. Norwich and Kelly (2004) examined the views of 101 boys and girls 10–11 years of age with moderate learning difficulties and reported far more "bullying" by other students. It would appear that it can be an unpleasant experience to be identified as a special education student.

Add to the above situation the following "drawbacks" to being in special education:

1. Teachers who may be inadequately or improperly prepared;

2. Polices that are more concerned with regulations and legal requirements than with individual achievement;

3. A curriculum that ignores post-school outcomes and successful independent adult living;

4. Programs that are underfunded, lack resources and are more concerned with "political correctness" than individual success;

5. A system that is contentious, inefficient and bureaucratic, and that focuses more on winning "turf wars" than on educating children.

With all of this it is easy to see why special education does not work for many students and why many of them end up with an unpleasant and unsuccessful school experience. We have too often veered off the course we first started on over 30 years ago and, at times, have lost our focus. The political and legal processes have erected barriers that have been difficult to overcome and we have provided our teachers and our students with too little resources to do what needs to be done. If we are to insure that the bright promise launched in 1975 of a successful, satisfying, appropriate and relevant education for all children is truly fulfilled, we have a lot of work left to do.

References

Barbour, B. (2005). A problem-solving model for special education's "storms." *School Administrator* 62(2): 544.

Brownell, M.T., Sindelar, P.T., Bishop, A.G., Langley, L.K. and Seo, S. (2005). Special education teacher supply and quality: The problems, the solutions. In T.M. Skrtic, K.R. Harris, and J.G. Shriner (Eds.), *Special Education Policy and Practice: Accountability, Instruction, and Social Challenges.* Denver, CO: Love Publishing Co.

Center for the Future of Teaching and Learning (2004). Special education: Not so special for some "qualified" teachers in short supply for special education students. *CenterView*, August, 2004, 1–6.

Edgar, E. (2005). Bending back on high school programs for youth with learning disabilities. *Learning Disability Quarterly* 28: 171–173.

Ferri, B.A. and Connor, D.J. (2005). In the shadow of Brown: Special education and overrepresentation of students of color. *Remedial and Special Education* 26(2): 93–100.

Finn, C., Rotherham, A.J., and Hokanson, C.R. (Eds.) (2001). *Rethinking Special Education for a New Century.* New York: Fordham Foundation and Progressive Policy Institute.

Gloeckler, L.C. (2002). IDEA reauthorization: It's time to simplify and focus on performance. In *A Timely IDEA: Rethinking Federal Education Programs for Children with Disabilities*, Washington, D.C.: Center on Education Policy.

Individuals with Disabilities Education Act of 2004, P.L. 108-446.

Kilgore, K., Griffin, C., Otis-Wilborn, A., and Winn, J. (2003). The problems of beginning special education teachers: Exploring the contextual factors influencing their work. *Action in Teacher Education* 25(1): 38–47.

Kniveton, B.H. (2004). A study of perceptions that significant others hold of the inclusion of children with difficulties in mainstream classes. *Educational Studies* 30(3) 331–343.

National Education Association (2004). Special education and the Individuals with Disabilities Education Act. Downloaded November 10, 2006 from http://www.nea.org/specialed. Norwich, B. and Kelly, N. (2004). Pupils' views on inclusion: Moderate learning difficulties and bullying in mainstream and special schools. *British Educational Research Journal* 30(1): 43–65.

Pardini, P. (2002). Special education: Promises and problems. *Rethinking Schools Online* 16: 1–6.

Prater, M.A. (2005). Ethnically diverse rural special educators who are highly qualified: Does NCLB make that impossible? *Rural Special Education Quarterly*, Winter.

Roberson, T., Schweinle, W., and Styron, R. (2003). Critical issues as identified by aspiring, novice and experienced principals. Paper presented at the Annual Meeting of the Mid-South Educational Research Association, Biloxi, MS, November, 2003.

Sailor, W. and Roger, B. (2005). Rethinking inclusion: Schoolwide applications. *Phi Delta Kappan* 86(7): 503.

Skrtic, T.M. (1991). The special education paradox: Equity as a way to excellence. *Harvard Educational Review*, 61, 148–2006.

U.S. Department of Education (2002). To assure the free appropriate public education of all children with disabilities. *Twenty-Fourth Annual Report to Congress on the Implementation of the Individuals with Disabilities Education* Act, Washington, D.C.: Author.

U.S. Department of Labor (2006). Teachers-Special Education. *Occupational Outlook Handbook*, downloaded November 20, 2006 from http://www.bls.gov/oco/ocos070.htm

Whitaker, S.D. (2005). Supporting beginning special education teachers. In T.M. Skrtic, K.R. Harris, and J.G. Shriner (Eds.), *Special Education Policy and Practice: Accountability, Instruction, and Social Challenges*. Denver, CO: Love Publishing Co.

SUGGESTED ACTIVITIES

1. Interview two parents of children with disabilities regarding their experiences with special education.

2. Talk with a special education teacher and a school principal and make a list of pitfalls to avoid in the special education process.

3. View the video "The New IDEA," or "The Adventures of ARD Man." Write a two-page paper describing the historical and legal basis for the major provisions of the IDEA.

4. Brainstorm in groups reasons why it has taken so much legal activity to get school districts to allow students with disabilities to attend school and to provide appropriate services to these students.

5. Obtain statistics regarding the number of special education students that complete high school and either go on to college or obtain employment nationally. Compare these figures to those in your local community.

6. In groups, develop a description of the "Ideal School" that would provide a meaningful and successful education for all students. Share your descriptions with other groups.

7. View the video, "We're Not Stupid!" and write a reaction paper on this video and discuss your paper with other members of your group.*

8. Think about problems that you have had in your life that stemmed from other people's intolerance of certain behaviors or characteristics. How did you feel about that and how did you respond to it? Share your thoughts with members of your group.

9. Observe two special education classrooms in action. Describe the activities in the two classrooms. Include a physical description of the room. Discuss specific teacher behaviors that appear to be conducive to boosting self-esteem and learning in the classroom. Describe the behavior management system used by the teacher. (Remember not to identify the class, the teacher, or any of the students in your observations.)

10. Research one or more of the following topics and write a three-page summary of what you found out about the topic(s).

    a. Inclusion

    b. Attention deficit hyperactivity disorder

    c. Asperger Syndrome

    d. No Child Left Behind and Special Education

    e. Facilitated Communication

11. Investigate and report on how your state reconciles the accountability provisions of the No Child Left Behind Act with the IEP provisions of the IDEA.

12. Rent and view one or more of the following movies:

    a. Mr. Holland's Opus

    b. Dangerous Minds

    c. Stand and Deliver

    d. Goodbye Mr. Chips

    e. Teachers

    f. Music of the Heart

    g. Dead Poets Society

Discuss the strategies the teachers depicted in the movies used to teach students with special needs.

* *We're Not Stupid: Living with a Learning Difference*, Media Projects, Inc., 5215 Homer Street, Dallas, TX 75206.

Suggested Resources

Books

Special Education Policy and Practice, Tom Skrtic, Karen R. Harris, and James G. Shriner. Love Publishing Company, Denver, CO.

Addressing Over-Representation of African American Students in Special Education: The Prereferral Intervention Process, Council for Exceptional Children, Arlington, VA.

Guiding Change in Special Education Services: How to Help Schools With New Ideas and Practices, James L. Hamilton, Ronald G. Havelock. Corwin Press, Thousand Oaks, CA.

Special Education and the Law: A Guide for Practitioners, Allan G. Osborne and *Charles, J. Russo*, 2004, Program Development Associates, P.O. Box 2038, Syracuse, NY 13220-2038. *Critical Issues in Special Education*, James E. Ysseldyke, Robert Algozzine, and Martha L. Thurlow, 2000, Houghton Mifflin, Boston, MA 02116.

Taking Sides: Clashing Views on Controversial Issues in Special Education, MaryAnn Byrnes, 2002, McGraw-Hill Education, Hightstown, NJ.

Critical Issues in Special Education: Access, Diversity, and Accountability, Audrey McCray Sorrells, Herbert J. Rieth, Paul T. Sindelar, and Sindelar, 2003, Addison-Wesley, Boston, MA.

New Directions in Special Education: Eliminating Ableism in Policy And Practice, Thomas Hehir, 2005, Harvard Education Publishing Group, 8 Story Street, 1st Floor, Cambridge, MA 02138.

Videos

The Merrow Report: What's Special About Special Education? Learning Matters Inc. 6 E. 32nd Street, 8th floor, New York, New York, 10016.

Beyond F.A.T. City: A Conversation About Special Education. Public Broadcasting Service, www.pbs.org.

Educating Peter. Available through Direct Cinema Limited, P.O. Box 1003, Santa Monica, CA 90410.

Bittersweet Waltz. Produced by L. Safan. Available through National Down Syndrome Society, 666 Broadway, 8th Floor, New York, NY 10012-2317.

Emerging Issues in Special Education, EnableMart Sales Office

4210 E. 4th Plain Blvd. Vancouver, WA. 98661.

Articles

Greenwood, C. R. Abbot, M. (2001). The research to practice gap in special education, *Teacher Education and Special Education* 24: 276–289.

McLeskey, J., Tyler, N. C, Flippin, S. S. (2004). The supply of and demand for special education teachers: A review of research regarding the chronic shortage of special education teachers, *Journal of Special Education*, 38.

deBettencourt, L.U. (2004). Critical issues in training special education teachers.

Exceptionality 12: 193–194.

Billingsley B.S., McLeskey J. (2004). Critical issues in special education teacher supply and demand: Overview, *The Journal of Special Education* 38: 2–4.

Brownell, M. T, Hirsch, E., Seo, S. (2004). Meeting the demand for highly qualified special education teachers during severe shortages: What Should Policymakers... *Journal of Special Education* 38.

William L. H. (2003). Ten Faulty Notions about Teaching and Learning That Hinder the Effectiveness of Special Education, *Journal of Special Education*, 36.

Websites

http://www.ideapractices.org/ (Information about special education law and recent developments in special education.)

http://www.teachnet.com (An excellent source for teaching ideas and resources)

http://www.indiana.edu/~cafs/ (The Center for Adolescent and Family Studies at Indiana University. Excellent resources and links to other helpful sites.)

http://www.disabilityresources.org/

http://www.nichcy.org/ (National Information Center for Children and Youth with Disabilities)

http://www.cec.sped.org/ (The Council for Exceptional Children)

http://www.taalliance.org/centers/index.htm

http://seriweb.com/

http://www.ed.gov/about/offices/list/osers/osep/index.html?src=mr

MULTIPLE CHOICE QUESTIONS

1. The Individuals with Disabilities Education Act (IDEA) was originally called

   a. the Perkins Supported Education Act of 1973

   b. the Education of All Handicapped Children's Act of 1975

    c. the Americans with Disabilities Act of 1990

    d. the Children's Educational Improvement Act of 1987

2. The IDEA emerged from

    a. the "Space Race" of the late 1950s

    b. the Nation at Risk report of the 1980s

    c. the return of Vietnam War veterans in the 1970s

    d. the Civil Rights movement of the 1960s

3. The component of the IDEA which focuses on helping each child to reach his or her potential is the

    a. the Individualized Education Program, or IEP

    b. the Individual Transition Plan, or ITP

    c. the Student Learning Arrangement, or SLA

    d. the Individualized Accommodation Plan, or IAP

4. The person known as the "Father" of special education is

    a. Samuel Gridley Howe

    b. Horace Greeley

    c. Jean Marc Gaspard Itard

    d. Pedro Ponce de Leon

5. The first formal educational services in this country to individuals with disabilities were

    a. self-contained classrooms

    b. institutions for the sensory impaired

    c. asylums for the mentally ill

    d. private schools started by private citizens

6. The battle in the United States to win appropriate educational services to children with disabilities was based on

    a. the 14th Amendment to the U.S. Constitution

    b. the 22nd Amendment to the U.S. Constitution

c. the Americans with Disabilities Act

d. Brown vs. Board of Education

7. Most students receiving special education services in our nation's public schools are diagnosed having

a. attention deficit disorder

b. mental retardation

c. learning disabilities

d. speech and language disorders

8. The "underfunded mandate" criticism of the federal special education law grows out of what aspect of the law?

a. the individual transition plan

b. the least restrictive environment

c. the free appropriate public education provision

d. the excess cost provision

9. Reasons for the growth of alternative certification programs (ACP's) to prepare special education include which of the following?

a. confusion about how to prepare special education teachers

b. a perceived need to get teachers into classrooms faster

c. a perception that teachers need more "real life" preparation

d. the expense of most university-based preparation programs

10. The approach to special education that involves pulling students out of the system, "fixing" them, and then putting them back is known as

a. mainstreaming

b. inclusion

c. facilitated education

d. child pathology

Whatever Happened to Reading for Fun?

DEBBIE LANDRY, BONNIE GIESE, AND ROXANNE FILLMORE
NORTHEASTERN STATE UNIVERSITY

HOW WE GOT HERE

In the picture book, *Testing Ms. Malarkey* (Finchler, 2003), a class reverses roles with their teacher with thought-provoking results. Of course, thought-provoking incidences are not reserved for well-written fiction. In real life, sometimes things happen which cause us to ponder and look closely at the world. This is true of the writers of this essay. All of them have a strong literature and literacy academic background and each has a personal commitment toward best practices for children of all ages. The road by which they traveled to the contents of the essay is somewhat different, but share common points. The most common point was the observation that children no longer seem to enjoy reading.

Roxanne Fillmore completed her dissertation comparing Children's and Teachers' Choices Awards, looking, among other things, for those aspects of literature that entice children into a piece of quality literature. Consequently, she has several years' worth of the books selected for the two awards in her home library. As a mother of four children, she expected her children to explore the library collection and find joy reading most of the books. For the first few years of the older children's school life, this was the case. Then the family moved to a school district that had adopted the Accelerated Reader program (AR). Things changed abruptly. At first children would take the books out one by one and put them back. They would ask why there was nothing to read. The large library collection was only of use to them as long as it contained accelerated reader books. Once those few were read, the children were no longer interested in reading literature that had "no points" attached to them. If they could not take a test over the text, they were no longer interested in reading the book! She watched her children turn from avid readers, visiting the library every other day because they were reading books under their covers at night to no longer wanting to go. She asked herself, "Whatever happened to reading for fun?"

Bonnie Giese works with teacher candidates as an instructor in the children's literature and language arts classes. Motivating her students to read and in turn motivate the children they will ultimately teach is of high priority to her. As her students discuss their experiences as readers in the public schools, she has noted how pervasive the Accelerated Reader program has been in the lives of these future teachers. A direct tie presented itself between the type of motivation to read the Program uses and the lack of motivation to choose to read on the part of the teacher candidates. Developing life-long readers was the goal she hoped to instill in these candidates, and yet many of them were not readers by choice.

As a classroom teacher in an AR public elementary school, Debbie Landry was required to incorporate it into her curriculum. She experienced first hand the machinations the children would go to in order to accrue their points. Later, as a doctorial candidate, she would discover unexpected responses from parents as they responded to the influence of AR in the lives of the children—a subject her research was not directly testing.

These combined experiences led the authors to write this essay. What follows is a discussion of the purposes of computer-based literacy programs. This will lead directly into a discussion of what the Accelerated Readers Program is, some of its components and how motivational theory is (and is not) incorporated. Since AR claims to be based on Lev Vygotsky's construct of zone of proximal development (ZPD), a brief description of the ZPD will be included.

The essay will continue by presenting the criticisms of the AR from respected leaders in the field and from research. Finally, a seven-step recommendation is made for those districts who have already invested in AR to lessen the negative impact on children and to derive the best that the program does offer.

Purpose of Computer-Based Literacy Programs

Computer-based literacy programs are intended to integrate technology into the curriculum. Because the student can receive instant feedback, these programs excel in differentiated instruction for students, allowing them to proceed at their own rates. The instruction is carried out in front of a computer screen, with minimal interaction between student and peers or between teacher and student. Ability to move to texts deemed as more difficult is controlled by how well the student answers some form of assessment, usually a multiple choice test. There are several computer-based literacy programs in the market. Accelerated Reader is one of the most prevalent ones in the schools today.

What is Accelerated Reader (AR)?

Advantage Learning Systems and School Renaissance Institute (2002) originally published the Accelerated Reader program in 1986. It was sold to schools as a motivational tool in encouraging children to read. Presently Renaissance Learning, a NYSE company, owns and markets the Accelerated Reader Program. It provides pre-kindergarten through grade 12 reading software along with booklists and other optional services. Its purpose is to create better readers through interaction with computers. Most recent information finds AR programs located in approximately 60,000 schools (concentrated mainly in CA, FL, GA, NC, and TX) throughout the United States. Funding for AR comes from regular school budgets, PTA funds, grants, Title I and other sources.

What is STAR?

STAR is the Standardized Test for Achievement of Reading. It is a computer-adaptive, norm-referenced reading test given to determine the reading level of the student. In this test, a student chooses from a list of words the best word to complete a sentence. Once the question is answered, the software delivers the next question, until the entire battery is finished. Instructors can then access testing results that both diagnose reading ability and indicate courses of improvement. STAR also generates a grade-equivalent score that can be used to give a current approximation of a student's ZPD. In order to participate in the AR program, each student is administered the STAR several times during the year. The results are used to determine which books the student will be allowed to read (Reading Renaissance, 1999).

There are three major disadvantages of using STAR to determine reading ability. First, it does not incorporate oral reading comprehension. Oral reading provides a form of scaffolding for reading that is excluded by the format in which STAR tests. Thus, children could understand books at a different level which is not indicated by the test. Second, the testing situation itself provides a context for children that can confound results. To ameliorate the problem, teacher observations would provide additional information which would determine the child's reading level. Finally, reading behaviors of students are not taken into account by STAR and yet this attribute can enhance the child's ability to derive meaning from a text.

DEFINING THE ZONE OF PROXIMAL DEVELOPMENT

Lev Vygotsky (1986) defined the ZPD as a dynamic continuum of independent and assisted activities. It describes learning by any child that can be accomplished with support. This learning often takes place in a social context, such as shared language activities. It includes the child's own structuring of the situation to help in learning, such as using pictures in a picture book or self-speech. While Vygotsky himself did not coin the phrase, educators commonly refer to such support as scaffolding. Working within the child's ZPD is considered to be the ideal learning environment. According to Vygotsky, the less scaffolding the child requires, the closer that knowledge or skill becomes learned and the child, in that area of learning, is moving out of ZPD into what he termed as "Independent Performance." Intensive scaffolding, with minimal learning, means the child is not yet ready for a new knowledge or skill.

The Accelerated Reader Program (Renaissance, 2002) claims ZPD as a basis for their scientific research. As defined by AR, the ZPD is the range of book readability levels suitable for a student, based on his or her responses to a set number of vocabulary words. AR determines readability levels of the trade books incorporated in their program by using an automated Flesch-Kincaid Reading Index. The results are then used to determine which books in the AR program are suitable for the child. The child then selects a color coded book from the correct level. Movement to a different color coded book depends on the retaking of STAR and a resulting score indicating that the child can move to another level.

This method of determining ZPD precludes all other forms of scaffolding. Vygotsky (1978), himself, refuted the idea that testing alone determines what a child is capable of doing because it only measures independent performance.

EVALUATING COMPREHENSION

Accelerated Reader (Renaissance, 2002) relies on testing for comprehension on each book the child reads. It determines this by a computer-generated multiple-choice test. These questions are easily quantifiable, but require a low order of thinking on the part of the child, as determined by Bloom's Taxonomy.

Comprehension studies counter-indicate the reliance on such tests for determining a child's comprehension of reading matter. Much of the research shows that interest in the reading material has a positive impact on comprehension. Further, students with a high interest in a topic are able to read more difficult material than a test would otherwise indicate. Conversely, students with little interest in a topic will demonstrate low comprehension. This is problematic for AR, which does not consider the use of written responses, extension activities, or repeated interaction with the text. In addition, no text-to-text or text-to-self connections are required of students using AR. All of these techniques have been shown to increase comprehension in students and are effective scaffolding techniques.

AR's Plan for Reader Development

The Accelerated Reader Program is designed to start in pre-kindergarten classrooms. These beginning readers are "read to"– listening to stories read to them by their teacher or another adult. Following the story, each child takes a test on the computer to determine how well he or she understood the text. There is an optional program that will read the test to the child which can be acquired at an additional cost.

Developing readers are "read with." This constitutes the children sitting with a teacher, peer, or cross-age peer to read a selection out loud together. "Reading to" experiences gradually move toward "reading with" experiences. During this phase, students are beginning to make connections between letters and sounds and speech to print. These emergent readers make the shift to more difficult books by practicing reading more difficult texts with someone else. Other suggested strategies from this phase are echo reading and repeated reading (Reading Renaissance, 1999).

Eventually, students become "independent" readers—required to read the books on their own and take tests as they complete the books. Time is given during the school day to specifically read books and take the tests. Children are expected to move to "reading independently" as the last step in the program. According to the Reading Renaissance program (1999). When "reading independently," students begin to perfect reading skills and higher order thinking skills according to the Reading Renaissance program (1999). Movement from one type of reader to the next is determined by the way in which the child performs on the tests.

By contrast, studies dating back from 1980 to the present time show that reading achievement occurs at higher rates when free reading time provided for the children is truly free choice (Fillmore, 1992). This free reading time block is scheduled in the day separate from direct reading instruction and reading extension activities.

Motivation Theory and Reading

Motivation theory looks at those aspects that motivate one to change. In the case of reading, one looks at those aspects that cause a child to desire to read. Generally, motivation is divided into two categories: extrinsic and intrinsic. Extrinsic motivation is anything that is created by someone other than the learner and often is done using rewards or punishments. It is the writers' observation that most schools consider extrinsic motivation a reasonable way to get children to exhibit desirable behaviors such as reading. Often such behaviors diminish once the extrinsic motivators are removed. Intrinsic motivation is developed within the learner. While adults set up learning environments that foster such motivations, the learner adopts the motivation as their own and it continues to motivate long after the child is out of the original learning environment.

AR focuses on external motivation that is strengthened by the reward and competitive point system. The company's literature refers to pizza lunches, skating parties, AR stores to shop for rewards, recognition buttons, and other behavior-related privileges. Because AR uses such a heavily infused extrinsic motivation, children run the risk of losing the motivation to read once the rewards are withdrawn. In fact, studies show that students who are motivated by such techniques do indeed show a high degree of reading avoidance, particularly outside school, once the rewards are removed or no longer desirable.

Particularly problematic is the research that indicates that a significant number of children participating in AR leave the program without the normal internal motivators to read. In the Tahlequah public schools, AR is phased out in sixth grade and the district recently added a required literacy class for the seventh and eighth grade because the children stopped reading on their own without the AR present and, when they do continue reading on their own, they lack the ability to analyze the literature. This is proving problematic with passing state tests and even obtaining desired scores on college entrance exams such as the ACT.

The reasons for this lack of motivation to read once AR is no longer a requirement for the child can be traced to the consequences of the AR system. AR discourages teachers' praise when effort on the part of the student is not significant. For example, if the student is not earning enough AR points, the teacher does not include the child in the group that receives the reward. The number of words in a book calculates the points possible and the student's test performance determines how many of those points the child may receive. If the child does not earn at least half of the points, the test will not count at all. Consequently, picture books are worth very few points and large chapter books are worth considerably more points. In such a system as AR, this seems to make sense, but remember that the child can only read those books that are within what is dictated by STAR's determination of the child's ZPD. The 'low-ability' student who is working very hard cannot achieve a point score equivalent to his or her counterpart who has been allowed to test on the chapter books. The child is placed in an impossible situation. Without acknowledging effort, it is easy to see why discouragement and reading avoidance become prevalent with many students. What should be a pleasure (internal motivator for life-long readers) has now become work.

AR's Role of the Teacher

A teacher in a classroom implementing AR has four basic responsibilities. First, (s)he models reading behavior for those students who are in the "read to" and "read with" categories. In the AR program, teachers are expected and encouraged to read and take tests along with students.

The teacher is required to identify sources for external rewards, such as funds for pizza parties or fast food coupons. The reward system is incorporated into the teacher curriculum and classroom management plan. This is to ensure that the students are provided motivation to read and test within the AR system. It also helps motivate each student to read the books designated by AR to be within his or her ZPD.

In addition to motivation, the teacher provides guidance for book selection within the ZPD for each student. The students are made aware of what books they can read in order to accrue points within the system. In many cases, only AR books are available in the class library for the students to read.

Finally, the teacher is required to maintain records of the status of individual students and of the entire class. The last is particularly true if the motivation being used by the teacher requires the entire class to succeed at a goal to get the reward. In some schools, classes need to accrue a certain number of points in order to get the reward. Such a system is usually well intended since some children are not able to accrue the same number of points as others. But the children themselves are well aware of who is contributing points (and who is not) and so the system can backfire with encouraging classroom environments of those who can and those who cannot. Obviously, the teacher must deal with such consequences.

Role of the Library Media Specialist

Since the Accelerated Reader program is primarily housed in the school Media Center, the Library Media Specialist plays a critical role in the administering of the program. The Specialist is expected to generate and distribute copies of AR reading lists for specific grade levels. These lists are made available to both teachers and students. Because the books are central to the students' success within AR, it becomes a selection tool. In other words, if a book has a test, then it should be added to the shelves. With limited funds for building the book collection, the AR lists can easily become the selection criteria for the school Media Center. As a consequence, the traditional role of media specialist/advisor to the reader diminishes with little room for selecting or evaluating books outside of the AR lists. Instead, the media specialist, having pre-coded the books into readability levels by placing a colored dot on the books, directs the students to the books with the color-coded dot that coincides with his or her reading-level group.

As a consequence of working within the AR system, library media centers have achieved reported success in circulation statistics. However, one wonders whether it is worth the cost. The library media specialist has diminished discussions with students regarding theme, underlying messages, character development, or symbolism. In fact, the media specialist is no longer encouraged to participate in the development of higher-level thinking skills in the students which was traditionally part of their role. Will these students who are able to select materials for no other reason than a tangible reward or for the points that are listed on the spine become life-long learners? What is the likelihood that as an adult, the student would even choose to utilize the public library, with the removal of rewards for motivation and coded dots as a selection tool?

ROLE OF THE STUDENT

The AR student has four basic responsibilities in the AR program. (S)he is required to submit to a continuous series of tests. The STAR is taken several times during the school year and is intended to determine which books are available to the student. As books are read, the student takes a multiple-choice test on details from the book. The student reads from a predetermined list of books—books which have been designated by AR as appropriate for that student and that have computerized tests developed for them. The student is expected to be motivated to read by the rewards or punishments that have been chosen by the teacher. Finally, the student is expected to submit to public acknowledgement or obvious lack thereof during assemblies, award nights, or other gatherings.

CRITICISMS OF ACCELERATED READER

It is interesting to note that the major purpose of AR—that of motivating children to read is, in fact, its greatest failure. While children do read copious quantities of books, the long-term outcome for the student is very different. AR's entire system results in de-valuing reading. Pavonetti (2002) found that although children participating in AR schools read more books, once the program is over, they read no more books than before. Chenoweth (2001) found an absence of well-designed and supportive research for AR and suggested that it may turn reading into an empty contest and actually discourage reading in its participants. Pavonetti also found a negative effect in some programs, meaning students read fewer books after participating in AR than before.

Part of the reason that reading is de-valued lies in the way in which the program is structured. Motivational techniques rely on external rewards and, inadvertently, punishments. Such techniques are fairly powerful for a short period of time, but often backfire. Alfie Kohn (1993) cautions against using tangible rewards as motivation because they often lead to diminished motivation. Jim Trelease (2006), one time supporter of the program, now criticizes the mandatory participation aspect, comparing the students to draftees, having no choice as opposed to enlistees, who do have a choice. He is adamant that performance in AR should not be tied to academic grades, a common practice in AR schools, though not one intended by the program.

Experts have pointed out the fallacy of emphasizing testing rather than finding ways to key into the students' needs or interests, both powerful internal motivators. Quizzes do not test critical thinking, or higher-level thinking, but tests the details of a book. Stephen Krashen (2002) suggests that before purchasing AR, and submitting students to these tests, a school should adopt a prudent policy to ensure that high-interest reading material is easily available to students, along with time to read and a place to read. Accelerated Reader discourages independent selection of books by students, denying them access to books outside their range or designated levels. In addition, the program narrows the definition of reading and literature by ignoring comic books, magazines, graphic novels, poetry, songs (Krashen, 2002).

A further irony is the impact of the time spent in reading instruction. AR requires a large block of time to administer, time that is structured into the school week and follows an AR format. It is questionable as to whether AR improves reading fluency, comprehension, or positive attitudes (Krashen, 2003). There is little mention of encouraging the teacher to provide direct instruction in reading strategies as is done in a balanced literacy program. AR does not promote the use of literature circles or engage students in reading extension activities. Extensive research clearly demonstrates that when elementary readers are provided good quality books and access to materials, they read more and do better on measures of reading comprehension and vocabulary (Routman, 1994).

In contrast to what is good practice, Alfie Kohn (1993) points out that students involved in AR skim the book for the facts needed to answer questions on the tests, which is different from the thoughtful engagement students should adopt when they open a book. True free reading time, the one determinate agreed upon by the reading experts and the United States Reading Commission (Fillmore, 1992), disappears. Frank Smith (1978) stated the importance of giving children time to read and to read books of their own choosing. This reading should be independent and within a supportive social context in the classroom. He reminds us that being able to read is one of the basic reasons we become literate. It is how we become life-long readers. Jerome Bruner (1984) maintains that literature is an instrument for entering possible worlds of human experience. This is the driving force in language learning. The teacher invites students into the world of literature through using literature in many contexts—contexts precluded by the AR experience. Consequently, the instructional role of the teacher is minimalized and the contextual learning environment for reading is diminished.

The Media Center is also impacted by the demands of the AR program. The program limits title choice, thus restricting materials selection on the part of both the student and the teacher. Consequently, the teacher fails to make the best use of resources that may be available. In building the AR program, the Media Center restricts collection development, concentrating on those books on the AR lists. For individual schools, the cost of the program is prohibitive enough that after purchasing STAR and the AR CD-ROM's for network systems there are no monies for other materials.

While AR does have the books on their lists sorted out by readability, it does not consider the other aspects of a book that may or may not be appropriate for children. AR does not review books for age-appropriateness or objectionable content. The media specialist, having committed the library funds to the AR program will find books in the collection that may not have been chosen had the ALA recommended policies for book selection been implemented.

No Child Left Behind requires that reading practices in the public school come from scientific research and thus follows certain guidelines. On all of the points required, AR does not meet the criteria of scientifically-based research. In searching for research to support the program, the authors found that much of the favorable research has been conducted by the Renaissance Group itself, or someone closely tied to the group. The empirical or observable data supporting the program is minimal and measures how successful children are in taking the AR type tests rather than external assessments which measure the broader range of literacy. The program has not successfully tested its product with experimental and control groups. Further, there is no statistical analysis to support the AR program. What research has been used to support the program either does not consider the long-term effects of the program, uses their own tests to measure success, or measures minutia such as increased circulation without considering the underlying cause and effect.

The program has claimed Lev Vygotsky's work on the zone of proximal development as the research base on which it stands. This is a shaky base for two reasons. First, the AR program's definition and use of ZPD is far removed from the ZPD concept that was developed as part of Vygosky's theoretical model. Second, in developing a curriculum based on this model, the curriculum itself is a separate model and needs to be researched on its own.

Moats, from the National Institute of Child Health and Development (1995), summarized the reason Accelerated Reader has been so popular in the public schools. She feels educators want to accomplish a quick and easy solution to the reading problem by using computer technology instead of investing in teacher training. Teachers and media specialists, through AR, minimalize their own role as educators by allowing the program to take a prominent part of the learning environment as a stand-alone program rather than a supportive one.

Parents Add their Thoughts

Landry (2005) had unexpected results when parents began to write to her expressing their thoughts on AR. In the following quotes, parents echo many of the concerns of this essay and give a human immediacy to the issue:

- A great deal of pressure for such young students

- I think the AR level and point levels are too public. I think this factor has the potential to make the lower readers feel even more of a failure than they already do because they are not reading at the same level as their peers, and haven't achieved as high an AR level.

- The only concern I have is that sometimes my son wants to read a book that is not an AR book and then he won't or can't read it because he needs more points. I worry that he is not learning to read for the pure joy of reading.

Summary of Criticism

The criticisms of Accelerated Reader fall within three categories. First, its long-term effects on the participants is directly opposed to its mission – that of motivating children to read. This is done through devaluing the reading process and through developing a motivational process which has short-term effectiveness but in the long run creates non-readers. The system makes reading work and only done when required to do so. This is in direct contrast to life-long readers who have intrinsic reasons to read and thus choose to read without external motivation. The second criticism of AR lies in the way it impacts the learning environment for the students. Originally meant to be a supplement to the curriculum, it has been accepted as a stand- alone program. It requires major modification in the schedule, in the Media Center, in budgets and in curriculum. It impacts on how the teacher chooses to motivate students, in the psychological safety of students and in the autonomy afforded the media specialists, teachers, and students. Because of the proscriptive nature of the program and the way it tends to be implemented by schools, it discourages the literacy instructional practices central to higher order thinking and development of internal motivations to read.

Finally, the research supporting the program does not bear close scrutiny. It has a strong internal bias with the researchers too close to Accelerated Reader or the Renaissance Group. Poor research design has been implemented with no control groups or matched groupings. The claim of having Vygotsky's work on the zone of proximal development as the theoretical basis of AR is inadequate since the application of the theory goes contrary to Vygotsky's work and since the entire program, as applied, should be measured for long-term success. External research is much more critical of the program, exposing the failure of the program to motivate children to read on a long-term basis and pointing out inappropriate practice adopted by schools that have purchased it. Further, the research used to support the program fails to meet the standards for scientific research as put forth by No Child Left Behind.

REACHING BEYOND AR

It is the opinion of the authors that the AR program was established with the best intention in mind. Certainly, encouraging children to read is an important educational goal. Somewhere along the way, that goal was lost in a maelstrom of technique and gimmicks. Topping and Sanders (1999) reiterates that what the company offers is a good tool to be used as feedback on student progress–not as a stand-alone program.

In an era where technology entices the child's attention, far too many children choose passive activity as a major way to occupy their time. Unlike watching television, during the reading experience, a child automatically creates mental pictures of the setting and plot described, something not available to the child watching a screen. In addition, the media narrative cannot be stopped for a literary discussion, therefore giving no scope for children to become involved in grand conversations (Tompkins, 2006). Video/television screens do not allow the opportunity for the shared experiences real literature provides and AR does not remedy this problem.

With the large financial investments that schools make into this program, it is reasonable to assume that some classroom teachers will need to work within the constraints of the program. Therefore we suggest some steps, perhaps a seven-step approach, to developing life-long readers. We begin by suggesting that the program be used as a tool or a supplement to a literacy program, and not as a stand-alone system.

Teachers could use the program as a management tool for keeping track of reading amounts and as the motivation that some children might need. This tool could also be used with special education and remedial programs to monitor the reading habits of these students. The feedback could then be used to plan instruction based on the needs and strengths that the program provides.

The AR suggested titles could be used when making decisions about a media center collection. For the most part the books are good quality pieces of literature, but they have been stratified by vocabulary and language use and do not encourage children to browse and select titles based on interest. The titles list could be used as a starting point when selecting materials.

We would also suggest the use of points assigned to specific books be minimized (if you cannot omit them altogether) in order to allow children to select books based on interest. This would allow them to continue to read for enjoyment rather than any extrinsic reward that might be offered. The focus on intrinsic motivation should be encouraged in order to allow interest, pleasure, vicarious experience, the completion of personal goals, and many other motivators to be reached. This focus on the pleasure of reading is directly tied to becoming a life-long reader.

As many of the current researchers have indicated, children need access to good quality literature (Krashen, 2006). In addition to quantity and quality, children need a variety of genres in order to meet their varying interests. Non-fiction is frequently ignored in classroom and library collections, so an added emphasis in this genre would be an important consideration.

Once a collection is in place, it is important to provide the time for leisure reading. That will require some creative scheduling for many teachers. If AR is a requirement for a school or district, this will be even more difficult. This leisure reading time should follow all the guidelines for free reading, especially student choice in materials. The student's choice should not be determined by the teacher or any other person. It is also important that the teacher model the reading activity, and in some cases, share his/her reading enjoyment. While children may not understand all the content in adult reading, they need to know that teachers also read for pleasure in addition to reading for information.

A final step to ameliorate the effects of AR is to incorporate assessments that require higher-order thinking on the part of the reader. Relying on AR's lower level questioning techniques, as incorporated in its tests, suggests to readers that minutia are important, not the theme suggested by the author. Children enjoy becoming involved in the problem-solving aspects of good stories, and assessment should allow them to develop this skill. Bloom's Taxonomy encourages the development of logico-mathematical knowledge. In taking ideas and information and generating new thoughts and conclusions, the reader moves from being a passive learner to one that makes sense of the world not just as a reader but as a learner in many venues. In this final step, the teachers and administrators at AR schools take control of testing and use assessments that not only give data most pertinent to the child as a developing life-long reader, but set the stage for learning at a higher level throughout the child's life.

IN CONCLUSION

In conclusion, we ask again, "Whatever happened to reading for fun?" A program such as the Accelerated Reader takes a potentially satisfying act and makes it automated and joyless. Far too many children choose only to read when the system rewards or punishes them. Far too few of them are becoming life-long readers —individuals who find intrinsic value in reading. It is our hope that teachers and administrators take into account the broad picture of their students as readers and learners throughout a lifetime instead of allowing a program that saps such time, money and effort to permeate a classroom, school, or district with little long-term reward. A literate adult finds reading satisfying, joyful, worth the investment and even fun. Our children should, too.

REFERENCES

Chenoweth, K. (2001). Keeping score. *School Library Journal* 47 (9): 48–51.

Fillmore, R. M. (1992). A comparison of certain literary elements found in the children's and teachers' choices awards for the middle grades for the years 1985, 1986 and 1987. Unpublished doctoral dissertation-name of university not given.

Finchler, J. (2003). Testing Ms. Malarky. NY: Walker Books.

Kohen A. (1993) *Punished by Rewards: The Trouble with Gold Stars, Incentive Plans, A's, Praise and Other Bribes.* Boston: Houghton Mifflin.

Krashen, S. (2002). Accelerated reader: Does it work? If so, why? *School Libraries in.Canada* 22: 24-26.

Krashen, S. (2003). The (lack of) experimental evidence supporting the use of accelerated reader. *Journal of Children's Literature* 29(2): 16–30.

Krashen, S. (2005). Home run research. *Knowledge Quest* 33: 48–49.

Landry, D. (2005). Teachers' perceptions of students' behaviors during standardized testing. No UMI number listed: Proquest.

Moats, L. C. (1995). The missing foundation in teacher education. *American Educator* 19(2): 43–51.

Pavonetti, L. M. (2002). Accelerated reader: What are the lasting effects on the reading habits of middle school students exposed to accelerated reader in elementary grades? *Journal of Adolescent & Adult Literacy* 46: 300–311.

Renaissance Learning. (2002). *How Scientific Research Supports The School Renaissance School Improvement Resources*. Madison, WI: Renaissance Learning, Inc.

Routman, R. (1994). *Invitations*. Portsmouth, NH: Heinemann.

Smith, F. (1978). *Understanding Reading*. NY: Holt, Rinehart and Winston.

Topping, K.J., & Sanders, W. (2000). Teacher effectiveness and computer assessment of reading: Relating value added and learning information systems data. *School Effectiveness and School Improvement* 11(30): 5–37.

Trelease J. (2006) *The Read-aloud Handbook*. NY: Penguin Books.

Vygotsky L. S. (1978). *Mind in society: The Development of Higher Psychological Processes*. Cambridge, MA: Harvard University Press.

SUGGESTED ACTIVITIES

1. You are a first year teacher in a school that mandates the use of AR, but does not support the use of extrinsic rewards. Describe ways that you will use AR in your room with positive results and how you will maintain student motivation.

2. How has the Accelerated Reader impacted your media center?

3. Interview a student, a teacher and a librarian from an AR school. Based on the chapter's content, develop a set of at least five open-ended questions to ask each person. Some questions you might consider asking could be:

   Student: How do you feel about Accelerated Reader?
   What do you like best about it?
   What do you like least about it?
   What makes a person a reader?
   Do you consider yourself a reader? Why or why not?

   Teacher: How do you feel about Accelerated Reader?
   What do you like best about it?

What do you like least about it?
What makes a person a reader?
Do you see your students as readers? Why or why not?

Librarian: How do you feel about Accelerated Reader?
What do you like best about it?
What do you like least about it?
What makes a person a reader?

MULTIPLE CHOICE QUESTIONS

1. Accelerated Reader software is prepared for grades

    a. PreK–12

    b. 1–8

    c. 3–12

    d. PreK–3

2. A criticism of Accelerated Reader Program is

    a. open choice of books

    b. independent selection

    c. limited choice based on levels

    d. low cost of the program

3. Computer-based literacy programs

    a. provide instant feedback to those using them

    b. allow users to proceed at their own rate

    c. result in minimal interaction between the teacher and student

    d. all of the above

    e. none of the above

4. The stated purpose of the Accelerated Reader Program is to

    a. introduce computer-based learning to the child

    b. create better readers through interaction with computers

    c. respond to developmental differences in attention spans

d. all of the above

e. none of the above

5. Accelerated Reader uses which assessment to determine the reading level of those children participating in the Program?

    a. STAR

    b. BEAR

    c. DIBELS

    d. all of the above

    e. none of the above

6. The method used by Accelerated Reader to determine reading level

    a. is predictable and flexible

    b. is optional for the schools

    c. is used to determine which books students will be allowed to read

    d. all of the above

    e. none of the above

7. Motivation for reading is encouraged by the Accelerated Reader program through the systematic use of

    a. free choice of reading material

    b. intrinsic motivational techniques

    c. positive acknowledgment of the child's effort

    d. all of the above

    e. none of the above

8. Criticisms of the Accelerated Reader Program include all of the following except

    a. AR creates life-long readers

    b. discourages the development of internal motivations to read

    c. large amounts of the library budget are required to purchase the program

    d. the program does not provide grade equivalent reading selections for students

9. Motivation theory can be divided into which two types of motivation:

    a. intrinsic and supplemental

    b. extrinsic and intrinsic

    c. extrinsic and extroverted

    d. extrinsic and supplemental

10. The students' role(s) in the Accelerated Reader Program include(s)

    a. submitting a continuous series of tests

    b. reading from a predetermined list of books

    c. submitting to the motivational techniques endorsed by the program

    d. all of the above

    e. none of the above

Why Do Students Hate to Read? Researching the Reading Attitudes and Coping Strategies of University Students

SUSAN ANNE CARLSON
PITTSBURG STATE UNIVERSITY

As an English professor, I've always assumed that my students read what I assigned, whether it was a six-hundred-page novel or a five-page short story. For fifteen years I've assigned quizzes to make sure that students had read, and they usually passed, confirming my illusion that they were reading carefully. But when I asked my students whether they read the assignments, the answer (by the majority) was a resounding "no"; they might read *SparkNotes*, they might skim, but they rarely engage in close readings of the required texts. To study this further, I surveyed 305 Pittsburg State University students and came to the following conclusions:

- Over half the college students in the survey group read only 50% or less of the readings assigned for their classes.

- Students use a variety of strategies, including gathering data from class discussions, grilling the few students who have read, and relying on Web sites (like SparkNotes) to get enough of the reading material to pass their classes.

- What many students call "reading" is really skimming. Only 9% of the students surveyed engaged in active reading in courses not required for their majors.

The purpose of this paper is to explore the gap between what we (as instructors) assume university students read, and what they actually read. This research is just a glimpse into uncharted territory, a survey of three hundred and five students at a small Midwestern college. But this research project also integrates the findings of recent national studies: the ACT College Readiness Report, the National Endowment for the Arts "Reading at Risk" Report, the Spellings Report (published by the Department of Education), and the 2003 findings of the National Assessment of Adult Literacy. After describing the survey, the paper will focus on the following four questions regarding the Pittsburg State University survey subjects:

1. How much do these students actually understand of what they read?

2. What percentage of assigned readings do these students read, in classes related to their majors and in general education classes?

3. Why don't these students read the required texts, and what stops them from reading?

4. What strategies do these students use to avoid reading and still pass their classes?

DESCRIPTION OF SURVEY SUBJECTS AND SURVEY

Pittsburg State University is a small, regional university in Pittsburg, Kansas, with 6,859 students (Bryant, 2006). Since the Fall of 2001, the school has changed its policies from open to restricted admissions: now students need an overall ACT score of 21, or grades of a "C" or better in pre/college high school courses, and/or graduation rankings in the top third of their high school class (*Freshmen Admission Requirements*, 2006). Most of the students come from rural communities in Southeast Kansas and Southwestern Missouri, and are, for the most part, white and middle class. A small percentage of students come from larger urban areas like Kansas City and Wichita.

In October 2006, a twenty-question survey was given out to 305 students in sixteen sections of General Literature, a basic education class required for all Pittsburg State students. The survey focused only on how students completed required reading for their classes.

Because this is a class most students take early in their college careers, the breakdown of survey subjects were mostly freshmen and sophomores, though 23% of the survey subjects were juniors, and 13% were seniors. The survey was designed on the basis of information gathered from three student focus groups. The surveys were kept anonymous, and instructors had no access to individual results. The students were informed of this before taking the survey, so they would feel comfortable enough to tell the truth.

HOW MUCH DO STUDENTS ACTUALLY UNDERSTAND OF WHAT THEY READ?

The survey subjects had trouble understanding their required texts. Overall, 29% said that they felt overwhelmed with the amount of required reading 60% or more of the time. When asked directly how much they understood, 23% of the students said that they comprehended 50% or less in the required readings for General Literature, and 18% said that they understood half or less of the material in their other classes. Roughly then, about one out of every five students is only understanding half or less of what they read in their college classes.

This result seems to reflect the larger nationwide problem of low reading comprehension skills for university students. In the report *Reading Between the Lines: What the ACT Reveals About College Readiness in Reading*, the authors concluded that only 51% of the approximately 1.2 million high school seniors who took the ACT Reading Comprehension Test scored a 21 (the highest score is 36) (ACT Inc., 2006). The *Reading Between the Lines* report shows that the figure was lower for various groups: only 21% of African-American students, 36% of Native American students, and 33% of Hispanic students scored a 21 on this test. (See Figure 1; *Reading Between*, 2006, p. 1.)

These numbers have more of an impact after a description of what the test looks like, and what a score of 21 actually means. The ACT Reading Comprehension Test is a "40-question, 35-minute test" (*Reading Test*, 2006) that requires students to read and interpret various passages from history, psychology, natural sciences, the arts and social sciences (*Content Covered*, 2006). The theory behind the test is that a student who does well will succeed in comprehending college textbooks. A student who scores a 21 on this test could answer about half

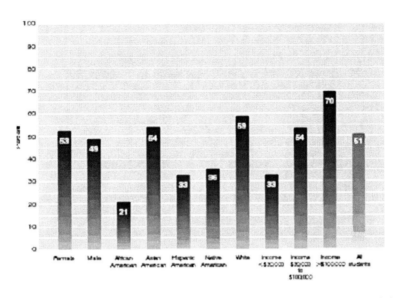

Figure 1: *2005 ACT-tested High School Graduates Meeting ACT College Readiness Benchmark for Reading*[1]

the questions right. This score means that the student reader can get the main idea in a paragraph, locate important details, and draw simple generalizations in "uncomplicated passages" (*College Readiness*, 2006).

This type of student will probably have trouble with complex reading assignments, and may have trouble in demanding classes. According to a 2005 ACT Report, a student with a score of 21 has about a 75% chance of getting a "C" in a college course, and a 50% chance of getting a "B" (*Issues in College*, 2005). An ACT score of 28 is required to show higher-level comprehension and the ability to understand complex texts.

The national ACT study may give us a glimpse into what might be a larger, unexplored problem. If a large percentage of students have lower-level comprehension, then they may not be able to fully comprehend the textbooks, and especially the more difficult primary works, that they are asked to read in university classes. The next question to ask then is *how* our students read.

Many of the questions on the survey were designed to find out what strategies students use when they are reading on their own. Sophisticated readers tend to be active readers—they interact with the text; their books are full of underlines and comments in the margins, questioning or combating the writer's thoughts. It's interesting, then, that in the PSU survey, only 27% of the students used active reading strategies in required readings for their majors, and even less(9%) used active reading strategies for general education courses. That percentage did not increase for juniors and seniors. In other words, three-or four-year students were using the same strategies as the freshmen.

Most of the students (42%), skim briefly, just to get the main points for their assignments in general education classes. Students have different strategies for required reading in their majors: 40% read every word, usually without taking notes, while 26% skim for main points. Another percentage just limit reading to headings and key words: 7% used this strategy in courses required for their majors, and 12% used this strategy in other classes.

Comments on reading were fairly negative. One survey subject commented: "If it doesn't have anything to do with my major, I don't read it!" Another student suggested that instructors "maybe not have us read so much. Reading for my major is difficult. Very boring, in all actuality I haven't read any of it, and have not failed a quiz, it's just so BORING to read!" These and other comments seem to suggest that one reason students find textbooks boring is that they are hard to understand. One implication is that many of the students in this survey group may be struggling to read, or may have already given up.

WHAT PERCENTAGE OF ASSIGNED TEXTS DO STUDENTS ACTUALLY READ?

The Pittsburg State University survey showed that most of the survey subjects start with good intentions: 93% of students buy the books before classes start, or a few days into the semester, and 89% felt that it was very or somewhat important to complete the required reading in courses related to their majors. A large majority, 65% of the students, felt the same way about courses not related to their majors, which would include general education courses.

However, the students' scores were much lower when they discussed the percentage of required reading that they actually completed: 60% of the students read 50% or less of the readings required for their majors. Over half the students in the survey group, 56%, also read only 50% or less of the readings in classes not required for their majors (See Figure 2). A small group of survey participants, 18%, said that they understood 50% or less of what they read for their college classes.

Percentage of Required Reading in Major

		Frequency	Percent	Valid Percent	Cumulative Percent
Valid	0–20%	73	23.9	24.2	24.2
	30–40%	47	15.4	15.6	39.7
	50%	62	20.3	20.5	60.3
	70–80%	79	25.9	26.2	86.4
	90–100%	41	13.4	13.6	100.0
	Total	302	99.0	100.0	
Missing	9.00	3	1.0		
Total		305	100.0		

Figure 2: *Percentage of Required Assignments Students Read*

Percentage of Required Reading not in Major

		Frequency	Percent	Valid Percent	Cumulative Percent
Valid	0–20%	53	17.4	17.5	17.5
	30–40%	55	18.0	18.2	35.8
	50%	64	21.0	21.2	57.0
	70–80%	76	24.9	25.2	82.1
	90–100%	54	17.7	17.9	100.0
	Total	302	99.0	100.0	
Missing	9.00	3	1.0		
Total		305	100.0		

Figure 2: *Percentage of Required Assignments Students Read (contd.)*

WHY DON'T STUDENTS READ THE REQUIRED TEXTS?

Before I received the survey results on this response, I had assumed that most students would say that they didn't read because of shortage of time; many of our students work their way through college, or marry young and start families. It's not unusual, for example, for students to work 40 or more hours per week, on top of a full class load. But surprisingly, lack of time was not the primary reason why students didn't complete their reading assignments. Figure 3 shows the five most common reasons students don't read, in order of their popularity on the survey.

Reading is too boring (36%)

Work hours (25%)

Social life (16%)

Reading is too confusing (10%)

Family commitments (6%)

Figure 3: *Reasons Students Don't Read*

The prevalent reason that the survey population wasn't reading was a dislike for reading *itself*. It's unclear, however, how those two terms "boring" and "confusing" are linked in the students' minds. The students may have just found the required texts dull, or they might have had trouble reading any type of complex text, and so they categorize college reading as "boring."

This disinterest in reading is also reflected nationally. In 2004, the National Endowment for the Arts (NEA) published the results of a national survey taken in 2001–2, in which they reported the leisure reading habits of over 17,000 Americans (*Reading at Risk*, p. viii). The NEA was interested in two issues: in a year's time, how much literature do Americans read for fun, and how many books do they read overall, in any category (p. ix). For the purposes of the study, the NEA defined literature as any type of fiction, drama and poetry, without any distinction as to the quality of the material (p. 2).

What this study found was depressing, though not surprising. Less than half of Americans read any kind of literature (p. ix). The group that was reading the least, after adults over 75, were the youngest adults (18–24) (p. xi). Only 42.8 percent of this group reads literature, a "rate of decline 55 percent greater than that of the total adult population," and a significant drop from the first year of this study in 1982 (p. xi). The study showed however, that this group had maintained their interest in television, and increased their interest in new media like the Internet and video games. According to Dana Gioia, the Chairman of the National Endowment of Arts, this is a worrying trend, since young people seem to be avoiding the more complex task of reading for video games and the Internet, which "foster shorter attention spans and accelerated gratification" (p. vii). Gioia concludes that "at the current rate of loss, literary reading as a leisure activity will virtually disappear in half a century" (p. xiii).

If the NEA study is accurate, then our college students are consistently choosing electronic media over literary reading. And they are also, on a national level, losing the ability to process complex texts. The National Assessment of Adult Literacy (NAAL) has just published their 2003 assessment of 19,000 Americans aged sixteen and older (White, 2006, p. iii). Though the literacy study was designed to find out Americans' ability to research issues into their physical and mental health, the study still remains one of the most recent and detailed literacy surveys. The news is not good. In their survey, the NAAL found "fewer adults" with the highest level of literacy in 2003, compared to their survey in 1992 (Demographics, 1996).

To understand "complex and challenging" texts, the adults surveyed would have had to reach the level of "proficient" in prose literacy (White, p. 5). The NAAL defines prose literacy simply as the ability to "search, comprehend, and use information from texts that were organized in sentences or paragraphs" (p. iv). A "proficient" score would mean that students could read and infer information in "lengthy, complex, and abstract prose" (p. 5). Only 27% of survey participants with a bachelor's degree could reach a level of "proficient" in prose literacy (p. 4). Of this group 60% had a lower level of literacy in the "intermediate category" (p. 14)— a category where the participants can understand "moderately dense" prose texts, and make simple judgments from the language (p. 5). For example, someone in this level could follow directions on a graph to "determine a healthy weight range" for a person on a body mass index (BMI) scale, but could not evaluate "which legal document is applicable to a health care situation" (p. 5).

What do all these studies mean for our students? The larger studies suggest that many of the young people in our university classes may not have the complex literacy skills required to understand what they read, especially when the required reading moves from textbooks to more difficult primary texts (a novel by Charles Dickens, for example, or *The Communist Manifesto*). Many of our students are not learning, in the sense that they are not processing difficult ideas in texts on their own time. In other words, many of our students may not have the reading skills to actually acquire a real university education.

WHAT STRATEGIES DO STUDENTS USE TO AVOID READING AND STILL PASS THEIR CLASSES?

If students have lower literacy levels and follow ineffective reading strategies, then they must be using some techniques to avoid reading, while gathering enough information via other means to pass their classes. The survey from Pittsburg State found that students do use a variety of strategies to avoid reading and still do well in class. In one of the focus groups we used prior to the survey, the students said that their primary goal was to get the *essential information* (what will appear in the test), the *bullet points*, without having to read the required texts. The following are the methods used by the students in the Pittsburg State Survey.

Using Technology to Avoid Reading

The most popular Web sites that the students use regularly are the following: Google sites (39%), SparkNotes.com (16%), Wikipedia (13%), and Yahoo (12%). All of these Web sites are designed to give a superficial overview of the text quickly, defining key terms and ideas. SparkNotes, for example, now owned by Barnes & Noble, served 10 million registered users as of January, 2005. Their summaries have expanded from literature, and now include detailed entries on subject areas like economics, psychology, health, and music (Wikipedia, 2006). Though originally designed as an introduction to texts, students now often use these sites (often offered free on-line) as replacement texts for the original works. In the English Department at Pittsburg State, for example, instructors have often heard complaints from students when they are asked to read a text that is not summarized on SparkNotes.

Using In-Class Activities to Avoid Reading

Students seem to rely most heavily on in-class strategies. They take notes in class, or rely on student comments during class discussion to collect basic information about the texts. Students especially like PowerPoint demonstrations for this purpose, whether the software is used during class, or displayed on corresponding Blackboard sites. Several students in the focus groups said that class information, not reading, was the way they gathered information to pass the classes, and this was one reason why they found it especially annoying when professors did not talk about the tested material in class.

Relying on Other Students to Avoid Reading

Finally, a popular strategy is to rely on the few students who do read to gather information quickly. Students said they often e-mailed the student who did read before class to get the basic information for quizzes or tests, or grilled the student in the minutes before class began. One group of international students had a more complex system: they would choose one student who had read all the material and had understood it. They would all get their content information from that student, either through e-mails or group discussion. That student was then rewarded throughout the semester with free meals.

RAMIFICATIONS OF THE STUDY

As this article stated earlier, this research project (and survey) is just a glimpse into the reading habits of university students. But if, as the national studies suggest, poor reading is a national trend for university students, then the situation is more serious. If there is a systematic avoidance of complex reading at the university level, then many students are not really developing complex thinking skills. Many of these students may be graduating without the ability to write or think beyond a simplistic level, despite earning a college degree.

This has serious ramifications for these students' futures in the job market. According to one of the leading experts on U.S. employment, Dr. Phil Gardner, employers are searching only for the best graduates, a small group of candidates who are "better-educated, ambitious, team players, technically adept, able to seek a balance in their lives and highly confident" (Michigan State University, 2005).

With competition from recent graduates, boomers looking for new careers, and displaced or laid-off workers, the recent college graduates have to prove themselves to be the most competent in order to stay in the running (Michigan State University, 2006). This would include a high G.P.A. and the ability to problem-solve by synthesizing complex material, whether that material is business-related (sales reports), or technological (instruction manuals for new types of software). The companies at career fairs, says Gardner, are planning on "only hiring a limited number of highly competitive students from each campus" (Michigan State University, 2006). Students who don't have the critical thinking skills to work at this level, and who haven't prepared with internships, may be left out in the cold.

THE FEDERAL GOVERNMENT COMES TO THE RESCUE

The U.S. Department of Education, aware of the same recent national studies, has decided that American university students are not ready for the global marketplace. On September 26, 2006, Margaret Spellings, Education Secretary for the Bush Administration, issued the findings of the Commission on the Future of Higher Education (a one-year commission headed by Mr. Charles Miller, the architect of the first No Child Left Behind program in Texas) (Marklein, 2006, p. 1A; Field, 2006). The Commission, which included five corporate executives and three professors, decided that the university system needs "urgent reform" (U.S. Department of Education, p. ix). According to the report, "…there are also disturbing signs that many students who do earn degrees have not actually mastered the reading, writing, and thinking skills we expect of college graduates" (p. x).

The Commission's solution is to create a "robust culture of accountability and transparency" (Kingsbury, 2006). It has requested that the Fall 2006 Session of Congress consider connecting the $80 billion of federal student aid (Friel, 2006) to "accountability standards," which would include creating a database to track anonymous individual students throughout their college years. Though the report has called for "increased accountability through assessment" (Field, 2006), Ms. Spelling has stated that she is not calling for standardized testing, and that the report simply starts the conversation on improving the ways colleges train students. Ms. Spelling has asked Congress to create legislation that would put the intentions of the report into policy. The Department of Education has encouraged the Fall 2006 Session of Congress to discuss the Commission's report, but impending legislation and debate on this issue is still unclear (Marklein, 2006).

FINAL COMMENTS

The gap between our expectations of university students' literacy and the reality cannot be ignored. It's clear from the recent Spellings Report that the U.S. Federal Government is intent on fixing the problem, and has little confidence in the ability of the universities to fix poor student achievement on their own. I end this article with three suggestions for actions that individual universities and faculty can take to begin dealing with the issues of student literacy.

1. Find and share preliminary research on student reading. Universities could use a survey to gather data on student attitudes toward reading at their own institutions. If an institution

finds that its students are reading required class texts, and reading at a "proficient" literacy level, then there's no reason for concern. If not, I'd suggest that professors consider the next two options.

2. Teach sophisticated literacy strategies in the classroom. Instructors should no longer assume that college students understand what they read. Instructors should include "active reading" training sessions as part of class periods. This would include showing students how to mark up a text, how to comment in the margins, and how to summarize and react to what they read. Faculty should also ask students openly if they do read their textbooks, and if they understand what they read.

3. Incorporate complex reading texts into classes of all subject areas. This is a suggestion for high schools by the ACT Study, but it also is relevant to university classes. Students learn how to read sophisticated texts with constant practice. This would also mean however, that instructors would have to test students in ways that ensure that the students have understood the reading materials in a way that goes beyond surface knowledge.

This article is just a small glimpse into a larger nationwide problem in college campuses. My hope is that this article may begin discussions that lead perhaps to more research on an issue that, up to now, has not garnered enough attention.

REFERENCES

ACT, Inc. (2006). *ACT Corporate Home Page*. Retrieved October 10, 2006, from http://www.actstudent.org/testprep/descriptions/readdescript.html

ACT, Inc. (2006). Content covered by the ACT reading test. *ACT Corporate Home Page*. Retrieved October 10, 2006, from http://www.actstudent.org/testprep/descriptions/readcontent.html

ACT, Inc. (2006). College readiness standards: Reading. *ACT Corporate Home Page*. Retrieved October 10, 2006, from http://www.act.org/standard/planact/reading/index.html

ACT, Inc. (2006). High school reading not challenging enough, says ACT. *ACT News*. Retrieved November 30, 2006, from www.act.org/news/releases/2006/03-01-06.html

ACT, Inc. (2005). Issues in college readiness: What are ACT's college readiness benchmarks? *College Readiness*. Retrieved December 5, 2006, from http://www.act.org/path/policy/pdf/benchmarks.pdf

ACT, Inc. (2006) *Reading between the Lines: What the ACT Reveals about College Readiness in Reading*. Iowa City, Iowa. ACT, Inc..

Bryant, Tom (2006). Message from President Tom Bryant. Retrieved November 28, 2006, from http://www.pittstate.edu/admit/why.html

Field, Kelly (2006). Uncertainty greets report on colleges by U.S. panel. *Chronicle of Higher Education*, 53, p. 1-1. Retrieved October 10, 2006, from Academic Search Premier database.

Friel, Brian (2006). Spellings turns to higher ed. *National Journal*, 38, p. 80. Retrieved October 10, 2006, from Academic Search Premier database.

Kingsbury, Alex (2006). A federal fix for highered? *U.S. News and World Report*, 141, p. 44. Retrieved October 10, 2006, from Academic Search Premier database.

Marklein, Mary Beth (2006, September 27). College overhaul called 'overdue': Spellings proposes national data tracking. *USA Today*. p. A1.

Michigan State University (2005, November 16). College job market poised to expand in 2005-06. *newsroom.msu.edu*. Retrieved December 7, 2006 from http://newsroom.msu.edu/site/indexer/2575/content.htm

Michigan State University (2006, November 17). Motivated collegians can expect more job opportunities in 2007. newsroom.msu.edu. Retrieved December 7, 2006from http://newsroom.msu.edu/site/indexer/2911/content.htm

National Center for Education Statistics (2006). Demographics. Retrieved December 7, 2006 from http://nces.ed.gov/NAAL/index.asp?file=KeyFindings/Demographics

National Endowment for the Arts (2004). Reading at risk: A survey of literary reading in America. *Research division report #46*. Washington, D.C.: National Endowment of the Arts.

Pittsburg State University (2006). *Freshmen Admission Requirements*. Retrieved December 5, 2006, from http://www.pittstate.edu/admit/fradm-req.html

U.S. Department of Education (2006). *A Test of Leadership: Charting the Future of U.S. Higher Education*. Washington, D.C.: U.S. Department of Education.

White, Sheida (2006). *The Health Literacy of America's Adults: Results from the 2003 National Assessment of Adult Literacy*. Washington D.C.: U.S. Department of Education.

Wikipedia (2006, December 5). Sparknotes. Retrieved December 6, 2006, from http://en.wikipedia.org/wiki/SparkNotes

SUGGESTED ACTIVITIES, PROJECTS AND READINGS

1. Read the 2004 *Reading at Risk* Report published by the National Endowment of the Arts. (You can download this report at http://www.nea.gov/research/ReadingAtRisk.pdf.) After reading the report, please consider the following questions: If the reading of literature is declining so quickly in the American population, are we then headed towards a new kind of literacy, one that is visual, for example? Will the arts follow this, and develop visually (in video games, Internet sites, and film) rather than in books? How do you think this might change the way people process information, the way they read, and the way they think? Write a five-page journal in which you summarize the report in two pages, and then respond to the questions on the next three pages. You can work alone, or with a group of up to two other students.

2. Read the 2006 *Reading Between* the Lines Study published by ACT, Inc. (You can download this report at http://www.act.org/path/policy/pdf/reading_report.pdf.) After reading the report, please discuss how the

results of this study reflect on education challenges in your state. If only 51% of the high school seniors could reach a score of 21 on the ACT, what does that seem to imply about the reading levels of students in your state's high schools, or colleges? How would this lack of reading proficiency affect teachers at both the high school and college levels in your state? Write a five-page journal in which you summarize the report in two pages, and then use the next three pages to describe the results of your discussion. You can work alone, or with a group of up to two other students.

3. The article has a copy of the survey instrument used as an attachment. As an activity, revise the survey to suit the needs of students in your school, and survey a group of students in a class, or a smaller group of students. After the survey, have the students gather in a circle, and ask some general questions to gauge the students' reactions towards the survey, and towards their own reading habits. After holding the focus group, write a 3-page reaction paper where you respond to both the survey results, and the opinions of the focus groups. Did any of the comments surprise you? Why or why not? How do these results change your assumptions about these students' reading abilities and habits?

4. The article discussed the plans of the U.S. Department of Education to "reform" the university system, based on the findings of the Commission on the Future of Higher Education. At the time of the article, the U.S. Congress had just been asked to consider these reforms. What's the current status of this situation? Has Congress acted on any of the Commission's findings? Write a five-page paper in which you discuss the current reform suggestions of the U.S. Department of Education. The paper would also track what, if any, changes have been acted upon by the U.S. Congress. Finally, discuss whether any of these changes will have an impact on the public schools and/or universities in your state.

MULTIPLE CHOICE QUESTIONS

1. What percentage of the students surveyed read only 50% or less of the readings assigned for their classes?

    a. less than 10%

    b. about 25%

    c. about 40%

    d. over 50%

2. How many students at Pittsburg State University participated in this survey?

    a. 53

    b. 100

    c. 305

    d. 2000

3. What percentage of students understood 50% or less of their readings for General Literature?

    a. 10%

    b. 23%

    c. 50%

    d. 81%

4. What was the main reason students in the survey said that they didn't read their textbooks?

    a. Their social lives were too active

    b. Reading textbooks is too boring

    c. Reading textbooks is too confusing

    d. They have too many family obligations

5. The 2004 National Endowment for the Arts study tracked the personal reading habits of 17,000 Americans. After the group over 75, the adults reading the least literature were in the following age bracket:

    a. 18–24

    b. 25–35

    c. 36–45

    d. 60–74

6. In 2004, when did Dana Gioia, the Chairman of the National Endowment for the Arts, expect leisure reading of literature to "virtually disappear" in the United States?

    a. 10 years

    b. 50 years

    c. 100 years

    d. 200 years

7. Why do the survey subjects use sites like SparkNotes for literature classes?

    a. To gain essential details of plot information without reading the original text

    b. To get key terms and ideas from a text summary

c. To pass exams and quizzes without reading the original text

d. All of the above

8. What other strategies do students use to pass their classes without reading the required texts?

    a. Take notes in class

    b. Get basic information from students who did the reading

    c. Rely on PowerPoint lectures or Blackboard sites

    d. All of the above

9. Who was the Secretary of Education in the Bush Administration at the time of this article?

    a. Dr. Phil Gardner

    b. Ms. Margaret Spellings

    c. Mr. Charles Miller

    d. Mr. Michael Chertoff

10. What are some ways that university faculty can improve student literacy on campus?

    a. Teach the students more effective ways to use SparkNotes and Google

    b. Teach sophisticated writing strategies in the classroom

    c. Incorporate complex reading material into classes

    d. Encourage students' abilities to interpret nonprint media

How We Help Hapless Students Hate School

UNIVERSITY OF MISSOURI-COLUMBIA

Education, learning and manipulating symbols are often regarded as something done by someone else—those who somehow "get it" or "know more than we do."

Robert Caro's biography of Lyndon B. Johnson (1982) describes how the young Texas congressman and his wife, Lady Bird, attended parties at the Washington home of Alice Longworth Roosevelt in the 1930s—cocktail parties populated with writers, artists, literati, policy wonks, and politicians. Lady Bird felt inferior when she listened to people talk about books—books she had not read or even heard of—so, she began going to the library and reading the volumes she heard discussed over martinis. She soon discovered that the glittering literati at the cocktail parties knew far less of what they were talking about than she did. *She* had actually read the book, the whole book—and often they seemed not to have done so at all. Lady Bird conquered her feelings of being "hapless," of being unaware, even intimidated. Her listening and thinking generated more cycles of reading, speaking, and listening—all the while developing her own critical thinking. She conquered her haplessness. Legions of people never do.

Is this representative of what teachers hath wrought? I do not know. But I do know that, after 36 years as an English educator and teacher of teachers, and after decades of advancements in teaching and learning, the "critical mass" of distaste for school remains more robust than we like to admit. In this context, I view most students as "hapless" because they dislike school for reasons that should not exist in the first place. That is, most students are "right" in the reasons for their hatred of school; it's just that they are not yet able to articulate their reasoning in detail. In this chapter, I will explore some of those reasons why students "hate" school, when in fact, they should love it. My comments are based on my own experiences as a secondary school teacher and occasional teacher of middle and elementary students; as a faculty member of a university English Department (directing its Campus Writing program) and as a faculty member and department chair at a large, research-extensive university. Most of my comments will focus on the teaching and learning of thinking, reading, and writing, which are crucial for success in most endeavors. I also hope that these observations will apply to most subjects and grade levels.

Regardless of what anybody thinks, the fact remains that writing, reading fiction and nonfiction texts, exploring language, reading and composing electronic media—affect all school content areas, as well as students' ability to use language and other symbols for professional/career purposes. Even more important is the fact that students' abilities to process and use symbols affect their own identity development and personal growth (Csikszentmihalyi, 1991). In short, symbols not only reflect the world, but also *create* it.

Of course, in spite of these powerful qualities, too many students somehow manage to hate writing, reading, speaking, and language study for many reasons. I have categorized these reasons into the following three, overlapping groups: 1. We (educators, administrators, et al.) often neither explain, nor demonstrate why and how language and other symbols are important to students; 2. we often do not provide students with choices in their work; and, 3. we often emphasize products over processes.

STUDENTS HATE SCHOOL BECAUSE WE DON'T EXPLAIN OR DEMONSTRATE ITS IMPORTANCE

We have long failed to articulate and demonstrate—convincingly—why English benefits people. Here, I will note only the five most important reasons. Firstly, students fail to understand the importance of school because we do not sufficiently emphasize writing and reading in all subject areas. While we are in better shape here than we were thirty years ago, we are still failing to *systematically* address "reading and writing across the curriculum." Such writing instruction has to be applied in all content areas, reinforced through consistent teacher development, and supported by administrators through spirit as well as funding. Not doing so, or only paying lip service to writing across the curriculum, prohibits students from seeing how and why literacy matters in their other classes. If reading and writing are defined as important only in one class—and students cannot see the transfer of these skills to other courses—then it becomes an isolated anachronism of the English class. If students write regularly in all their courses, then fluency will more likely be developed. If they write regularly in all their courses, then they are more likely to use writing as a way to explore and internalize course content—to solve problems. For this to occur, teachers in all disciplines need to accept the fact that writing and language are integral to thinking and learning—but too many teachers still do not believe this. They believe that their field, say chemistry or math, is cleanly apart from and separate from language. The old adage remains true: *If you are a teacher IN English, then you are a teacher OF English.* I have never believed this. I could have learned college algebra if my instructor could have explained to me *why* X happened to have a value of 3. He could not. In frustration, he would yell, "It just *does!*"

However, humans are obligated to use language to demystify the world. We've long practiced this. In ancient times, inventing and telling creation myths helped us demystify the great unknown. In early American history, telling stories around the camp fire or around the stove or fireplace helped demystify the perils of life, helped create an internal light with which to face common fears. Today's problems must be "processed" the same way, by using language to demystify, to clarify, and to solve problems, whether they are college algebra, poverty, or AIDS.

Secondly, students fail to understand the importance of school because we only focus on the "what" of language—not on the "how" . Reading, writing, and language are seldom taught in terms of general semantics, which focuses on *how* people interact with symbols. General semantics is a systematic approach to rationality and sanity through attention to language. Here are a couple of basic examples. One principle of general semantics is "either/or" thinking, also referred to as two-valued orientation vs. the multi-valued orientation. Two-valued orientations presume that there are only *two* very different possibilities or options in most situations—one is either a Democrat or a Republican; water is either hot or cold; literature is either intriguing or boring. On the other hand (itself a two-valued phrase!), a multi-valued orientation acknowledges all the many shades of gray between polarities.

Another, larger principle of general semantics is the map/territory analogy, which states, "the map is not the territory; the word is not the thing itself " (Korzybski, 1933). The founder of general semantics, Alfred Korzybski, developed this principle as a result of his work in World War I, where he counseled soldiers suffering from "shell shock" or trauma induced by the terrors of battle. He found that these soldiers had entered the war with idealized notions of what war was—that they were full of what Twain calls "gunpowder and glory"—that they had heard and sung patriotic songs, such as *Over There* and heard speeches glamorizing the battle for democracy. Hence, many soldiers went into war with a "mental map" of what war was going to be—but when they experienced the real territory of actual war (friends killed, mustard gas, etc.), they realized that the two did not match up very well. Their map did not reflect reality,—did not reflect the territory, so they had to come to terms with this major difference. Our language can create idealized or false maps of reality—but when we check it against reality, they may not be very accurate. If teachers gave this—rationality and sanity and connection to reality—as one purpose of language, then students would better comprehend why they are in a language class in the first place.

Maybe more importantly—and even communicated less often to students—is the fact that people's abilities in using symbols affects their own identity development and personal growth. In short, language and other symbols help to *create* our reality. Here is a case in point: writing can be used as a way of healing. Counselors, psychologists and psychiatrists, and teachers of all kinds have used writing as a way for people to define, frame, analyze, and "distance themselves" from such problems as drug abuse, the emotional and physical abuse of women, gender identity issues, cancer therapy, grief over the loss of loved ones, and post-traumatic stress disorder. In a class focused on the teaching of writing and healing, my students wrote about divorce, adoption, death, crime victimization, anorexia, sibling and parental relationships, and rape. Psychologists Pennebaker (1997), Smyth (1997) and others have researched how writing affects our physical, mental, and emotional health.

We now know that writing has positive physical effects on people. For instance, writing can lower anxiety levels, blood pressure, heart rate, and the number of trips to the doctor's office. Writing can help people "re-frame" and re-define experiences that have bedeviled them, giving them more distance and objectivity, which often allows them to see *multiple reasons—not just one*—for why something occurred. Writers explore alternative scenarios and flesh out the *larger contexts* of their experiences. One student who had unresolved issues about her adoption, researched this issue as a general or national issue—its statistics, its multiple causes and effects, its varying perspectives. Doing so, allowed her to place her own "problem" into a much larger context, which, reduced her anxieties over her own particular situation.

Thirdly, students fail to understand the importance of school because we do not clarify the links between the uses of symbols and creativity. Our collective failures to link school work with creativity and imagination leads to students' inability to solve problems, an inability to think creatively. Considerable research has demonstrated that American students are far better at following directions than they are at "creating something out of nothing" or thinking creatively (Healy, 1990; Golde, et al. 2006). In any problem situation, if students cannot *imagine* options and possibilities, other than those that are literally in front of their face, then they cannot think creatively. The principle of "plurality" or "multiplicity" is crucial here in two equally important ways.

First, successful thinkers must generate as many solutions as possible, because, if one idea fails, they can modify it and try it again—or, they can try one of the other options in their repertoire. Second, students must be able to freely manipulate symbols of all kinds, to "move" or to "shuttle back and forth" between levels and types of symbols, as Gruber (1986) describes: "These incessant dialectical movements—between process and product, person and society, one modality and another, intention and expression—are the core of the creative process" (p. x).

Fourthly, students fail to understand the importance of school because we focus on form more than content. For eons, students have studied literature and history. However, when test time rolls around, students are often directed to memorize elements of form, such as, "What are the literary elements of the short story?" and "On what date was the *Magna Charta* signed?" Never mind about what the short story author is trying to communicate to readers, or what meaning the *Magna Charta* offers to its readers, then and now. Form and facts are indeed important—but not at the expense of the "larger" and more important meanings and purposes.

For decades we have drilled students on grammar and punctuation rules, that is, rules written and exemplified in textbooks—a "read it and learn it" approach. Therefore, grammar and punctuation are usually taught *divorced* from their concrete referent—the human voice. Why learn an abstract rule if you never hear it in action, never see it applied? In this example, if teachers supplied the content (the human voice), then students could hear the differences that alternative options can make, thus understanding the importance of this school work.

Form rules over ideas in many other ways—in correct outlining form ("The Roman numeral comes before the letter."); in correct bibliographic format and endless piles of note cards. It's not the note cards that are important—it's the quality of the topic you choose—if indeed you are allowed to choose a topic; it's the substance of the points you raised—if indeed you did not rehash what others have already stated.

We have snuffed the spirit of inquiry and research—the fun of finding things out that can lead us down many unknown paths—that many English teachers, themselves, are fearful of it and avoid it whenever possible. Since 1992, many of the superb English teachers who participate in The Missouri Writing Project, have feared the word, "research." The best way I have found to ignite English teachers' spirit of inquiry and research is through teaching the genre of Creative Nonfiction, where research becomes personal and purposeful. Nonetheless, the killing of the spirit of inquiry—replacing it with an anal retentive focus on note cards and MLA format—is just plain pitiful.

A focus on form contributes to students' lack of fluency in reading and writing. No matter what or how students read and write, they simply do not generate enough and hence lack fluency—the most "basic" element in writing. The same is true for reading. Fluency in writing is coordination with eye, hand, and brain—it means how many words per minute can you generate? Students never compare writing with other skills that demand constant practice, such as shooting free-throws in basketball—a skill, which requires hours and hours and hours or becoming a good driver or stone mason. Overall, Americans' sense of quantity or volume of writing and reading is different. If we have a history of not asking for much, then when we ask for a little more, it sounds like a whole lot! Students often write 3 papers per semester and they think that it's a heavy load. It is not. Students in other countries (Great Britain, New Zealand, etc.) generate far more writing than American students. I know that classes are large in America, but not every piece of writing has to be read by the teacher or even graded.

There is another important variable in fluency—"flow"—psychologist Mihalyi Csikszentmihalyi's concept of a highly pleasurable and challenging activity, in which people become so immersed and focused that they lose track of time, lose a sense of self, and lose awareness of their surroundings (1991). Our student readers and writers are seldom allowed to find flow in their reading and writing activities. If they did, then fluency would not be an issue. That is, immersion in generating language—on topics that writers are truly interested in and care about—generates a higher number of words per minute. This situation creates a chain reaction, in that the more frequently writers write longer pieces without censoring themselves, the longer those pieces become, over time. It is likewise true that writers who truly care about the topics in which they are engaged in are also investing *all* of their knowledge and "multiple intelligences" (Gardner, 1985). Hence, they are bringing in not only cognitive ways of knowing to their task, but intuitive and emotional ways of knowing, as well.

A focus on form leads teachers to ignore or trivialize the importance of emotion and intuition in thinking, reading, and writing. Emotion and irrationality have long played a major role in human thinking and development, including decision-making and the forming of public policies. (To be convinced of this, you only need to look at any of our public policies.) In my view, policy makers often use the rational to "explain" or to "justify" policies that have been arrived at irrationally. However, our culture has seldom acknowledged that emotion and intuition play important roles in how we interpret symbols and how we record and respond to the world (e.g., see John-Steiner, 1985). This stoic refusal of our education and government establishments to allow for emotion and irrationality—even to place it on the table for exploration—is, in itself, an irrational act.

Finally, students fail to understand the importance of thinking, speaking, reading, and writing because they have few adult models engaging in these activities. What is crucial to most teaching and learning is the "concrete referent"—the actual thing or process that we are trying to teach; "learning by doing," as Dewey taught us (1910). To teach thinking, speaking, writing, reading, and listening, the best concrete referents are 1. students observing adults or other more advanced students engaged in these acts; and, 2. students actually doing these activities with adults or others more advanced. Students then need to reflect upon and critically evaluate these experiences. For example, students need to see adults "thinking out loud" as they engage in reading and writing or engaging in a science experiment or whatever. This activity helps students to demystify such processes that appear unattainable to them; we have to model how we really think and write—in all of its faulty logic, misfires, muddles, confusions, false starts, and dead-ends. When students experience real people thinking aloud as they engage in the actual processes we are teaching, students invariably think, "Oh, that's what I do! So I'm not so dumb, after all?!" This requires that teachers strengthen their egos and demonstrate what they really do during the acts of reading and writing—bumble and fumble around like everyone—and eventually emerge from the chaos with an effectively shaped message or product that works.

STUDENTS HATE SCHOOL BECAUSE THEY HAVE FEW CHOICES IN THEIR WORK

Students have few choices in their thinking, reading, and writing. We often do not allow students to write for real audiences and purposes. Instead, they write to the teacher in order to be tested and evaluated. They are, essentially, "writing in a vacuum." Therefore, students seldom witness the effects that their words can have on real people. Can you imagine a playwright never seeing the effects of her play on a real audience?

Nor are students often encouraged to select their own reading or to read for their own purposes—from fixing a carburetor, to escaping to the fantasy world of Mordor. Research has told us for a long time that boys prefer nonfiction over fiction, but they are often not allowed to read nonfiction. To make matters worse, standardized tests tend to focus on the reading of fiction, again penalizing boys. Giving people choices, (even if it's a choice of which poison to drink) gives people some control over their destinies and hence fosters autonomy and independence. *Not* providing students choices keeps them dependent upon others.

Students often cannot link their personal world of popular culture to their school world. We do not help students to connect their "personal world" of music, film, and television, to their "school world." However, these two worlds share much in common. Electronic and popular media have been called "the hidden curriculum," because it can teach students more than the school curriculum (Postman, 1984). When we fail to use television, film, music, and advertising to teach the reading and writing of print (regardless of content area), we miss out on a fertile and *level* playing field, because most students bring to school a broad and deep knowledge of electronic media. We also need to teach students about media persuasion because advertising and propaganda have infiltrated nearly every venue imaginable—classrooms, government, textbooks, gas pumps, even churches.

Students often cannot connect verbal processes and products with those that are visual— we divorce them . The truth is that most of today's texts employ multiple modes, and research tells us that visual and verbal processes are interdependent. In a writing and healing class for teachers, my students wrote about divorce, adoption, death, armed robbery, anorexia, sibling and parental relationships, and incest. The theory and research of Arnheim (1986), Karl (1994), Paivio (1996), Kosslyn (1983), and many others demonstrate that words elicit other words—but also images—and that images elicit other images—and also words. Too many "struggling" writers and readers—and I have worked with them, one on one—believe that mental imagery has no place in a writing or English class—that imagery is irrelevant or somehow "outlawed" when dealing with words. Nothing could be further from the truth. Ironically, it's often the most struggling students who have excellent imagistic abilities—for scenes, for description, for detail, for imagination. These are the same students who have been deeply nurtured by visual media. However, in school we manage to cut these students off from using their imagistic abilities to create meaning in and through language.

Students often cannot "talk out" their ideas with others. They are often not allowed to talk in class. How can you learn to use language if you're not allowed to speak? Douglas Barnes (1990) and others have demonstrated the powers of talk—presentational talk (which happens once in a while when students "recite" book reports or something in front of the class)—but even more important "exploratory talk"—hypothesizing and venturing guesses and taking risks and getting feedback, so that you can modify what you're thinking and saying. If students cannot talk out their ideas, then they cannot test them and further refine them.

Students Hate School because we Emphasize Products over Processes

We often do not focus on thinking when teaching reading, writing, viewing, and discussion. Instead, what we do is rely upon deduction or "thesis-statement-driven," formulaic writing (which has its value—it's just that it often militates against exploratory thinking and writing, where we make connections). The hardest mold to break in any academically-trained or "educated" writer is *chronology*—breakfast to bed narratives. Narrative itself is great—but strict chronology restricts both readers and writers. *Show examples of each, noting the element of passive reading of texts vs. participating in reading.*

We also emphasize the written product over the *processes* of thinking, reading, and composing, and, sometimes, err in the opposite direction by devaluing the written product. After a quarter century of the extremely effective National Writing Project's work, too many teachers remain unaware of what it takes to produce effective writing. Many have never had a course in the teaching of writing. Many test out of freshman composition courses and their skills become rusty if they do not complete much writing in other courses.

A far smaller number of teachers become so engrossed in the processes of writing (or other topics in other disciplines) that the final products receive short shift. That is, final products may not receive equal emphasis in grading, may not receive individualized feedback, may not be "celebrated" by publishing it or displaying it, etc. The effect is the same, regardless of the direction in which teachers may err: students are restricted in letting either the process or the product generate further thinking and work. For maximum effect on students, processes and products must be emphasized equally.

We often do not allow students to experiment with language and other symbols. American students are very good at following directions, but compare poorly with students from other countries in invention and creativity—in making something out of nothing; in seeing multiple options in situations; in constructing and building meanings for themselves. My top notch undergraduates are fearful of taking risks—and they are all English teaching majors. When I ask them to use dialogue, a common response is, "I've never used dialogue before and I'm not sure about it. I'm nervous...." They are very hesitant over something that does not really warrant caution.

Here is one more example about not allowing students to experiment. One of my long-standing convictions has been that students seldom engage in real and thorough revision of their writing because they do not see the purpose in it. They do not see any purpose in it because, for starters, they've already written it down—they think of writing as being something like baking a cake: if you've already baked the cake and taken it out of the oven, why put it back in?! Another more important reason they don't see the purpose in revision is because they do not have *other versions* of the same message to compare it to. Not having two or more versions of the same message discourages students from *concretely seeing how one version is more effective than the other.* They don't revise because, if they are comparing it to anything at all, it's some very vague notion of "good writing" that floats around in thin air. Students need concrete comparisons to actually see that one version is better than the other.

We often fail to teach the processes involved with using the Internet. Students can unconsciously hate school because they believe that technology can provide more help than school can ever deliver. Corporations and technologists have long "over-sold" technology as being the answer to everything. No one can deny that computers, emails, I-Pods and everything else have made writing and communicating more accessible. On the other hand, "messing around with technology" is a time-soaker and can easily become an end in itself, displacing time that could be devoted to language and literacy activities. Being facile with technology is too often confused with being facile with language. Although one can help the other, they are not the same thing. Back in the 1980s when we first set up a computer writing center on our campus, students thought that typing it up and printing it off made it a wonderful paper—even though they had not revised anything. They did not yet understand the "garbage-in/garbage-out" concept. Today's students are beyond this, but they still believe too much of what they read on the Internet, which leads to my next point: Internet "information" is not equal; in fact, not all internet information is even information.

This fact, often hidden to students, greatly confuses them. In 1948, the Shannon-Weaver model of communication (they worked for Bell Labs) re-defined "information" as being virtually anything but "static"—the kind of noise that interferes with an electronic signal, such as when your TV set's channel dial is stuck between two stations. It is amazing how widely-accepted and influential this transmission model has been! For half a century now, we have defined any kind of lies or nonsense—anything but static—as "information." In the electronic world of the Internet, Shakespeare's play, *King Lear* is "information,"—just as is a Web site brimming with propaganda, embedded sales pitches, half-truths, mistakes, innuendoes, and lies. Shakespeare and the Aryan Nation Party's Web site is not the same thing—but they are both equally classified as "information" under the umbrella of the all-knowing and god-like Internet. How many people fail to make such distinctions, how much of the time?

We often fail to teach certain topics and processes, because we have been inoculated to believe that students are clinically impaired and/or "are not yet at that developmental stage." In our summer institutes for teachers, we tell them that they are not allowed to say, "My students cannot do that, because they are too young/old/not-at-that-developmental-stage/etc." The theories of Jean Piaget, as valuable as they have been, may have caused an equal amount of harm, by teachers "locking" students into various, labeled "stages of development," e.g., "concrete operations."

From another direction, the discipline of special education is overloaded with labels and categories—from "dyslexia" to "emotional behavior disorder" to "attention deficit disorder" to "gifted."). These are, of course, excellent terms and diagnoses, for many individuals. On the other hand, I have worked with too many students who had been, at an early age, labeled with such terms. Fortunately, many find their way out of the self-fulfilling prophecies that such labeling can inflict.

Students have to pass a writing exam before they were eligible to graduate. Over a twelve-year period, as a Director of Writing at an open-admissions university, I had countless mature adults come into my office who had failed to pass the exam. Their body language was inevitably downtrodden: their eyes focused downward, their shoulders slumped, as they would say, "I cannot ever pass this exam, because, uh . . . well . . . when I was a kid, I was diagnosed as dyslexic" (or whatever term). I would then sit down with them and I would talk them through the exams, both objective and written. Most of them passed quite easily. The opposite has held true with my other students. Those who had been labeled as "gifted" often discover, later in life, that they are no more gifted than anyone else they know. This requires an adjustment on their part.

CONCLUSION

When the young Lady Bird Johnson found herself feeling dumb or ignorant at those Washington D.C. cocktail parties, if she had believed herself to be "gifted," she would not have followed up on the books and art she heard being discussed. Nor was she carrying the weight of a label, such as "learning disabled." Nor were there other obstacles in her way to hinder her from learning the truth— from escaping her haplessness. It is astonishing what students can do if we simply *allow* them to do it.

REFERENCES

Arnheim, Rudolph. (1986). *New Essays on the Psychology of Art.* Berkeley, CA: University of California Press.

Barnes, D, James Britton & Mike Torbe (1990). *Language, the Learner and the School.* Portsmouth, NH: Boynton and Cook.

Caro, Robert. (1982). *The Path to Power: The Years of Lyndon Johnson.* New York: Alfred A. Knopf.

Csikszentmihalyi, Mihalyi. (1991). *Flow: The Psychology of Optimal Experience.* New York: HarperPerrenial.

Dewey, John. (1910). *How We Think.* Boston: Heath.

Gardner, Howard (1985). *Frames of Mind: The Theory of Multiple Intelligences.* New York: Basic Books.

Golde, Chris and George Walker (eds.) (2006). *Envisioning the Future of Doctoral Education.* San Francisco: Jossey-Bass.

Gruber, Howard (1986). "Foreword." In *Notebooks of the Mind: Explorations of Thinking.* Albuquerque: University of New Mexico Press.

Healy, Jane. (1990). *Endangered Minds: Why Children Don't Think and What We Can Do about It.* New York: Simon and Schuster.

John-Steiner, Vera. (1985). *Notebooks of the Mind: Explorations of Thinking.* Albuquerque, NM: University of New Mexico Press.

Karl, Herb. "The Image is Not the Thing." In *MediaSpeak: Three American Voices*. Roy F. Fox (ed.). Westport, CT: Greenwood Press.

Kosslyn, Steven. (1983). *Ghosts in the Mind's Machine: Creating and Using Images in the Brain*. New York: Norton.

Korzybski, Alfred. (1933). *Science and Sanity*. Lancaster, PA: Science Press.

Paivio, Allan. (1991). *Mental Representations: A Dual-Coding Approach*. New York: Oxford University Press.

Pennebaker, Steven. (1997). *Opening Up: The Healing Power of Expressing Emotions*. New York: Guilford Press.

Smyth, J. M., Stone, A., Hurewitz, A. and A. Kaell. (1999). Effects of writing about stressful experiences or symptom reduction in patients with asthma or rheumatoid arthritis: A randomized trial. *Journal of American Medical Association*. April 14:281(14): 1304–0.

Shannon, Claude. (1948). A mathematical theory of communication. *The Bell System Technical Journal,*. 27, 379–422.

"Science Phobia?" Could No Help With Spatial Skills Be a Factor?

JILL (ALICE A.) BLACK

MISSOURI STATE UNIVERSITY

It is generally recognized that very young children are "natural scientists" with great curiosity about the natural world around them and a love of exploration. What happens as children get older? A number of questions arise. Does society, or do schools, or feelings of frustration in studying science discourage much of this curiosity in some children? What types of exploration do teachers encourage? As they get older, do all children tend to explore in the same way?

To address the latter two questions, one might consider the cover of a popular book for teachers and parents. The cover of *Boys and Girls Learn Differently!* (Gurian, 2001) depicts three children, all approximately 11 years old, in a classroom setting. Information about the abacus is written on the board; a girl is shown reading a book about earlier times, while two boys are excitedly working with two abacus calculators. Is this difference in mode of exploration typical? Which of those two methods of exploring uses more three-dimensional spatial skills? Obviously, the actual physical manipulation of a three-dimensional object does so, in comparison to a two-dimensional printed page (or computer screen). Which method is more prevalent in our elementary classrooms? Jones, et al., (2000) studied the use of science equipment by elementary children and found that boys tended to use tools in exploratory, inventive ways, while girls strictly followed teachers' directions and did little playing or tinkering with tools. Tracy (1987) associated male superiority at spatial tasks with use of tools and toys involving spatial relationships.

The implications are quite important, partially because spatial abilities are statistically related to performance in science, including Earth sciences (Lord & Rupert, 1995; Pallrand & Seeber, 1984), and mathematics (Fennama & Sherman, 1977). They are also very important because many prominent Americans think our country is losing its predominance in science (American Association for the Advancement of Science, 2006), because the great majority (98%) of elementary teachers, who can foster a love of science at an early age, are female (United States Department of Labor, Bureau of Labor Statistics, 2003).

Spatial abilities tend to be a function primarily of the right brain hemisphere, and females tend to have more difficulty with the spatial tasks measured in science education studies, on average (Halpern, 1992; Levine, Huttenlocher, Taylor, and Langrock, 1999). Linguistic abilities are found in the left hemisphere, and males, on average, have more problems learning language arts (Hyde & Linn, 1988).

Children with trouble in language arts receive a great deal of encouragement, practice, and instruction, especially in the early school years. Traditional schooling, however, provides little or no attention to children who may need remediation of spatial weaknesses. Geary (1998) and Moir and Jessel (1991) think that this situation may be related to the tendency of students, often girls, to drop out of spatially-related courses, such as math and science, when those subjects become more complex in higher grades. This can be termed "science phobia." Leaving the development of spatial abilities to chance may, then, primarily hurt females. Ironically, elementary teachers tend to be female, and tend to continue the emphasis on linguistics with which they are comfortable often avoiding teaching science (Tilgner, 1990).

It is important in today's world that citizens understand the planet on which we live and the interrelationships between Earth systems. Many conceptual problems in the Earth sciences have been reported (Schoon, 1995). It is possible that continued failure of students to understand science concepts may contribute to "science phobia." Many Earth science conceptual problems appear to have a spatial component (Piburn, et al., 2002), yet relatively few studies have considered relationships between spatial ability and Earth science conceptual understanding.

Therefore, although it is recognized that many factors may contribute to science concept understanding, the possible role of spatial abilities should not be overlooked. This study investigated spatial ability, a factor that has been shown to be statistically related to performance on a test of Earth science concept understanding, at the level of performance on individual concepts rather than the test as a whole, with university non-science majors as subjects.

PREVIOUS STUDIES

Science standards are based on constructivist philosophy, but learners may not be able to assimilate new information with previously held concepts if their previous concepts are not consistent with the ideas of scientists. Misconceptions, or alternative conceptions, have been reported in many science disciplines, including Earth science (Schoon, 1995; Philips, 1991; Henriques, 2002; Lee, Eichinger, Anderson, Berkheimer, & Blakesless, 1993). Some reported misconceptions are presented as factual statements or are related to the cause of phenomena, such as gravity and Earth's shape, cause of seasons, cause of earthquakes, Earth's internal structure, location of origin of lava, weather, including gases and phase changes, and cause of moon phases. Others are of a broader nature and can be called conceptual difficulties. Downs and Liben (1991, p. 306) wrote of "cognitive limitations and misconceptions", and Lawson (1995, p. 301–302) stated that "some misconceptions may derive from students' lack of thinking skills or cognitive deficiencies or differences." Examples include understanding or interpretation of: map projections (Downs & Liben, 1991); geologic block diagrams (Kali & Orion, 1996); topographic mapping (Repine & Rockey, 1997); way-finding (Richardson, et al., 1999); geologic time (Dodick & Orion, 2002a); and model interpretation (Dyche, McClurg, Stepans, & Veath, 1993). Misconceptions and conceptual problems often appear very resistant to change (Zeilik & Bisard, 2000).

Many conceptual problems involve scale (distance, area, volume, and time) or visualization of: a.) unseen objects, such as Earth's layers or shape, b.) the relative positions of moving objects, such as Earth/moon/sun positions or molecules in the kinetic molecular theory (KMT), which are basic concepts of meteorology, and c.) three-dimensional structures represented by two-dimensional images (map projections, contour maps, air photos, block diagrams, or astronomical diagrams).

Although scientific literacy for all is our national goal, it is also acknowledged that not all humans possess identical intellectual abilities (Petrill & Wilkerson, 2000). One of the areas in which differences have been noted is the subset of intelligence broadly termed spatial ability, which has been linked to high performance in science and math, but has been undervalued or ignored by traditional education (Matthewson, 1999; McCormack & Mason, 2000). This situation may be due in part to the association of spatial abilities with mechanical vocations during America's industrial age. Researchers have not reached consensus about spatial ability factors or tests that measure those factors (McGee, 1979; Halpern & LaMay, 2000; Eliot, 1980). One widely sited classification system is found in the meta-analysis of Linn and Petersen (1985), who described three spatial ability factors or types.

Spatial perception is described by Linn and Petersen (1985) as spatial relationships with respect to the orientation of the subject's own body, in spite of distracting information. They state that "the other feature of spatial perception tasks is a focus on disembedding or overcoming distracting cues" (p. 1482). Mental rotation is a "Gestalt-like" process involving "the rotation of a two- or three-dimensional figure rapidly and accurately" (p. 1483). While mental rotation tasks can be solved with an analytic, part-by-part strategy, they can be solved much more quickly by those who can mentally rotate the entire figure as a whole. Spatial visualization is described as the "analytic combination of both visual and nonvisual strategies", and involves . . . "complicated, multistep manipulations of spatially presented information" (p. 1491). Linn and Petersen also write that a "flexible adaptation of a repertoire of solution strategies" is necessary (p. 1485), and that "these strategies are more characteristic of general ability than of spatial ability" (p. 1491). Therefore, spatial visualization appears to be characterized more by use of strategies rather than as a separate type of spatial ability, and tests described as measuring this ability seem to vary greatly.

Males often score higher on several types of spatial ability tests (Maccoby & Jacklin, 1974; Linn & Petersen, 1985; Halpern & LaMay, 2000). The greatest male advantage is in mental rotation, with a lesser advantage on spatial perception, and little or no male advantage in spatial visualization (Kimura, 1999).

University non-science majors often become public leaders and educators, and may therefore greatly influence public policy about Earth resource issues. Non-majors, however, have been shown to lag behind science majors in science content understanding (Nordvik & Amponsah, 1998), spatial ability (Lord, 1987), cognitive level (Maloney, 1981) and study habits (Ryan, 1989). It is important for our nation's future that these students have an understanding of important Earth science concepts upon which they can base knowledge of ongoing problems and situations.

Although complex bodies of literature exist concerning both Earth science misconceptions and spatial abilities, relatively few researchers (Kali and Orion, 1996; Piburn et al., 2002) have considered the relationship between specific spatial abilities and Earth science conceptual understanding. No research has been found that relates specific Earth science misconceptions to specific spatial abilities.

Evidence exists that spatial ability can be improved (Lord, 1995, 1997; Bezzi, 1991; Kyllonen, Lohman, & Snow, 1984; Piburn et al., 2002; Pallrand & Seeber, 1984). Therefore, if a relationship exists between Earth science conceptual understanding and spatial ability, curricula may hopefully be developed to facilitate both spatial abilities necessary for Earth science conceptual understanding and understanding of spatially-related Earth science concepts that are associated with misconceptions and other broader conceptual problems.

In previous research, the Earth Science Concepts (ESC) test was developed and field tested for two years to test student misconceptions and broader conceptual difficulties (Black, 2005). It was also used to investigate relationships among conceptual understanding and spatial abilities. Significant positive relationships at a moderate level were found between scores on each of three types of spatial ability and Earth science conceptual understanding scores of university non-science majors. Students who scored higher on any of the tests of spatial ability also tended to score higher on the overall ESC test. Mental rotation was the type of spatial ability that was most highly correlated to ESC score, and stepwise regression showed that mental rotation score was the independent variable that best predicted ESC score.

THE STUDY

The purpose of this study was to investigate the relationship between scores on the three types of spatial ability tests and performance on individual test items, and to determine the various Earth science concepts associated with those individual items. Do students who score higher on a specific type of spatial ability tend to have greater understanding of specific Earth science topics, such as the cause of seasons or topographic maps? This study is considered a preliminary study; additional data is being collected and a larger study with results from a larger number of subjects will be published.

Mental rotation (PVOR score) was predicted to be the spatial ability factor that was most related to performance on specific items on the ESC, while spatial perception was predicted to be the factor least related to performance on specific items. The explanation, or hypothesis, that explains this prediction is that many items that are related to misconceptions and conceptual difficulties involve interpretation of object movement in three dimensions, and viewing of objects from different vantage points. Topics that were predicted to be related to mental rotation included the cause of seasons (Items 1, 11, and 18), KMT (items 3, 17, 12, 6, and 14), the astronomical event that occurs during one month (item 2), geologic block diagrams (items 8 and 19), cause of moon and phases (items 4, 15, 18, and 9), distance to moon, starts (item 10), and cause of tides (item 18). Spatial visualization was predicted to be related to a number of items due to the DAT test measuring ability to interpret two-dimensional to three-dimensional transformations and viewing of objects from differing vantage points. The ESC items predicted to be related to spatial visualization were geologic block diagrams (items 8 and 19), meteorologic block diagrams (item 7), air photo interpretation (item 20), topographic map interpretation (item 16), distance to molten material (item 5), and viewing astronomical objects from different vantage points (items 1, 2, 4, 9, 15, and 18). Items that were predicted to be related to spatial perception, due to their inclusion of disembedding and determination of angular distances, were air photo interpretation (item 20), topographic map interpretation (item 16), and position of the sun at noon (item 11).

METHODS

Selection of spatial ability tests was based on the three-category spatial classification of Linn and Petersen (1985). The Purdue Visualization of Rotations test (PVOR) (Guay, 1977) was used to test mental rotation. The Differential Aptitude Test - Space Relations (DAT) (Bennett, Seashore, & Wesman, 1991) test was chosen to test spatial visualization, and the Group Embedded Figures Test (GEFT) (Witkin, Oltman, Kaskin, & Karp, 1971) was administered to test spatial perception. Criteria for selection of spatial ability tests included published validity and reliability data, suitability for group administration, citations in science education literature, availability, and measurement of spatial tasks that appeared related to possible misconceptions or conceptual problems.

The 20-item multiple choice ESC test was based on the misconceptions and conceptual difficulties literature, and included all four areas of Earth science. Criterion validity was 0.595 and K-R reliability was 0.742. Each item offered five possible responses. Response (e), "I don't know", was intended to discourage guessing. The number of students who selected this response on each item ranged from 0 to 48.

To obtain a numerical value for use in correlation statistics, each possible response choice on all ESC items was assigned a value number indicating its approximation to the scientific explanation or thought processes used by scientists. The scientifically correct explanations were assigned values of 5. "I don't know" responses were assigned values of 0, as no thought was indicated. If one part of a distracter response indicated the scientific explanation, but the remainder of the explanation did not, the response was assigned a value of 2. If only ideas associated with misconceptions were evident, a value of 1 was assigned. In only one case was a value of 3 assigned; this was made to reflect the distinction made by Kali and Orion (1996) between penetrative and non-penetrative spatial thinking. Each item response by each participant was assigned its corresponding value. Mental rotation was hypothesized to be more related to scores on individual ESC items than the other two types of spatial ability and spatial perception the least related.

Tests were administered to 97 subjects who were enrolled in six undergraduate science classes at a Midwestern public university. Participants also completed a demographic survey and were administered the BEM Inventory (Bem, 1974), which determined psychological gender. Participants included 35 males and 30 elementary-middle school preservice teachers. Mean age was 24.4, and mean years of university study was 3.3 years. The percentage of subjects who had taken no high school Earth science was 73%.

RESULTS

Many Earth science misconceptions and conceptual difficulties were evident. Mean score was 6.82, or 34% (SD = 3.03). Results indicated that one or more spatial ability test scores were significantly correlated to nine of 20 ESC items, or 45% of ESC items. Persons who exhibited a lack of misconceptions or conceptual difficulties by choosing the scientifically accepted response on those items also tended to score well on specific spatial ability tests. Of 13 total significant correlations, four were at the .01 level and 9 at the .05 level. Of those, PVOR scores were responsible for three of the four .01 correlations and six total correlations, or correlations with 30% of all ESC items. Three of those 6 PVOR correlations were moderate, and three were weak. Of five significant correlations with DAT scores, one item was moderately correlated at the .01 level and four were weakly correlated at the .05 level. Two items were weakly correlated at the .05 level to GEFT scores.

The one topic that was significantly correlated to all three spatial abilities was the most complex of two geologic block diagram items. In this item (Item 19), a potential geologic block diagram was depicted within its stratigraphic layers. Two astronomical concepts (the astronomical event that occurs within one month (Item 2) and cause of seasons (Item 1), a topic also important in meteorology) and one KMT item concerning the evaporation of water (Item 17) were correlated with both PVOR and DAT scores. Topics that were correlated with one type of spatial ability were motion of molecules in ice, topographic map interpretation, relative astronomical distances, and a simple geologic block diagram.

Several demographic characteristics of subjects were also significantly related to individual ESC item responses. Three items, none of which were significantly related to spatial abilities, were related to number of university Earth science courses and one to number of high school Earth science courses. These were a moon phase diagram, the position of the sun overhead in southwest Missouri, and air photo interpretation.

Four individual items were significantly related to gender, although gender was not significantly related to any of the spatial ability scores or ESC scores in the earlier study, when the ESC test score as a whole was considered. In all four cases, males were significantly more likely to answer with the scientific response. Topics included interpretation of a weather block diagram, distance to stars, a combined diagram about tides, seasons, and moon phases, and the complex geologic block diagram.

One item was related to age (a moon phase diagram), one to psychological gender (psychological male persons tended to get a scale-related item about distances to stars correct more often than psychological feminine persons), and one to university grade level (combined diagram of tides, seasons, and moon phases). No items were significantly related to major (elementary/middle education major compared to other non-science majors) or number of completed university or high school science classes. Both ESC items with and without diagrams were correlated to scores on spatial ability tests.

Conclusions

This research is considered only a preliminary study, but a number of conclusions can be drawn from the results obtained thus far. The results support the hypothesis that specific Earth science concepts, including those associated with common misconceptions and conceptual difficulties, are related to specific types of spatial ability. They are consistent with earlier results concerning the relationship of ESC scores and spatial ability scores. They also support the proposed idea that mental rotation is most associated with a number of Earth science misconceptions and conceptual difficulties, followed by spatial visualization, and that spatial perception is least related. Both the PVOR and DAT have aspects of viewing objects from different vantage points. In addition, the strongest correlation between spatial tests was between PVOR and DAT scores ($r(97) = 0.57$, $p < 0.01$). Also, the GEFT, used to measure spatial perception, does not involve motion, viewing phenomena from different vantage points, or two-dimensional to three-dimensional transformations.

It is not surprising that the more complex geologic block diagram was statistically related to all three spatial test scores. The task involved disembedding the block from surrounding rock layers (GEFT). It concerned visualization of interfaces between the two figures (DAT). This may be a penetrative ability like that described by Kali and Orion (1996). Distracters B and D exhibit no penetrative ability. Also, to choose between correct answer A and distracter C, one must realize that to produce C, the block would have to be tilted, or rotated at an angle from the position in A (PVOR).

Several unexpected results were found. Surprisingly, only one weak correlation between understanding of the cause of moon phases and PVOR scores was found. A greater relationship was expected due to the predicted strong moving spatial component and necessity to view objects from different vantage points. Conversely, the strong relationship found between the astronomical event that occurs once a month and both the PVOR and DAT was unexpected. This was one of the lowest difficulty items, and might even be memorized verbally. Perhaps students who visualize celestial bodies and revolution, rather than memorizing words, tend to be those who score higher on the PVOR and DAT. Also, the relationship of the air photo interpretation question with the GEFT, although stronger than with the other two spatial tests, was not significant. It had been predicted that the result would be significant due to disembedding skills needed to distinguish drainage patterns from the air photo.

The initial study, which considered the relationship of the three types of spatial ability and ESC scores as a whole, found no significant relationship between sex and test score relationships (although males outperformed females, but not to a significant degree, on all tests except the DAT). In this study, however, when individual items or Earth science topics on the ESC were considered, significant results favoring males were found for four individual ESC items. One involved astronomical scale, and was also the only item significantly, and inversely, related to femininity (T-score on the BEM). Two were block-type diagrams, one geologic and one meteorologic. Three were fairly complex items, although two of the three were not particularly high difficulty value. Perhaps students who had studied very little Earth science (73% of subjects had no pre-university Earth science courses) found complex questions involving both Earth science and spatial skills overwhelming. Additional studies will focus on the past study of and interest in Earth science by subjects, and their relationship to all test scores, including individual item scores. Interviews with subjects concerning reasons for their answers are also planned.

Although, certainly, many factors influence learning of Earth science concepts and the "science phobia" exhibited by some students, including preservice teachers and practicing elementary teachers, the significant contribution of spatial ability should not be overlooked and left entirely to chance. This study suggests that perhaps individual concept understanding might be facilitated by the development of spatially-oriented curricula or activities that address specific misconceptions or conceptual difficulties. One note of caution is necessary however: Mental rotation appears to be a type of spatial ability that may be somewhat more difficult to improve with interventions than are other types (Zavotka, 1987; Piburn, et al., 2002). Much additional study in all related areas is indicated.

NOTES

1. There are many animated computer programs that depict three-dimensional objects from different sides. An interesting question may be to what extent learners need to have previous experience with similar actual three-dimensional objects and situations before the two-dimensional computer representations have significant meaning (e.g. steep topography or caves in Earth science).

REFERENCES

American Association for the Advancement of Science. (2006). Experts at AAAS Forum Urge U.S. to Renew Its Commitment to S&T Innovation. On line. http://www.aaas.org/news/releases/2006/0502 innov.shtml. Accessed November 20, 2006.

Black, A. (2005). Spatial ability and earth science conceptual understanding. *Journal of Geoscience Education*, 53 (4): 402–414.

Bem, S. (1974). The measurement of psychological androgeny. *Journal of Consulting and Clinical Psychology*, 42: 155–162.

Bennett, G.K., Seashore, H.G., & Wesman, A.G. (1991). *Differential Aptitude Test for Personnel and Career Assessment: Space Relations Technical Manual*. San Antonio, TX: The Psychological Corporation.

Bezzi, A. (1991). A Macintosh program for improving three-dimensional thinking. *Journal of Geological Education* 39: 284–288.

Dodick, J., & Orion, N. (2003). Cognitive factors affecting student understanding of geologic time. *Journal of Research in Science Teaching* 40: 415–442.

Downs, R.M., & Liben, L.S. (1991). The development of expertise in geography: A Cognitive-development approach to geographic education. *Annals of the Association of American Geographers* 78(4): 680–700.

Dyche, S., McClurg, P., Stepans, J., & Veath, M.L. (1993). Questions and conjectures concerning models, misconceptions, and spatial ability. *School Science and Mathematics* 93: 191–197.

Eliot, J. (1980). Classification of figural spatial tests. *Perceptual and Motor Skills* 51: 847–851.

Fennama, E., & Sherman, J. (1977). Sex-related differences in mathematics Achievement, spatial visualization and affective factors. *American EducationalResearch Journal* 14: 51–71.

Geary, D.C. (1998). *Male, female: The evolution of human sexual differences*. Washington, DC: American Psychological Association.

Guay, R.B. (1977). *Purdue Spatial Visualization Test: Rotations*. West Lafayette, IN: Purdue Research Foundation.

Gurian, M. (2001). *Boys and Girls Learn Differently!* San Francisco: Jossey-Bass.

Halpern, D.F. (1992). *Sex differences in Cognitive Abilities* (2nd edition). Hillsdale, NJ: Lawrence Erlbaum Associates.

Halpern, D.F., & LaMay, M.L. (2000). The smarter sex: A critical review of sex differences in intelligence. *Educational Psychology Review* 12, 229–46.

Hawkins, B. (2000). Young children's interpretations of aerial views as it relates to their ability to understand the Earth as spherical. Paper presented at the meeting of Association for the Education of Science Teachers Annual Meeting, Akron, OH.

Henriques, L. (2002). Children's ideas about weather: A review of the literature. *School Science and Mathematics* 102 202–15.

Hyde, J.S., & Linn, M.C. (1988). Gender differences: verbal ability, A meta-analysis. Psychological Bulletin, 4(1), 53-69.

Jones, M.G., Brader-Araje, L., Carboni, L., Carter, G., Rua, M.J., Banilower, E., et.al. (2000). Tool time: Gender and students' use of tools, control, and authority. *Journal of Research in Science Teaching* 37: 760–783.

Kali, Y., & Orion, N. (1996). Spatial abilities of high-school students in the perception of geologic structures. *Journal of Research in Science Teaching* 33(4): 369–391.

Kimura, D. (1999). *Sex and Cognition*. Cambridge, MA: MIT Press.

Kyllonen, P.D., Lohman, D.F., & Snow, R.E. (1984). Effects of aptitudes, strategy training, and task facets on spatial task performance. *Journal of Educational Psychology* 76: 130–143.

Lawson, A.E. (1995). *Science Teaching and the Development of Thinking*. Blemont, CA: Wadsworth.

Lee, O., Eichiinger, D.C., Anderson, C.W., Berkheimer, G.D., & Blakesless, T.D. (1993). Changing middle school students' conceptions of matter and molecules. *Journal of Research in Science Teaching* 30: 249–270.

Levine, S.C., Huttenlocher, J., Taylor, A., & Langrock, A. (1999). Early sex differences In spatial skill. *Developmental Psychology* 35: 940–949.

Linn, M. & Petersen, A.C. (1985). Emergence and characterization of sex differences in spatial ability: A meta-analysis. *Child Development* 56: 1479–1498.

Lord, T. R. (1985). Enhancing the visuo-spatial aptitude of students. *Journal of Research in Science Teaching* 227: 395–405.

Lord, T. R. (1987). A look at spatial abilities in undergraduate women science majors. *Journal of Research in Science Teaching* 24 757–767.

Lord, T. R. & Rupert, J. L. (1995). Visual-spatial aptitude in elementary education majors in science and math tracks. *Journal of Elementary Science Education* 7: 47–58.

Maccoby, E.E., & Jacklin, C.N. (1974). *The Psychology of Sex Differences*. Stanford, CA: Stanford University Press.

Maloney, D.P. (1981). Comparative reasoning abilities of college students. *American Journal of Physics* 49: 784–786.

Mathewson, J. H. (1999). Visual-spatial thinking: An aspect of science overlooked by educators. *Science Education* 83: 33-–4.

McCormack, A.J., & Mason, C.L. (2001). Visual/Spatial thinking: A forgotten fundamental for school science programs. Paper presented at the meeting of the Association for the Education of Teachers of Science, Akron, OH.

McGee, M.G. (1979). Human spatial abilities: Psychometric studies and environmental, Genetic, hormonal, and neurological influences. *Psychological Bulletin* 86: 889–s 918.

Moir, A., & Jessel, D. (1991). *Brain Sex: The Real Difference between Men and Women*. New York: Dell Publishing.

Nordvik, H., & Amponsah, B. (1998). Gender differences in spatial abilities and spatial activity among university students in an egalitarian educational system. *Sex Roles, 38*, 1998.

Pallrand, G.J., & Seeber, F. (1984). Spatial ability and achievement in introductory physics. *Journal of Research in Science Teaching* 21: 507–516.

Petrill, S. A., & Wilkerson, B. (2000). Intelligence and achievement: A behavioral genetic perspective. *Educational Psychology Review* 12: 185–199.

Philips, W.C. (1991). Earth science misconceptions. *The Science Teacher* 58: 21–23.

Piburn, M.D., Reynolds, S.J., Leedy, D.E., McAuliffe, C.M., Birk, J.P., Johnson, J.K. (2002, April). The hidden Earth: Visualization of geologic features and the subsurface geometry. Paper presented at the annual meeting of the National Association for Research in Science Teaching, New Orleans, LA.

Repine, T., & Rockey, D. (1997). Constructive contours: Build a life-size topographic map on school grounds. *The Science Teacher* 64: 26–29.

Richardson, A.E., Montello, D.R., & Hegarty, M. (1999). Spatial knowledge acquisition from maps and from navigation in real and virtual environments. *Memory and Cognition* 27: 741–750.

Ryan, J. (1989). Study skills for the sciences: A bridge over troubled waters. *Journal of College Science Teaching* 373–377.

Schoon, J. K. (1995). The origin and extent of alternative conceptions in the Earth and space sciences: A survey of pre-service elementary teachers. *Journal of Elementary Science Education* 7 27–46.

Tilgner, P.J. (1990). Avoiding science in the elementary school. *Science Education* 74:421–431.

Tracy, D.T. (1987). Toys, spatial ability, and science and mathematics achievement: Are they related? *Sex Roles* 17: 115–138.

United States Department of Labor, Bureau of Labor Statistics. (2003). Online. http://www.bls.gov/cps/cpsaa9.pdf. Accessed June 16, 2003.

Witkin, H.A., Oltman, P.K., Kaskin, E., & Karp, S.A. (1971). *A Manual for the Embedded Figures Test*. Palo Alto, CA: Consulting Psychologists Press.

Zavotka, S. (1987). Three-dimensional computer animated graphics: A tool for spatial Instruction. *Educational Communications and Technology Journa*, 35: 133-–44.

Zeilik, M., & Bisard, W. (2000). Conceptual change in introductory-level astronomy Courses: Tracking misconceptions to reveal which and how much concepts Change. *Journal of College Science Teaching* 26: 229–232.

SUGGESTED ACTIVITIES AND READINGS

1. View the video *A Private Universe* (Schneps, M., & Sadler, P. (1989). Pyramid Films, Santa Monica, CA.,) which depicts Harvard graduates in their graduation gowns being asked about several common Earth science misconceptions. Survey class members about their answers to the same questions before showing the film.

2. Ask class members what their perceptions are of their spatial abilities. Ask if these perceptions have affected their choices of high school classes, college major, or career choice.

3. Ask students if they think their spatial abilities could be improved, and if so, describe what specific abilities could be improved and how they think the improvement could be accomplished.

4. Go to the Web site http://www.ldeo.columbia.edu/edu/DLESE/maptutorial/Title_page.html. Proceed through the on-line tutorial. Discuss with the class individual differences between students in interpreting maps. How do you think problems with map interpretation encountered by the class relate to spatial abilities described in the article?

5. Discuss the possible causes of some of the most common Earth science misconceptions and conceptual difficulties described in the chapter.

6. Read Gurion's book concerning different learning styles of boys and girls (Gurian, 2001) and Howard Gardner's book *Frames of Mind* on multiple intelligences (Gardner, 1983). Discuss the relationship of this research to the ideas in those reading.

Multiple Choice Questions

1. This chapter described which type of research?

    a. qualitative – grounded theory

    b. quantitative – cause and effect

    c. qualitative – case study

    d. quantitative – correlational

2. Which of the following correctly describes the subjects of this research?

    a. Almost 2/3 had taken no pre-university Earth science courses

    b. Most were elementary preservice teachers

    c. Most were university freshmen

    d. Subjects scored well on the test of Earth science conceptual understanding, with an average score of 85%

3. Which is TRUE regarding spatial ability?

    a. Past research suggests that spatial ability cannot be improved

    b. Researchers generally agree on definitions of spatial ability types

    c. Researchers generally agree on which spatial ability tests measure certain types of spatial ability

    d. Spatial ability is statistically related to achievement in the sciences and mathematics

    e. Spatial ability is primarily a function of the left hemisphere of the brain

4. Which type of spatial ability is described as a spatial relationship with respect to orientation with the subject's own body?

    a. spatial visualization

    b. spatial perception

    c. spatial orientation

    d. mental rotation

5. Which is NOT described as an example of a broader conceptual difficulty?

    a. interpretation of map projections

    b. analysis of geologic block diagrams

    c. Earth science model interpretation

    d. understanding of Earth's shape and gravity

6. The type of spatial ability that was most often correlated with responses to individual ESC items was

    a. spatial visualization

    b. spatial perception

    c. spatial orientation

    d. mental rotation

7. Which is TRUE regarding the results of this research?

    a. There were no significant relationships between gender and spatial ability test scores and scores on the ESC, but there were significant relationships between gender and scores. Females scored better than males on several items

    b. The type of item that was significantly correlated to all three types of spatial ability was a moon phase diagram

    c. The DAT was least correlated to individual ESC items

    d. Females scored higher than males on two items on which there was a statistical correlation between spatial test scores and scores on the test of Earth science conceptual understanding

8. Which of the following does NOT accurately describe mental rotation?

    a. Research shows that interventions may be more likely to favorably change scores on this type of spatial ability test, in comparison to the other two types

    b. Scores of mental rotation were least related, of the spatial ability types, to overall ESC score, but were most highly related to individual ESC item scores

    c. Males tend to score higher, on average, than do females

    d. It involves doing a spatial task *quickly*

    e. It involves viewing objects from different vantage points

9. The type of spatial ability that was the best predictor of ESC scores as a whole was

    a. spatial visualization

    b. spatial perception

    c. spatial orientation

    d. mental rotation

10. Which of the following ideas was NOT related in the chapter concerning science phobia?

    a. It may be related to a tendency to feel inadequate at understanding spatially-related concepts

    b. Students may drop out of spatially-related courses when those subjects become more complex in higher grades

    c. Many elementary teachers tend to avoid teaching science

    d. Of the two genders, females are given the most opportunity in traditional education to improve the type of intellectual ability at which they tend to be weakest

SECTION VI

Final Thoughts and Future Directions

Yes, I can honestly say I hate school and I can also say I hate my teachers besides a few of them and I can not even ask a question without making myself look like a idiot in front of the other 26 students who are trying to learn with our teacher who honestly should not even deserve the right to be called a teacher until they learn that they got to give respect to get it and then maybe school will be fun for me. But until that day, school is my living hell…and I'm the only one not afraid to say it.

—13-YEAR OLD MISSOURI MIDDLE SCHOOL STUDENT

I dropped out of high school English teaching (the first time) after just one year. Outside the school, students were terrorizing subway passengers, buying and selling dope, having babies. Inside, we gave departmental exams on Tennyson. Even when I did manage to figure out ways to supplement the curriculum, I had to sneak in early so that I could steal ditto paper and other supplies. In the ensuing two decades, things have not gotten better, but steadily worse.

—SUSAN OHANIAN, HUFFING AND PUFFING AND BLOWING SCHOOLS EXCELLENT (1988)

Finally, it is not new [in this latest frenzy about education] that we hear so little from people who work in schools. Where are the teachers' voices? Their absence eases the official debate; it subtracts many complications from the argument; it avoids many difficulties that cannot be solved by a new curriculum requirement, another test, or merit pay. But if this makes life easier on the commissions, it has a dreadful simplifying effect on what Americans learn about schools from these reports.

—DAVID K. COHEN, THE CONDITION OF TEACHERS' WORK (1984)

Proposals for educational reform usually proceed from the assumption that the train is on the tracks and just needs to go faster, more smoothly, or to new destinations—improvements that are straightforward and relatively minor. But, what if that assumption is incorrect? If the train is derailed, the work needed is major indeed as it is known in the midst of the living of it?

—JOHN I. GOODLAD, TEACHERS FOR OUR NATION'S SCHOOLS (1990)

Twelve Questions We Must Ask about Why Kids Hate School

STEVEN P. JONES

MISSOURI STATE UNIVERSITY

DIRECTOR, ACADEMY FOR EDUCATIONAL STUDIES

Teachers can't help but be discouraged when they look up during a lesson and see that some students, even a significant number of them, don't look like they're at all interested in what's being said or taught to them—as if they "hate" the whole experience of being with and learning from the teacher. Most teachers, I think, have three instinctual reactions when such moments occur or when they have time to reflect on such moments. Failure in the classroom demands explanation, even blame. One instinct teachers have is to blame themselves for the failure; a second instinct is to blame students; and a third instinct is to blame some circumstance that has ruined the learning experience—a circumstance, or set of circumstances, that, if removed, would restore the proper environment or productive relationship required for effective, spirited learning. If I'm right about this, the discouraged even disconsolate teacher who reflects about a failed lesson—or a series of failed lessons—gets a full helping of guilt about his or her own ineptitude, a shot of anger and resentment aimed at his or her students, and a feeling of helplessness about circumstances over which he or she has no control. They say things come in threes. Guilt, resentment, and helplessness are a terrible threesome with which the committed, conscientious teacher must contend.

I think this tri-partite division of blame passes the test of common sense. It probably is the case that kids hate school because of mistakes teachers make, because of attitudes, background, or interests students do or do not bring with them to the classroom; and because there are school, school district, state, national, and cultural realities that do not help students to want to learn. At least I assume so in what follows.

As clear as this three-part division might be, it cannot solve the problem of the disinterested, "hateful" student. For that I suggest we need to answer some serious questions, and in what follows I suggest twelve such questions spread across a three-part discussion of our contemporary educational situation. The committed conscientious teacher struggling to hold the interest of students—and anyone who wants to help that teacher and his or her students—needs to consider (and reconsider) contemporary political issues surrounding education, the structures of schooling that shape educational experiences, and the day-to-day instructional and curricular choices teachers make.

THE POLITICAL LANDSCAPE

State Assessment Tests and No Child Left Behind (NCLB)

Politics, or the involvement of politicians in things educational, is one of those circumstances over which teachers have little or no control. The central manifestation of political involvement in schools, teaching, and learning is the presence and pressure of high-stakes assessment tests tied to NCLB legislation. This is a natural place for the frustrated teacher to turn his or her thoughts when faced with recalcitrant, reluctant and "hateful" students:

Questions:

1. Wouldn't it be easier to keep students interested in learning if teachers didn't need to worry about and "teach to" high-stakes achievement tests?

2. Why don't we get rid of those achievement tests and let teachers teach in the lively, personal, interesting, and challenging ways of which they are capable?

We are now more than a decade into the political legitimization and full flourishing of high-stakes testing, with the many implications that testing brings to students and teachers in classrooms. For many teachers, administrators, and teacher educators, the scope and fervency of this political intrusion into educational matters in the form of high-stakes testing is a critical even crippling limitation on teachers that does not help them teach in a manner that encourages students to like school (See Ohanian, this volume). Teachers, knowing the sanctions involved with No Child Left Behind (NCLB) legislation, feel an unrelenting pressure from local school and school district personnel to raise scores on the state tests used to measure Adequate Yearly Progress (AYP). They read all signals sent to them by their superiors—all the beginning of the year talks, staff development activities, evaluations of areas of weakness identified in previous assessments—as mandates for what and how they are to teach. Teachers come to know that teaching in ways that interest students is less important to score-keeping administrators and politicians than teaching in ways that raise student scores in standardized tests.

However, this is not quite the story that those same score-keeping administrators and politicians tell about high-stakes testing, teaching and learning. The story they tell in defense of themselves has two intertwined parts—one part that tells an "accountability" story and argues for a need to measure how well teachers and the schools are doing; and a second part that argues for a need to reform and improve teaching, and a way to make sure that change happens. Here is a brief recap of their story.

The story begins in 1983 when the National Commission on Excellence in Education published *A Nation at Risk*. This landmark report claimed "the educational foundations of our society are presently being eroded by a rising tide of mediocrity that threatens our very future as a Nation and a people" (p. 5). This report, and others like it, inspired professional and public debate about the state of our schools. In the early eighties, continuing complaints of a failing school system were impossible for either politicians or educators to ignore. If local schools were failing—and the public perception, given the evidence, was that they were—then they must be made to improve. In most states the criticism levied by *A Nation at Risk* mobilized politicians and state education officials to create policies to improve the quality of schools.

One of the first things state officials started doing was unifying the curriculum. States controlled state curricula by using such things as curriculum frameworks, state tests, textbook adoption criteria, accreditation standards, university entrance content expectancies, and criteria for teacher evaluation (Kirst, 1995). Another way states could control local schools was to examine and accredit them in terms of "outcomes" rather than "inputs," and state departments of education took an increasing role in defining and enforcing the kind and quality of "performance" that would be acceptable. Mostly state accrediting agencies (and state legislators) were interested in the academic performance of students, as individuals and as collective groups, as these were demonstrated through tested achievement and observations. After all, the "outcome" that was foremost on the minds of legislators, educators, and the public at large at this time was what students actually knew and could do with the education they received in the public schools.

All this set the stage, of course, for state achievement tests. If the state creates or outlines a curriculum and delineates at each grade level exactly what students are to know and be able to do, then it has a basis for testing to see if all that has been mandated has been accomplished. This was the way state officials were to hold teachers and school officials "accountable" for what they were supposed to be doing: producing students who had a reasonable amount of knowledge and skill, enough so they could succeed in college, the military, or the "real world." Schools would be "held accountable" for their failure (or success) in producing such students.

The state achievement tests used to measure school success were to be "new and improved"—no longer just the old "bubble answer" tests that were supposed to measure what students "knew" in the different subject fields, but better tests that were also supposed to measure what students "could do" or "perform" in these fields. These tests, and the NCLB legislation that followed them, were designed to get teachers to do a better job in the classroom where "better" meant two things: to make sure more (even all) students acquired the basic skills and competencies necessary for a successful future; and to get teachers to teach in new and better ways. The implication in the first charge is that teachers had become too comfortable, if not too lazy, and that they were not pressing themselves to meet the educational needs of all students, no matter the skill level, interest, or background of those students. The implication in the second charge is that teachers had been teaching the wrong things and in the wrong ways. The new state tests that attempted to measure "performance" were intended to drive instruction in the classroom away from rote memorization and toward the application of knowledge to real life problems. State officials and educational leaders wanted to get teachers to move past and beyond the teaching of isolated bits of knowledge and memorized information. These state tests are now bound up with the NCLB legislation—legislation that adds a moral high ground to the demands of politicians for school accountability. Schools are to successfully educate not just some or most children, but "all" children.

So, we return to the questions posed above. It may be that it would be easier to keep students interested in learning if teachers didn't need to worry about and "teach to" high-stakes achievement tests. But it does not seem like those tests will be going away anytime soon—maybe not during the entire span of a teacher's career. This suggests another set of questions we should ask in addition to those above:

3. *Are there ways for teachers to teach in interesting, vibrant ways even while working within the pressure of high-stakes achievement tests? If so, can teachers be persuaded they can do this?*

4. *Are teachers ready to adopt, even embrace, the demand for accountability being made of them? Do they see that "leaving no child behind" is a good thing—a good and necessary part of their jobs?*

5. *Can politicians be persuaded to make achievement tests, necessary for "accountability," less decisive, or not wholly decisive, in the measurement of student achievement? Could these tests be augmented by other measures, thus limiting the high-stakes pressure of such examinations? If other accountability measures were in place, would teachers be freed to teach in vibrant, interesting ways?*

Choosing Sides: The Political Left or the Political Right

Beyond agreement between democrat and republican legislators about the value of NCLB and the high-stakes testing that goes with it lies a wide and unbridgeable divide about the conduct of public schooling. This divide has real implications for teachers.

If school is boring, distasteful, and hateful to students, say adherents of the political right, it's because public school personnel haven't been forced to reinvent themselves in ways students and their families might find attractive and meaningful. Subscribers to this view believe schools will be improved only when educators have to compete for students, a competition they would encourage by some sort of voucher system. Leftist critics not only believe the capitalistic, free market model is a wrong model for the public schools to follow, but they often distrust the motives of those who propose and support such changes (See, for instance, Emery and Ohanian, 2004). In its place they propose an entirely different language and set of intentions—intentions more caring than competitive, more democratic than capitalistic, more communitarian than global.

One must be careful about naming which different people or groups of people make compatible political "bed-fellows," but there are a variety of people seen to be in sympathy with a right-oriented vision of the public schools. These include not only those who argue for educational vouchers and charter schools designed to encourage educational innovation and prove the advantages of educational entrepreneurship; they also include those who worry about the economic best interests of the country (they would say) and the need for schools to produce students who will be effective participants in the new global economy. The recent report from the National Center on Education and the Economy, *Tough Choices or Tough Times* (2006), captures this worry and connects it to educational vouchers. The authors of this report note the continuing low scores of American students in mathematics, science, and general literacy, compared to students from countries that are global partners and global competitors. In 2007 the worry is not just the blue-collar industrial jobs we have lost to developing countries, but even more particularly the loss of white-collar jobs traditionally performed by college graduates in such fields as medicine, accounting, and engineering.

The authors chart ten changes, or "tough choices," they believe must be made in education if we are not to suffer the "tough times" that will occur if we do nothing. Among the changes is this one about the role of school boards:

> Schools would no longer be owned by local school districts. Instead, schools would be operated by independent contractors, many of them limited-liability corporations owned and run by teachers. The primary role of school district central offices would be to write performance contracts with the operators of these schools, monitor their operations, cancel or decide not to renew the contract of those providers that did not perform well, and find others that could do better....

> Parents and students could choose among all the available contract schools, taking advantage of the performance data these schools would be obligated to produce.... The competitive, data-based market, combined with the performance contracts themselves, would create schools that were constantly seeking to improve their performance year in and year out (p. 16, Executive Summary).

Just this sliver of text from the authors of *Tough Choices or Tough Times* suggests the magnitude of change right-leaning and market-driven proponents believe desirable for education. In this vision, the language of business and the free-market economy supplants the language that is usually used by citizens and school people alike to describe public schools, their purpose and function. High-stakes testing has a comfortable place in this vision as "data"—like profit and loss statements in the business community—that drives teachers and administrators to improve scores as a measure of the better "product" they can manufacture. Parents are now seen as consumers, wise enough to buy a better product for their children than an inferior one. Competition drives the producers of inferior, costly products out of business leaving the field open to those more driven and efficient.

Much of modern leftist critique of the public schools is aimed at the kind of thinking that lies behind such proposals as those made by the authors of *Tough Choices or Tough Times*. Jonathan Kozol (2005) criticizes what he sees at the heart of the agenda of President George W. Bush, his associates, and other right-oriented education critics. Education changes coming from those quarters, he suggests, are based on a scientific model of accountability and measurement "that consciously applies the practices of business management to guarantee efficiency in operation of a classroom, school, or district, while, in general, bypassing questions about inequality, to the degree that this is possible" (p. 209). When we view schools as factories that produce workers in response to a changing global economy, we tend to justify what Kozol calls an "apartheid" system of schooling in America. When finding and acquiring an education in a competitive world where advantage means everything, there is no need to apologize that the best get the best and the rest get the rest. This is unacceptable to Kozol and the school of leftist critics, and such thinking keeps them poles apart from those on the political and economic right.

As presented in this brief review, neither a middle ground nor a common ground between these two radically different understandings is readily apparent. Either educators need the pressure of having to compete for students before they create schools that engage students meaningfully and prepare them for life, especially an economic life in the global economy; or, they need to reject market models for schooling in favor of communal, caring, and egalitarian concerns. They feel the push and pull of these different poles as they prepare curriculum and plan lessons. Teachers feel the pressure from the right in the prescribed curriculum they are given to teach and the high-stakes test their students will take as a measure of their effectiveness as a teacher. They feel the pull from the left when they look in the faces of some of the students they teach, especially those from underprivileged families too poor to buy needed school supplies. Teacher education candidates hear one version of what they are supposed to do in classrooms from teacher education faculty members who have totally accommodated themselves to the view from the right. And they hear a call to arms from teacher education faculty members galvanized with a spirit of upheaval and revolution.

Of course, it might be that both camps offer false choices or critically limited perspectives that block out a common ground that might be found to exist. This might tempt us to ask the following question:

> 6. *Can't educators, on their own, be moved to create schools and classrooms where enlivened teaching and learning both prepares students for their future economic life and prepares them for life as a citizen who can participate in a critical discourse about important social, political, and economic issues?*

This question shows the way to the second section of this essay that inquires about the structures of schools and learning in schools.

THE STRUCTURE OF SCHOOLS AND LEARNING IN SCHOOLS

I think that if I were a principal in a public school I might be tempted to say the following to my faculty as we met together for the first time before school started in the fall:

"What if I told you (even though I knew it was not true) that effective next year the parents of our students would be given full educational vouchers that they could take and spend anywhere they pleased—at the Catholic school over by the parish, the private school across town, or the next public school down the street. Or they could plan and spend those vouchers on a homeschool curriculum of their own choosing. Competition for students is on. We have one year to figure things out—one year to come up with some compelling reasons why our parents would be crazy to spend their vouchers at any other school than ours. If we cannot convince ourselves that our school is so good that this would be true, then we won't be able to convince our parents. So, let's take stock of ourselves. Let's capitalize on our strengths, work on our weaknesses, and, if necessary, radically re-invent ourselves. Let's get busy and do it now."

If I said such a thing to teachers—even in the light of the section on politics, above—it would be in hopes of stimulating them to re-examine themselves and their school, and, if necessary, to re-structure or re-invent themselves, their school, their priorities, their purposes, and their practices. And it would be precisely so as to make the school and the teaching and learning that happened within it so invigorating and important that neither the students nor the parents would "hate" the school or anything about it. This suggests another question:

7. *What structures involved in the conduct of schooling and of learning in school make it difficult if not impossible for (some) students to learn in meaningful and interesting ways? Or, to put it another way: Is there a better way to structure schooling, or teaching and learning, so students can learn in meaningful and interesting ways?*

To speak of the "structure" of schooling and the "structure" of teaching and learning in school is to speak of several things at once. Three aspects of structure will be touched on here: organizational structure, the structure of knowledge with its implications for the structure of learning in classrooms, and the physical structure of school buildings themselves.

Why are schools organized the way they are? Are schools organized so teachers can effectively teach and students effectively learn? Or are schools bogged down by an organizational structure that almost guarantees teacher frustration and student apathy? Every political or social institution has a history, a story of its reasons for coming to be and reasons why it came to be organized in a certain way. Educational historians such as Carl Kaestle (1983) and David Tyack (1974) help tell that story. Beginning in the early 1980s and extending well into the nineties, "school re-structuring" was a predominant theme in educational literature. Organizational change was a central theme in this literature. For Murphy (1991) school re-structuring generally involved systemic changes in such things as work roles, organizational and governance structures, and connections among the school and its larger environment. For Newman (1993) re-structuring proposals "suggest major changes in students' learning experiences, in the professional life of teachers, in the governance and management of schools, and in the ways in which schools are held accountable." Re-structuring advocates spoke and wrote about such things as teacher empowerment, decentralization, site-based management, and shared decision-making—ideas that had the potential to reorganize schools in less bureaucratic, less controlled ways. This talk still exists, but now it exists alongside talk of how to satisfy political pressure to increase scores on high-stakes achievement tests. Teachers may be empowered, but primarily in how to realize the demands for accountability issued from above.

A second aspect of organizational structure has to do with time and how the school, the school calendar, and the school day are organized. Teachers are with the students seven hours a day for about half a calendar year—but how shall that time be filled? (Or, is that too much time together, or not enough?) What principles should organize their time together? Should students be sorted by age? By grade? By ability level? Should the traditional divisions of curriculum into subject matter be maintained, or are there other more engaging ways to orient student learning? Teachers (and/or administrators) must decide academic requirements, length and organization of class periods, curricular scope and sequence, and the school calendar (See Sawyer and Gregg in this volume who report how a simple delay in school starting time would help some students to like school more). Teachers and administrators must decide about extra-curricular activities that might be offered and extra programs that might be needed for students who require more help. (Should high schools provide day care, information about birth control, extended family counseling services, other health services?) They decide grading policies, attendance policies, and disciplinary policies. Some of these things may be decided at bureaucratic or political levels beyond the reach and influence of local teachers and administrators, but others may be decided at the local level. Sometimes such decisions are made just out of "tradition" or habit. What real change in teaching and learning, and in the academic interests of students, might happen if such organizational issues were re-visited and changed?

Of course, given the presence of mandatory standardized testing imposed from above, thinking about change is not so simple as teachers sharing local talk about the needs of students and how best to teach them. This is the essential "contradiction" pointed at by such people as Linda McNeil (1986) and others who note that control policies like standardized testing serve to structure "school knowledge" in certain ways, and not others. As we recall from the earlier section of this essay, officials from state departments of education fully intend to control the curriculum and do so by instituting goals, curriculum frameworks, and standardized achievement tests. These serve to structure knowledge and teaching and learning activities in classrooms at all levels and in all subject matters. In feeling the pressure of these mandates, and especially the pressure to raise test scores in accordance with NCLB, teachers often resort to such things as worksheets, list-filled lectures, and short-answer tests, making school knowledge often disjointed, fragmentary, and temporary—this despite the intentions of education critics and politicians who envision better practices (as mentioned above). Standardized tests can often make school knowledge seem far removed from the knowledge of our everyday experience (McNeil, 1986).

A final aspect of structure is the structure of the physical plant—the school building itself. They say you can learn a lot about a culture by examining the architecture of its courthouses, churches, and schools. Why are schools designed and built the way they are? Would teaching and learning be improved if school buildings were designed differently? Powell, Farrar, and Cohen (1985) point out that most high schools are laid out just like shopping malls. Like merchants wanting to attract buyers into their shops (often with sales and "easy payments"), teachers try to lure students into "buying" what they have to sell in their little stores just off the main mall area. There is even a game area (the gymnasium) and a food court (the cafeteria). And like the mall, school is a great place to "hang out" with your friends.

But do high schools (or middle schools and elementary schools) require this traditional physical lay-out? What are the alternatives? In his book *The End of Education* (1995) Neil Postman writes what he calls a "fable" where he envisions a very different kind of education for students—one where they come to care about and serve their local communities by being *out* of their "dreary classrooms" and away from their "even drearier lessons." In the fable, one of the protagonists remarks, "It is not written in any holy book that an education must occur in a small room with chairs in it" (p. 96). But, even if we are charmed by the idea of breaking away from traditional classroom structures, we must ask: if we are not to meet students in a small room with chairs, then where will we meet them? What is the proper, most necessary space for students to meet those who will teach them?

There are, in this section on the "structure" of schooling, a spate of questions that demands the asking of two more:

8. *Where shall we go for answers about how to better structure schooling?*

9. *How willing are we—as teachers, administrators, teacher educators, politicians, and community members—to put into doubt the structures of schooling that we hold to be valuable, necessary, or essential? How open can we be to the new ideas we might find? How willing are we to look?*

It is not hard to answer the first of these questions. The short answer is that we have some reading to do. We have to pick up the contemporary books written by such people as Postman and McNeil, mentioned above, and discover the ideas they have for us. But if we really want to be adventurous and put our modern ideas in doubt, we have to read beyond those who speak specifically about reforming contemporary public schools. We need to read in philosophy of education—people like Nell Noddings and John Passmore. We need to revisit the ideas of John Locke and Jean-Jacques Rousseau. Even the ancients—Plato, Aristotle, and Quintilian (see Pauline Nugent's essay in this volume)—await us, if we would only care to examine them.

It is, however, less easy to answer the second question. It is hard for us to put our self-understandings in doubt—to challenge all the assumptions that helped us make sense of our own experiences as students as well as those that help us make sense of ourselves as teachers. There is the question of having time enough, and support enough, for such an examination. And then there is the question of beating your head against the wall when, excited about new ideas, you see nothing but resistance around you.

CURRICULAR AND INSTRUCTIONAL PRACTICES

10. *What kind of curriculum and what manner of teaching will stimulate students, especially those students most inclined to "hate" school?*

11. *How willing are we—as teachers, administrators, teacher educators and others closest to the educational setting—to challenge our self-understandings about curricular and instructional matters? Are we open to new ideas we might find? (This questions echoes themes established in questions three and nine, above.)*

No one goes into teaching wanting to be a "bad teacher." Or, to put it in terms of the question at the heart of this book, no one goes into teaching intending to bore students to death, kill a student's interest in learning, or have students "hate school." No one wants to stand up in front of students and read ambivalence, avoidance, disgust, boredom, or resentment in the faces of his or her students. At the very least, teachers want to teach well, effectively and efficiently. At the very least, teachers want students to learn something that they, the teachers, believe is important for students to know or be able to do. This does not mean that there aren't bad teachers, that there aren't people who should not be teachers, that there aren't people unwilling to expend the effort or have the commitment to become excellent teachers. And it does not mean that there aren't teachers who get misled, mixed up, or confused about their purposes—like Jean Brodie, in "The Prime of Miss Jean Brodie," who becomes more interested in creating "Brodie's girls" than helping students as she should have (Spark & Kermode, 2004).

And it does not mean that there aren't teachers who make curricular and instructional choices that end up boring students. There are boring and inept teachers, and students suffer because of them.

One can get dizzy very quickly thinking about why teachers fail to interest students in what it is they have to teach and what can be done to remedy the problem. Indeed, the literature on teachers and teaching is so full of analyses of the problem and proposals to fix it that it's difficult to know where to begin one's sorting through.

244

In this volume, Thomas Deering begins his thinking about this subject by remembering that the typical five- or six-year old child has some sort of innate drive to know and understand the world. That child has to know "why" something is the way it is, and he or she won't be satisfied until some answer is made. In *The Disciplined Mind: Beyond Facts and Standardized Tests, the K-12 Education that Every Child Deserves*, Howard Gardner shows where those innocent "why" questions can lead. Gardner argues for an education inspired by what he calls "a set of *essential questions*" (italics in the original), and he offers the following as examples:

> Who are we? Where do we come from? What do we consider to be true or false, beautiful or ugly, good or evil? What is the fate of the earth? How do we fit in? What is the earth made of? What are we made of? Why do we live, and why do we die? Are our destinies under the control of God or some other "higher power"? What is love? What is hatred? Why do we make war? Must we? What is justice and how can we achieve it (p. 216)?

Such questions are the real "stuff" of the disciplines, and, according to Gardner, the task of the teacher is to offer students access to the best answers to these human questions.

> The rationale and the reward for studying the disciplines should be enhanced access to, and stronger purchase on, the major questions of human life. If you want to understand what it means to be alive, study biology; if you want to understand the composition and dynamic of the physical world, study chemistry, physics, or geology; if you want to understand your own background, study national history and immigration patterns and experiences; if you want to gain intimate knowledge of the feats of which human beings are capable, study and participate in art, science, religion, athletics, and perhaps even developmental psychology (p. 218).

But can the beleaguered biology teacher look at his 10th grade students and honestly believe that **they** care about the question "What does it mean to be alive?" Can he believe they (his students) think this is an "essential" question that motivates them to a year-long study of biology? Can the history teacher honestly believe students care about what hatred is, why human beings make war with one another, and what justice is and how we can achieve it? Why aren't these just exactly the kinds of questions that lead students to disengage from school, to "turn off" what the teacher is saying, and to quit caring about school at all?

Kieran Egan, in his recent book *An Imaginative Approach to Teaching*, offers some help to us here. Egan suggests that the passion of the young—the kind of wonder that inspires the child Deering writes about, and that same wonder revisited in the essential questions Gardner suggests—can be continued or recaptured even in later years. Egan writes:

> Students don't need a throbbing passion for learning algebra or a swooning joy in learning about punctuation, but successful education does require some emotional involvement of the students with the subject matter. All knowledge is human knowledge and all knowledge is a product of human hopes, fears, and passions. To bring knowledge to life in students' minds we must introduce it to students in the context of human hopes, fears, and passions in which it finds its fullest meaning (p. xii).

Egan also writes:

> The soul of teaching has to do with meaning. Everyone concerned with education, from the beginning, has recognized that the task is not simply to teach facts and skills that can be reproduced when required. The trick is to tie the facts and skills to their deeper meaning in human experience (p. 211).

According to Egan, the curricular and instructional task is to open up space for students to have an emotional and imaginative involvement with the subject matter—to tie facts and skills to their deeper meaning in human experience. He offers suggestions to teachers for how this can be done. For instance, he suggests teachers of young children to ask such questions as "What is emotionally engaging about the topic? How is it meaningful? Why should it matter to us?" These questions (and others—see Appendices to the text) are placed at the center of the teacher's plan for teaching a given topic. Egan suggests teachers make use of such things as metaphors, binary opposites (good/bad, right/wrong, love/hate, etc.), mental images and play in telling the dramatic story connected to the subject matter under discussion. Where a more advanced literacy is the goal with students in the middle years of their education, Egan suggests, among other things, that teachers help students explore the "heroic" qualities attached to a topic, and that teachers ask how students can understand the human hopes, fears, passions, or struggles that have shaped how we know a particular topic. When older students require a more theoretic or "philosophic" understanding, Egan hopes teachers help students understand the great organizing and causal principles that are used to explain a topic, but also help them understand what gives the events or ideas around this topic an importance far beyond their own particulars. What features of the world pose the problem to be investigated and explained? What does this way of thinking imply about the nature of the world and our relationship with it? These are the kinds of questions Egan believes teachers must put at the forefront of their teaching.

Both Howard Gardner and Kieran Egan provide specific examples of curricular material that can be energized by the approaches they suggest. To repeat: "Students don't need a throbbing passion for learning algebra or a swooning joy in learning about punctuation," Egan suggests, "but successful education does require some emotional involvement of the students with the subject matter." It's good that in his approach, and that of Gardner, students don't need "throbbing passion" and "swooning joy" because those are things a teacher sees far too infrequently in students. But how frequently do we see teachers committed to organizing their curriculum and instructional approaches so as to draw out the emotional and imaginative involvement of the students with the subject matter? In the ways we prepare teachers, and in our support of them once they are in the field, do we help them identify the human questions, and the human connections, in the disciplines they are teaching? Do we help them, as Egan does in his text, construct learning goals, build lesson plans, and construct assessment activities around the emotional involvement of students with the subject matter? If we did, would fewer students hate school?

So, the final question this essay will ask:

12. *Are we optimists or pessimists when it comes to thinking about why kids hate school? That is, do we believe teachers can, with the right training and support, teach in ways that will interest or invigorate even those students who are now most inclined to hate school? Do we believe that even those most disinterested students, given excellent and inspired teaching, can be brought to a successful engagement with important subject matter in schools? Do we believe that this can happen even within the confines of NCLB inspired, and crushingly important, standardized testing?*

CONCLUDING REMARKS

Why do kids hate school? Why, when the teacher looks upon the students in her class, does she see looks and behaviors that show that some students couldn't care less about what learning might be available to them in the classroom? Should she blame herself, her students, circumstances beyond her control?

The essays in this volume help answer these questions—hopefully, this last one, too. Questions are at the center of this final essay not to suggest that there are no answers to why kids hate school and what we can do about

246

it. The questions suggest our continuing need for discussion, dialogue, and debate about how to respond to student disinterest and hatred of school. The questions and the discussion of political, structural, and curricular and instructional aspects of education are intended to give some form to this continuing conversation. That conversation happens in many different ways and in many different places—in public spaces (as it did in the Academy for Educational Studies Conference); in print (as it does in this book); in professional development workshops in schools across the nation; in teacher education programs; and in the talking to oneself—the inner-dialogue all teachers have—at the end of a long day or a long week when students have taken all a teacher has to give..

There probably isn't a more important conversation to have.

REFERENCES

Egan, K. (2005). *An Imaginative Approach to Teaching*. San Francisco: Jossey-Bass.

Elmore, Richard F, Charles H. Abelmann, and Susan H. Fuhrman. (1996). In Helen F. Ladd (Ed.), *Holding Schools Accountable: Performance-based Reform in Education*. Washington, D.C.: The Brookings Institution.

Emery, K. & Ohanian, S. (2004) *Why Is Corporate American Bashing Our Public Schools?* Portsmouth, N.H.: Heinemann.

Gardner, H. (1999). *The Disciplined Mind: Beyond Facts and Standardized Tests, The K-12 Education that Every Child Deserves*. New York: Penguin Books.

Kaestle, C. (1983). *Pillars of the Republic: Common Schools and American Society, 1780 – 1860*. New York: Hill and Wang.

Kirst, M. (1995). Who's in charge? Federal, state, and local control. In Diane Ravitch and Maris A. Vinovskis (Eds.), *Learning from the Past*. Baltimore, MD: The Johns Hopkins University Press.

Kozol, J. (2005). *The Shame of the Nation: The Restoration of Apartheid Schooling in America*. New York: Crown Publishers.

McNeil, L. (1986). *Contradictions of Control: School Structure and School Knowledge*. New York: Routledge Press.

Murphy, J. (1991). *Restructuring Schools: Capturing and Assessing the Phenomena*. New York: Teachers College Press.

National Center for Education and the Economy. (2006). *Tough Choices or Tough Times* (Executive Summary). http://skillscommission.org/pdf/exec_sum/ToughChoices_EXECSUM.pdf

National Commission on Excellence in Education. (1983). *A Nation at Risk: The Imperative for Educational Reform*. Washington D.C.: U.S. Department of Education.

Newmann, F. (1993). Beyond common sense in educational restructuring: The issues of content and linkage. *Educational Researcher* (22/2): 4–13.

Postman, N. (1995). *The End of Education: Redefining the Value of School.* New York: Alfred A. Knopf.

Powell, Arthur, Eleanor Farrar, and David K. Cohen. (1985). *The Shopping Mall High School: Winners and Losers in the Educational Marketplace.* Boston: Houghton Mifflin Company.

Spark M. & Kermode, F. (2004). *The Prime of Miss Jean Brodie.* New York: Everyman's Library Contemporary Classics.

Tyack, D. (1974). *The One Best System: A History of American Urban Education.* Cambridge, MA: Harvard University Press.

SUGGESTED READINGS

Egan, K. (2005). *An Imaginative Approach to Teaching.* San Francisco: Jossey-Bass

Gardner, H. (1999). *The Disciplined Mind: Beyond Facts and Standardized Tests, The K-12 Education that Every Child Deserves.* New York: Penguin Books.

Postman, N. (1995). *The End of Education: Redefining the Value of School.* New York: Alfred A. Knopf.

Each of these three books has something serious to say about how better to serve the students in our public schools. Egan's book offers "templates" to teachers of all levels that will help them think through the subject matter they are teaching and how to plan lessons for that teaching. Gardner argues that there are disciplines—fields of study, each with its own habit of thought. The teacher's difficult task is to bring students to some knowledge of those disciplines, but he offers help about how to do this in lively and interesting ways. Postman's book is a challenge to our thinking about the failed and failing purposes of schools that tend to kill learning with suggestions about other purposes we might pursue.

SUGGESTED ACTIVITIES

The twelve questions discussed in this essay might be used for small group discussion, large group discussion, classroom debates, or informal and formal writing assignments.

MULTIPLE CHOICE QUESTIONS

1. According to the author, a teacher who has failed to inspire students to learn might

   a. blame him or herself

   b. blame students

   c. blame circumstances that are out of the teacher's control

   d. all of the above

2. The use of standardized tests expanded and was legitimized when several reports critical of education were published. The decade when these reports started people worrying about schools and clamoring for change was

    a. the 1960s

    b. the 1980s

    c. the 1990s

    d. none of the above

3. State departments of education started controlling curriculum by

    a. devising curriculum frameworks

    b. creating state examinations

    c. changing accrediting standards

    d. all of the above

4. One of the reasons state officials and educational leaders want to control curriculum was to

    a. get teachers to use more worksheets and lectures in their teaching so students would learn more material

    b. get teachers to emphasize the learning of facts testable by "bubble sheet" kinds of tests

    c. get teachers to move away from the teaching of isolated bits of knowledge and memorized information

    d. get teachers to emphasize the different learning styles students use

5. The authors of *Tough Choices or Tough Times* believe

    a. schools would improve more, and faster, if they had to compete for students

    b. the capitalistic, free market model for schooling won't work

    c. the capitalistic, free market model for schooling is morally wrong

    d. all of the above

6. Leftist critics of school vouchers and capitalist-oriented thinking about the public schools believe

    a. an apartheid system of education is morally wrong

    b. we ought to worry more about caring than competition, democracy more than capitalism, and local communities more than global economic issues

c. all of the above

d. none of the above

7. Structural change refers to

a. how schools are organized

b. how schools structure school knowledge

c. the physical lay-out of schools

d. all of the above

8. The author believes the kinds of "essential questions" Gardner mentions

a. will probably not motivate students to care much about their studies

b. are not the kinds of questions teachers can realistically be trained to ask their students

c. seem to appeal to the natural questions human beings ask, even starting when they are very young

d. none of the above

9. Kieran Egan believes

a. knowledge is the accumulated facts and data currently known about the world—the kind accessible to students in encyclopedias or textbooks

b. knowledge is human knowledge and all knowledge is a product of human hopes, fears, and passions

c. knowledge is ever-changing due to scientific advancements and technological change

d. none of the above

10. The author

a. asks too many questions!!!

b. asks questions he hopes will lead to further discussion, dialogue, and debate about why kids hate school and what we can do about it

c. all of the above

d. (Note: "c" is the right answer)

CONTRIBUTORS

Jill (Alice A.) Black is an Assistant Professor in the Geography, Geology, and Planning Department at Missouri State University, where she teaches Earth Science for Teachers to preservice elementary and middle school teachers, as well as other geoscience and education courses. Her research and writing are in the areas of spatial ability and Earth science conceptual understanding and the instruction of the nature of science.

Stefan Broidy teaches in Wittenberg University's Education Department, where he is also Director of Graduate Studies. His research and writing are in the areas of professional ethics, philosophy of language, and educational policy issues. He is currently completing a monograph on kindness in the ethics of teaching.

Susan Anne Carlson has been a Professor of English at Pittsburg State University since 1991. Her main research interests are the Brontës and 19th century British Literature. She had several research assistants who contributed to this article: Melissa Smith-MacDonald, John Rodrigue, and J.P. Sloop.

Jeffrey H. D. Cornelius-White is Assistant Professor and Program Director for School Counseling at Missouri State University. Jeff is also editor of *The Person-Centered Journal*, and the associate editor of the *Journal of Border Educational Research*. His work typically focuses on person-centered and social justice issues in counseling and education.

Philip Cusick is a Professor in the Department of Educational Administration at Michigan State University. His research interests include organizational theory, secondary schools, and issues of social class as they relate to schools. His most recent book is *A Passion for Learning: The Education of Seven Eminent Americans*.

Thomas E. Deering is the Dean of the College of Education at Augusta State University. His areas of interest include philosophy of education and teacher education. He is editor of several Kendall-Hunt books, including *Essays in History and Philosophy of Education, Issues in Teacher Education,* and *Perspectives on American Education*.

Roxanne Fillmore teaches Early Childhood Education at Northeastern State University in Oklahoma. Her current work includes developing a literacy-based curriculum for Cookson Hills Community Action Head Start and research into the effectiveness of university education programs. Her interest in the Accelerated Reader Program stems from doctoral work comparing children's and teacher's choices in literature.

Roy F. Fox serves as Professor of English Education and Chair of the Department of Learning, Teaching, & Curriculum at the University of Missouri-Columbia, where he also directs the Missouri Writing Project, a site of The National Writing Project. His research focuses on the teaching and learning of writing, as well as media literacy—especially how people interact with television, film, and advertising messages.

Lynda George is an Assistant Professor at Central Connecticut State University. She taught in the Hartford Public School System for 23 years before joining the CCSU faculty in 2002. Research interests include moral development, the Socratic Method, and urban education.

Bonnie Giese teaches Elementary Education/Early Childhood classes at Northeastern State University in Tahlequah, Oklahoma. Her interests are in Accelerated Reading centers, on an involvement with literature-based curriculums, children's literature, and how literature can be used in thematic teaching units and cross-curricular areas.

Judy Gregg is the Coordinator of School Relations, Student Support Services in the College of Education at Missouri State University. She worked in Springfield R-XII School District as a teacher, curriculum facilitator, assessment coordinator and instructional specialist. She has also served as Assistant to the Director of Greenwood Laboratory School at Missouri State University.

Adam P. Harbaugh is an Assistant Professor of Curriculum and Instruction at the University of North Carolina at Charlotte. He is co-author (with Jeffrey H. D. Cornelius-White) of the forthcoming book from Sage entitled *Learner-Centered Instruction: Building Relationships for Student Success*.

Don Hufford is a Professor in the School of Education at Newman University. He has worked in diverse education and social work roles, including having been a teacher, principal of a residential school, director of a residential treatment program for adolescents, director of a settlement house (inner-city community center), director of a summer camp for inner-city children and youth, and youth director of a YMCA.

Steven P. Jones is a Professor in the Department of Reading, Foundations, and Technology at Missouri State University. He is the Director of the Academy for Educational Studies at MSU. His academic and research interests include philosophy of education, teacher education, and the teaching of great books.

Deborah Landry is an Assistant Professor of Elementary Education at Northeastern State University, Tahlequah, Oklahoma. She is a former early childhood educator in Oklahoma, having taught grades kindergarten and second. Her research interests include oral histories, veteran history projects, and Japanese early childhood education. She is also a retired U. S. Marine Corps Officer.

Pauline Nugent is a Professor in the Department of Modern and Classical Languages at Missouri State University where she teaches courses at all levels primarily in Latin, Greek, and Hebrew. Her research interests focus on Patristics—the study of the Church Fathers. She is currently writing a book entitled *Jerome's Commentary on Daniel*. She is interested in both ancient and modern pedagogy, with special attention to the art of teaching.

Susan Ohanian is a long-time teacher and prolific writer. She maintains a Web site (www.susanohanian.org) that offers a wide range of commentary on and critique of current educational practices. Her recent book, with Kathy Emery, is entitled *Why Is Corporate America Bashing Our Public Schools?*

David Owen is a Professor of Education in the Department of Curriculum and Instruction at Iowa State University. His work has centered on philosophy of education with a special interest in exploring the implications of Richard P. McKeon's work for education. He is co-editor of *On Knowing—The Natural Sciences*.

Cathy J. Pearman is an Assistant Professor in the Department of Reading, Foundations, and Technology at Missouri State University. Her research interests include the impact of technology on literacy acquisition, development of English language learning methodologies, and factors contributing to successful professional development schools.

Emmett Sawyer is Director of Special Programs and Accreditation for the College of Education at Missouri State University. A former public school administrator, he was also Director of Greenwood Laboratory School at MSU. He holds the rank of Assistant Professor in the Department of Educational Administration and teaches courses in EAD and in the Master of Arts in Teaching program.

Karen Scott is Director of Student Support Services for the Springfield, MO school district. She has 31 years experience in public schools as a classroom teacher, guidance counselor, and district administrator and is an adjunct professor for Drury University. She has worked extensively in the area of support for at-risk students and has helped create numerous programs in the area of drop-out prevention.

Eric Sheffield is an Assistant Professor of Educational Foundations in Missouri State University's Teacher Education Program in Springfield Missouri. Trained as a philosopher, his research focuses on educational practice and policy as a philosophical matter. He has written on service-learning, moral education, academic freedom, and the structure of philosophical inquiry.

Karla J. Smart-Morstad is an Associate Professor in the Department of Education at Concordia College, Moorhead, MN. She teaches general methods for secondary education and special methods for English education, as well as secondary reading in the content areas. Her research interests are in qualitative studies in education, particularly descriptive review.

Sara B. Triggs is an Assistant Professor in the Department of Education at Concordia College, Moorhead, MN. She teaches educational foundations, middle school education, elementary language arts, and elementary reading in content areas. Her research interests are in qualitative studies in education, particularly descriptive review.

Jerry Whitworth is Associate Dean in the College of Professional Education at Texas Woman's University. He is currently the Past President of the Texas Association of Colleges for Teacher Education and the President-Elect of the Texas Council for Exceptional Children. His research interests include the effective preparation of teachers, strategy instruction for students, and creating more inclusive schools.